IN
DEFENSE
OF
LOVE

IN
DEFENSE
OF
LOVE

AN ARGUMENT

RON ROSENBAUM

MELVILLE HOUSE
BROOKLYN • LONDON

In Defense of Love

First published in 2023 by Doubleday, a division of
Penguin Random House LLC, New York

First Melville House Printing: July 2024

Permissions credits can be found on page 247.
Portions of this work originally appeared in slightly different form in *Slate*.

Melville House Publishing
46 John Street
Brooklyn, NY 11201
and
Melville House UK
Suite 2000
16/18 Woodford Road
London E7 0HA

mhpbooks.com
@melvillehouse

ISBN: 978-1-68589-159-6
ISBN: 978-1-68589-160-2 (eBook)

Library of Congress Control Number: 2022048868

Printed in the United States of America
1 3 5 7 9 10 8 6 4 2

A catalog record for this book is available from the Library of Congress

For X with love:

You know who you are

And you know why.

Some men say an army of horse
And some men say an army of men on foot...
Is the most beautiful thing...
But I say it is what you love.

FROM SAPPHO, FRAGMENT 16,
TRANSLATED BY ANNE CARSON

Conscious subjects and their mental lives
are inescapable components of reality. But
not describable by the physical sciences.

THOMAS NAGEL

Contents

Preface

It was a cold October morning in New Haven and I, a naïve Yale freshman, duly reported to a room in the begrimed, Gothic-like fortress of Payne Whitney gym. I had received a peremptory invitation on Yale letterhead, but no description of what was to happen. Nothing had prepared me for what was about to take place. Yes, over breakfast, a couple of legacy preppies whose older brothers and sisters attended Yale and other Ivy League and Seven Sisters schools like Vassar and Smith could be heard snickering over "the stolen Vassar photos," but it was not immediately clear what that meant to me, a public high school–educated, suburban, non-legacy student.

I proceeded along the corridors of the cavernous gym, hung with large-scale Stubbsian portraits of hunting scenes—horses and dogs. I assumed all of this was part of some phys ed checkup and checked into the assigned room.

The lights were extra bright and there were men in white with large cameras I barely glimpsed before I was ordered to stand in the middle of the room and remove my clothes. At which point things began to get surreal. The white coats began affixing three-inch-long metal pins to me with surgical tape, one to each vertebra, so that they described the curve of my spine—a process that I was told would allow the camerawork to better capture said curvature, leaving me feeling a bit like a naked porcupine. After which there were sounds of buzzing and clicking as the men in white began photographing my nude form from every angle, while others used tape measures to compile my limb and neck circumferences, among other stats.

It didn't take long, and looking back I marvel at how unquestioning I remained about this strange procedure, which I learned was compulsory and was called the "posture photo"; because of the word "posture" I assumed it had some curative spinal purpose, though I never heard anything further about it during my time at Yale. It is now like a scene from a half-forgotten nightmare.

It was not until some three decades later that I would learn what it was really all about and the scandalous pseudoscience behind it, and what became of the nude photos, including mine, and why. Because of something I would write all those years later, they had to be burned, and some seven thousand remaining photos of naked Yalies went up in smoke.

A combination of circumstances had led to my embarking on an investigation of this strange—now even stranger-appearing—ritual for *The New York Times Magazine*. This is what I learned in a cover story published in 1995.

The "posture photo" ritual was not part of the phys ed program but rather something more widespread and dubious.

It seemed that beginning in the forties and lasting through at least 1971, a pseudoscience crank named William H. Sheldon, who had been influenced by Weimar-era German eugenics theories and made a splash in pop science media, succeeded in convincing almost every elite American college and university—Ivy and Seven Sisters alike—to make available the unwitting seventeen- and eighteen-year-old members of their incoming freshman classes to take part in a vast nationwide study of Sheldon's theories about the characterological implications of postural ratios. These included lengths of limbs divided by circumference of waist and neck, etc. Sheldon believed a study of these ratios could reduce each individual to a three-digit number. It was a continuation of the German (and later Nazi) quest to define the physical and psychological embodiment of the Master Race—and those physical specimens who did not fit the profile.

Sheldon was not a professed Nazi, but the posture photo procedures were human experiments that violated all sorts of ethical guidelines for use of human subjects, with no apparent concern about potential psychological effects. In fact, from the letters I received over the years after my story was published, it seemed that women in particular were subject to distress and shock, even trauma, at the time and especially upon learning they had been used, in effect, as experimental animals with little concern by the institutions that were supposed to act in loco parentis, yet made them the butt of jokes by Ivy League marching bands.

How did this happen? I still find it hard to believe. From what I could gather, Sheldon presented college administrators with the chance to participate in an important advancement of science in return for clandestinely sacrificing their student bodies and personal privacy to the greater glory of science. It was only in the aftermath of my *Times Magazine* story that some of these sacrificial lambs said they'd found it a disturbing experience and thanked me for pulling back the curtain on the mystery of what they'd gone through when, often, college bureaucrats would be of no help and often came close to denying any of it happened. A denial that became unsustainable when, after a long and complicated quest, I found thousands of the photos, mainly negatives, in neatly labeled caches in the archives of the Smithsonian Museum's anthropological wing. Images of the "best and brightest" of the American elite, among them future presidential candidates and a past president, all in file boxes along with nineteenth-century explorers' anthropological catalogs of Indigenous peoples' bodies. Photos of their alumni the elite institution rushed to claim and destroy probably before they could be sued.

The whole episode exposed the power and default reverence for "science" and its claimed ability to solve deep mysteries of human nature, and it came back to me when I was shaping this book on the "science" of love and the attempt to subject love to scientific explanation. Not just love, but, as we'll see, grieving, death, free will, poetry, and evil.

My title derives from a late-sixteenth-century defense of poetry by Sir Philip Sidney, a sonneteer contemporary of Shakespeare who wrote a once celebrated but now largely forgotten work called "An Apologie for Poetrie"; "apology" then used in the now largely archaic theological sense of church "apologetics"— discourse and debate over, for instance, the true metaphorical or metaphysical meaning of the transubstantiation of the communion wafer.

Like many hard-core English majors, I had enjoyed Sir Philip's spirited defense of poetry and his concept of its being "an other nature" and so I thought of titling this book "An Apology for Love." But, to avoid misleading prospective readers with "Apology," I retreated to "In Defense," having endured an overly subtle, potentially misleading title of a previous book, *Explaining Hitler*. Some took that title to be *my* explanation, rather than a study of the enterprise and the many attempts, often misguided, to explain Hitler. Akin to the many attempts, often misguided, to explain love. The Hitler book has been translated into ten or so languages, of which the Italian title, *Il Mistero Hitler*, was my favorite. You could consider this book *Il Mistero Love* or after the French title *Pourquoi Hitler?—Pourquoi Love?*, Why Love? Another way of looking at it is as an attempt to explore the question raised by the famous final line of Philip Larkin's poem "An

Arundel Tomb." The line "What will survive of us is love" asks the question "What is the what"?

And I tell this story of the posture photo fiasco both because I was an experimental subject of a misguided attempt myself and because—as will become apparent—it suggests an origin of my concern for many of the other misguided attempts to scientize the mystery described in the book that follows. And the persistence of the Mystery.

IN
DEFENSE
OF
LOVE

CHAPTER 1

Love Is in Trouble

A LL MY LIFE I have wanted to write about love. And I *have* written about love. To a certain extent. Up to a point. But it is only now that I feel the need to risk writing a book about love. A defense of love. It's only now that I've come to feel that love needs defending, love is under siege, love has powerful enemies. Love has deniers.

Only now do I feel that love needs rescue. Rescue from the reductionists. Rescue from those who want to see it not as a phenomenon but an epiphenomenon; a secondary effect, not a primary cause. Collateral damage from a sexual encounter, perhaps.

Love needs rescue from the fMRI (functional Magnetic Resonance Imaging) neuroscientists and their Big Mistake (confusing correlation with causation). The ones who want to reduce love to a lit-up stream that symbolizes synaptic connections. The ones trying to tell us there is no mystery, that love can be quantified by measuring differential blood flow, localized in the left ventral tegmental area and the right anteromedial caudate of the brain, recent fashionable foci in the brain. Neuroreductionism, it's been called.

Or as one astute observer puts it:

"Well this gets us into the question of whether we have a soul distinct from our electrical wiring and the flow of electrons that travel along it. They [the neuroscientists] don't seem to like that line of thought because it [love] can't be reduced to their limited imaginations of what being human is and means."

And love needs rescue from the neurochemists who want to reduce it to some molecular elixir (first phenylethylamine, most recently oxytocin, the multitasking miracle molecule hailed in all the pop-sci love lit not just as the "molecule of love," not just as "the molecule of postorgasmic serenity," or the "cuddle hormone," but as the world-bestriding "moral molecule," capable of bringing about both orgasms and world peace. (Not to be confused with OxyContin, the powerful synthetic opioid.)

And love needs rescue from the bonobo chimp–worshipping social anthropologists who want to eliminate love in favor of some Edenic pre-paleo primate polyamory that will eradicate what they seem to believe is the greatest scourge and curse of humankind: romantic jealousy (as the French say, "without adultery there is no novel"). Which they will accomplish by eliminating—apparently by fiat—monogamous love, the profound evil that is jealousy's source. If only Othello had known!

And love needs rescue from the simpering pop philosophers like Alain de Botton who want to reduce it to some mild, thin-blooded saccharine niceness. Here for instance is the most read quote on Google from his book *On Love:*

> Every fall into love involves the triumph of hope over self-knowledge. We fall in love hoping we won't find in another what we know is in ourselves, all the cowardice, weakness, laziness, dishonesty, compromise, and stupidity. We throw a cordon of love around the chosen one and decide that

everything within it will somehow be free of our faults. We locate inside another a perfection that eludes us within ourselves, and through our union with the beloved hope to maintain (against the evidence of all self-knowledge) a precarious faith in our species.

In other words, we "throw a cordon" of niceness around the other, which rules out mad passion. Think Johnny Cash's mega hit on the country charts, back in the sixties, "Ring of Fire." Not merely room-temperature warm, but burn-down-the-house fiery.

That's more like it for many.

Love is not always nice. Love is not always mild. Ask anyone. Ask Jane Austen, for god'ssake: "I have no notion of loving people by halves, it is not my nature." Read *Persuasion* and have your heart rent, if you have one.

And love needs rescue from Helen Fisher, the doyenne of the pop-sci industrial complex that feeds off quotes from Dr. Fisher, the Queen of Love Science, whose signal contribution has been to claim that her fMRI studies demonstrate that love is *not an emotion.* This is her big reveal! One she repeats ceaselessly in TED talks and venues such as *Psychology Today* and *Cosmo* online, even, as we shall see, *The Wall Street Journal,* and it seems every other pop relationship story you see, to the tune of millions of Google hits.

Love is not an emotion with all the exquisite nuances and variations that entails, Helen Fisher insists. No, love is a "drive." A crude indiscriminate mental motor function like hunger, thirst, and cocaine addiction, all mediated by the dopamine system in the brain. Which tells us precisely nothing about the infinitely variegated, subtly differentiated spectrum of human feelings, the five hundred shades of love, although we seem meant to be bowled over by the insight that love is basically no different from crack addiction.

An emotion is a lesser, more insubstantial, virtually trivial thing compared with a drive, Fisher's work implies. To which one should add the piquant pseudoscientific declaration about the true marker of an emotion: a facial expression. Yes, this is what Dr. Fisher's colleagues now have to say: We've got it backward, and every emotion is not merely expressed but defined by a singular facial expression (one of only six!), which may even be the secret cause of love. Love doesn't qualify as an emotion because it lacks an explicit facial expression associated with it and that gives rise to it. Be careful how you smile. This was told to me, firsthand, in person, straight-faced, by one of Fisher's coauthors—of a paper in the *Journal of Neurophysiology* that used fMRIs to study "Reward and Motivation in Early-Stage Intense Romantic Love" (ESIRL). Yes, they've "staged" love now—like cancer.

And love needs rescue from the evolutionary psychologists with their just-so stories that cram into a Procrustean bed of Darwinian just-so stories the origin of every human passion. Love by this analysis then is just a kind of speed dating app in the race for reproductive primacy of the selfish gene. "Squirrels are busy," one of Dr. Fisher's acolytes told me, gesturing down the hall of her lab at the Delphic fMRI machine in Albert Einstein College of Medicine. Love evolved as a way of expediting the squirrels' pairing off and reproducing process while the busy nut-gathering process goes on. Those romantic rodents! We are their heirs: the evolutionary taming of the shrew.

And love needs rescue from the DNA geneticists with their elevation to romantic preeminence the sense of smell, with the poetically named "histo-incompatibility" theory—the scratch 'n' sniff theory of love that argues that the nose knows all. Erotic—and romantic—attraction is all a matter of the ability to sniff out the olfactory spectrum of a potential mate's immune system, the "antigen palette." And to home in like bloodhounds on those whose spectra are most *incompatible*—and thus can supply missing antigens in potential offsprings' blended genome. And this sniffing can translate to, triggers, profound feelings of love.

And love needs rescue from the neo-Marxist dialectical materialists of eros such as Catherine Hakim, the British sociologist who made a splash around the turn of the century with her "preference theory," which argued that women make romantic choices based mainly on monetary calculation, and which some critics have called a Marxist update of Jane Austen. In any case, Hakim's "erotic capital" theory of mating reduces feminine allure to a rapidly depreciating currency. All relationships, then, are not matters of attraction so much as transactions.

And love needs rescue from Michel Houellebecq, one of its early enemies, the often brilliant but deeply cynical French novelist who spoke of the body as "capital," and sexual attraction as a commodity in the globalized economy. Although, in what seems like a change of heart, Houellebecq now also calls out the materialists as enemies of love. Although he verges on denying love exists anymore. Here he is in a *Paris Review* interview:

INTERVIEWER What is your concept of the possibility of love between a man and a woman?

HOUELLEBECQ I'd say that the question whether love still exists plays the same role in my novels as the question of God's existence in Dostoyevsky.

INTERVIEWER Love may no longer exist?

HOUELLEBECQ That's the question of the moment.

INTERVIEWER And what is causing its disappearance?

HOUELLEBECQ The materialist idea that we are alone,
we live alone, and we die alone. That's not very
compatible with love.

"The question of the moment." That's what I want to write about. I was struck at first just by how notable it is that one of the foremost novelistic diagnosticians of postmodern sexual culture felt the real mystery—"the question of the moment"!—was love, and was unashamed to ask the kind of question poets, philosophers, and lovers had been asking for millennia: Is it real? Was it ever? Will it disappear under the onslaught of its enemies?

But you will note in acceding to its potential "disappearance" that Houellebecq is at least conceding that it once existed and that such existence was something of importance—phenomenal, not epiphenomenal.

And once again, it's "the question of the moment." Materialism, determinism, scientism (not science itself) has called it into question. The question of the moment. The mystery of the ages. Meanwhile more enemies: Love needs rescue from a digitizing culture that has anachronized the pen and paper love letter in favor of the text and the sext and the dick pic. Tinder and Grindr. Now chatbots. No, I'm not a (complete) Luddite, but I know the difference that sending or receiving a real, non-virtual love letter can make.

And love needs rescue from porn, which seeks to monetize ("the money shot") eros. (Something that has been true long before: Columbia's Steven Marcus noticed the significance of the euphemism for ejaculation in Victorian porn: "spending.")

Not that eros is always or solely equivalent to love. The distinctions among love, eros, lust, and desire deserve to be preserved. And further refined. I personally, I should say, have never downloaded online porn (NSA can back me up on that), which I find anti-sexual.

And something else I know intimately, from years of irritated reading of literary theory: Love needs rescue from the literary theorists who "historicize" it into a "construct," a "product" that "instantiates the hegemony." Even worse are the literary theorists who claim that literature "invented" love. Again, love becomes a secondary effect.

And though I'll have more to say about them, I should note that there's at least one countervailing force in this multidisciplinary attack on love: the LGBTQ+ marriage movement—LGBTQ+ rights in general. Like many of us of all sexual orientations, I was heart-struck by the stories and pictures of same-sex couples at long last allowed to marry. They weren't (most of them) doing it for the health benefits ("civil unions" would serve in most states). It was clear from their facial expressions that they were doing it for love, they were doing it to celebrate and consecrate their love in a way that made many straight couples envious. In a way that should make the reductionists who deny love hide their heads in shame.

Like many New Yorkers in the eighties and nineties, I was a hopeless witness to the suffering and death from HIV/AIDS of people I knew, if not well. And witness, too, to the love for each other, known and unknown, that the epidemic inspired. There was nothing more real than that love. Allow me to mention just one person whose deathbed I visited, a fellow named Duncan Stalker, who was my editor at *Manhattan, Inc.* magazine, and the circle of love he inspired.

Nothing could make up for what happened, but the marriage

victory was at least a token, and perhaps a sign that love is love, married or not, same or different sex—something I've always believed.

It was literature that inspired the particular turn this book has taken—the poets versus the reductionists. The ancient debate was a question raised afresh for me when I found myself attempting to puzzle out Philip Larkin's poem "An Arundel Tomb," especially that mysterious, provocative last line: "what will survive of us is love." It's a question I delve into further in the later chapters of this book—the materiality, the ethereality, and the survival of love, all of which the reductionists reject. All of which led me to decide to write my defense of love in the spirit of Sir Philip Sidney's "An Apologie for Poetrie," his late-sixteenth-century response to the reductionists of his age, the philistines and puritans who dismissed as superficial and trivial that which they feared as a threat: the unsanctified spell of poetry.

No, Sir Philip said to those who would reduce poetry to a lesser form, to frippery, to unserious rhetorical décor at best, the stanzas of Satan at the worst—poetry could be as serious as death. Could not be tied down and quantified by the laws of nature and science. It was "an other nature." Not superficial, more profound. "An other nature," a level, a dimension, both higher, and deeper, not capable of being anatomized in body or reduced to logic in mind.

Sir Philip was the author of the love-drunk 108-sonnet-long sequence *Astrophil and Stella* (c. 1590), certainly an influence on Shakespeare's later sonnet collection. Though it is a little more over the top. I can never forget the moment when Sir Philip's poet goes into a fit of jealousy after his coy mistress tells him how much her dog loves her. "That cur!" he exclaims, "knows nothing / I burn, I burn for love." Foolish but touching. Love can warm the heart, yes, but it's not love if it can't burn it. Set it ablaze. Reduce it to ashes.

And there is something about the defense of love that is analogous to the defense of poetry. Both poetry and love are possessed of powers, powers beyond the control of church and state. Both create a realm capable of a sinister allure, a dizzying distraction that could tempt the vulnerable away from their true purpose in life: contemplation of the damnation of their souls, which should be all their study. It was more than fear of poetry, it was the terror of pleasure. The treachery of beauty: not only skin deep but sin deep.

Today love has a different spectrum of enemies than poetry had. But all with the same aim: Cut it down to size, nail that butterfly to the specimen case, etherize it on a table. Put it out of its misery. Do a postmortem on its corpse. Deny love any ontological primacy. Reduce its baffling complexity to elementary science, to an iron chain of causality, a collection of four neurochemicals, the algorithms of determinism. Reduce its sometimes unfathomable inexplicability to mundane solubility—a crossword puzzle.

Of course, a defense of love must go on the offensive as well, and will probably be offensive to some at times. I'm thinking of my discussion in my chapter on "Love in the Age of Oral Sex," and novelist Sheila Heti's thought-provoking aphorism: "We live in an age of really great blow-job artists. Every era has its art form. The nineteenth century, I know was tops for the novel."

But by going on offense, I mean I want to do more than debunk the debunkers who say that love per se, love actually, love factually, does not exist. In the following chapters, I seek to clarify the questions raised by Philip Larkin about love: If it "survives," just how and where—and for how long—does it exist? Is it a cloud that brightens and darkens the sky and then blows away?

To return to literature for a moment, the other love of my life, almost on a par with the love of good women, I will address the other enemies of love, but first I really must address...

A Digression on the Mad Delusion of Inventionism

This is closer to home for me. For years now I have followed the way literary theorists are recurrently drawn to the intellectually reductionist enterprise of "inventionism."

The persistent argument is made that the language of love is what has actually created love, that love was an invention of love rhetoric, that the rhetoric precedes the romance. It's astonishing how prevalent this reductive tactic of "inventionism" has become in the academic world. Indeed, it was an aspect of literary love-reductionism that changed my life. I've alluded to it in the past, but it has a special relevance to the origin of this book.

It happened at a seminar at Yale graduate school in the seventies. I had a graduate fellowship in English lit and was invited to a special seminar in which the graduate adjunct read a much buzzed-about paper on the subject of Chaucer's "Parlement of Foules." I know—probably not on your bedside table, a little difficult to get through the fourteenth-century Middle English, but once you do it's an enchanting extended fantasia: a debate about the meaning of love, about the very questions I've raised, a debate conducted with great classical erudition among some very articulate creatures of the air (birds if you please). It was a kind of avian love contest; the version I read at Yale (with great difficulty) gains from the archaicism of the fourteenth-century Middle English.

But the author of the buzzed-about seminar paper sought to

convince us that it was naïve to think that Chaucer's poem was about love at all. No, no, no. It was really about "the making of poetry," a then fashionable English department way of refashioning old texts into new doctoral dissertations.

At the close of this performance, I had the naïve temerity to ask what was clearly seen as a foolish question: What was Chaucer's attitude toward his ostensible subject, love itself? Love actually?

I could sense the uneasiness of the other graduate students around me at this faux pas. I recall, the scholar hung his head sadly—why try, why try?—and lifted his countenance to treat me to a mildly pitying sneer, took a draw on his Gauloise, and gestured Gallicly to the air with nicotine-stained fingers. Exhaling with the dramatized existential exhaustion of enduring the concerns of the simpleminded, he said, "But love is so uninteresting compared to the making of poetry."

Don't get me wrong. I like the discussion of the making of poetry (or I recalled thinking it an ingenious complexification at the time. After all, I'm an English major nerd).

But the bored, reductive dismissal of love crystallized my feeling that I was not meant to be a graduate student whose only future was to drive love out of more texts. I was out of there. The "invention of love" trope had become the new guise of the denial of love.

Inventionism. Name a phenomenon one thought was part of human nature, and some academic will have found a specific century, even a specific decade, usually a specific little-known text, in which it was "invented." Thus giving themselves credit for the invention of the invention. I devoted a chapter of my book on Shakespeare controversies to attempting to demystify and debunk the rank sophistry of Harold Bloom's claim that "Shakespeare invented the human." (Apparently something Sophocles and Homer neglected to do.) But however ludicrous, even as a hyperbolic metaphor, that the claim is, it has had a hardy vapidity that does discredit to Shakespeare's authentic uniqueness (he did invent "an other nature" at the very moment Sir Philip Sidney coined the phrase).

Of course, there's Michel Foucault and his cohorts who ignited a still ongoing controversy over whether both sex and gender were invented by language. And at this very moment as I was rewriting this passage and I was idly scrolling down the excellent 3 Quarks Daily website I came upon this: "How the Victorians Invented the Future." From a book that made the claim that "before the Victorian age the future was rarely regarded as a different place from the present." Oh, please. Yes, Jules Verne, sure, but what about Thomas More's *Utopia*? Virtually all of Renaissance English literature (including Shakespeare) is about the contemplation of the Greek and Roman past, historical and poetical. And if there's a past there's a future: the present. A "different place." But those useless doctoral dissertations don't write themselves and love has not been spared this smug donnish game. Oh, no, love has been a prime target of the inventionists. With so many claimants for the alleged invention, there really ought to be a Patent Office of Love.

Not necessarily the first, but the first claim about the invention of love I encountered was in reading C.S. Lewis's 1936 tome, *The Allegory of Love*. This book attempted to make the case that romantic love was an "invented" emotion, specifically an invention circa the thirteenth-century Provençal troubadour poets and their versified rulebook *The Lays of Courtly Love*. ("Lays," I hope I need not remind you, is a somewhat antiquated word for verse tales. No sniggering in the back!)

Not that one should disregard the Provençal troubadour lyricists! No, their claim that the only true love was unconsummated adulterous love merits attention if not allegiance. But they didn't "invent" love, even that variant.

And for the Christian believer C. S. Lewis's *Allegory of Love*, this was a kind of bait and switch: Romantic love was just an "allegory" anyway, a figure of speech for that Higher Love, the Love of God all should aspire to. Terrestrial love was, as usual, something secondary, something one got past. If one was lucky, learning the limitations of earthly love was a step along the path to real love, spiritual love.

The C.S. Lewis claim of a thirteenth-century invention of love actually ascribes a rather late date in the inventionist pantheon. I found Tom Stoppard's play *The Invention of Love* thrilling, all the more so because (though it often seems forgotten) I think the play regards "invention" ironically—yet paradoxically affirms love in all its uninvented, non-ironic nonbinary earnestness and comedy.

Stoppard's protagonist (or éminence grise) in the play, the late-nineteenth-century poet and classics pedant A. E. Housman, claims in the play that love was really "invented" nearly a thousand years before C. S. Lewis's Provençal troubadours. Housman argues, as if daringly, that love was invented by Catullus, the Latin lyric (and epic) poet who lived in the century before Christ. Yes, Catullus, that brilliant poet of the pain of love—"Odi et Amo" ("I hate and I love"). Catullus, Housman claimed, invented the love poem, which in turn "invented" love.

It's a claim I would like to believe since I sacrificed many headachy hours translating Catullus's elegantly twisted Latin syntax, whilst loving his anguished and acerbic obscenity. ("Irrumabo"!) But please: His "invention" was predated centuries before by the Song of Songs, that biblical text of eros, and by Sappho, and even Sappho (c. 500 BC) was likely predated by Archilochus.

Ah, Archilochus (c. 650 BC), we hardly know ye, only fragments remain from later classical manuscripts (it was he to whom was attributed the aphorism concerning the hedgehog and the fox: "The fox knows many things, the hedgehog knows one big thing"). But he is deservedly legendary (well, among a few classicists) for having written such a bitter, wrenchingly bereft, lost-love poem, a poem so powerful it caused the woman who was denied him—and her father—both (!) to kill themselves. Or so the story goes.

Now, that's a love poem. That's a lost-love poem. That's a poem that would have the wizards of Nashville weepers crying in their beer. The only country song fit to compete, I'd say, would be George Jones's masterly portrait of a man's grief for a woman who left him, decades ago: "He Stopped Loving Her Today." (Stopped loving her today, because he *died*.) But even Archilochus did not "invent" love.

Still—let's be serious, academics—did language and rhetoric really "invent" emotions such as love and romance? It sounds sophisticated to say it, but it may just be sophistry. And, needless to say, it's popular among male academics to look down one's nose at the idea that love has an independent, non–rhetorically induced existence. Because if romance were "real" in any meaningful sense, it might cause them to question the choice to spend their lives in dusty seminar rooms. Again, the enemies of love must reduce it to a secondary product, deny it independent ontology or esthetic, ecstatic primacy.

I'd almost forgotten that onetime staple of twentieth-century academic inventionism, Denis de Rougement's *Love in the Western World*, which subscribes to the Provençal thesis, until I came across a posting on a Nabokov LISTSERV that recalled Lionel Trilling's invocation of de Rougement.

Trilling, a mid-century literary critical demigod—who was wrestling somewhat obtusely with Nabokov's attitude toward love in *Lolita*—wrote that the book's subject matter "makes it unique in my experience of contemporary novels. If our fiction gives accurate testimony, love has disappeared from the western world, just as Denis de Rougement said it would. The contemporary novel can tell us about sex, and about sexual communion, and about mutuality, and about the strong fine relationships that grow up between men and women; and it can tell us about marriage. But about love, which was once one of its chief preoccupations, it can tell us nothing at all." (And come to think of it, can it tell us much about "strong, fine, relationships" at all?) Does it not leave some (nonbinary) relationships out entirely?

Literature itself as an enemy of Love! And the totalizing belief that if love has disappeared from Western literature, it must mean that "Love has disappeared from the western world!" Can that be true? Already? If one subscribes to one or another form of inventionism, one must be prepared to believe that such a fragile construct, such a secondary downstream effect as Love, could disappear.

While I can't help but agree with Trilling's dismissal of de Rougement's imperious prediction of the end of love after its brief Provençal flowering, there is certainly more to say on the question of love in the contemporary novel—and in the contemporary world.

Sex as an Enemy of Love

For instance—not to let the literary world off the hook—Bad Sex Writing can be implicated in the reductionist death of love. With all the sweaty, strained metaphors for body parts that attempt to rise to the level of literature and mainly make one embarrassed to ever have had sex—or anything that could be so badly verbalized—before. Or again. That's what I initially thought after getting a poor (male) intern from one of my NYU classes to assemble for me ten years' worth of the notorious London *Literary Review*'s Bad Sex Writing Prize's short list of egregious literary erotica. Reading one hundred bad descriptions of sex in a row can put you off sex. Not to mention love (which rarely is mentioned).

For those who wish a taste of what is considered state-of-the-art bad sex writing, I present the two winners of the 2019 *Literary Review* bad sex award. (The judges were unable to decide on just one winner and so named two writers.)

First there is:

Katsuro moaned as a bulge formed beneath the material of his kimono, a bulge that Miyuki seized, kneaded, massaged, squashed and crushed. With the fondling, Katsuro's penis and testicles became one single mound that rolled around beneath the grip of her hand. Miyuki felt as though she was manipulating a small monkey that was curling up its paws.

> [from *The Office of Gardens and Ponds* by Didier Decoin
> (MacLehose Press)]

And then there is this:

She was burning hot and the heat was in him. He looked down on her perfect black slenderness. Her eyes were ravenous. Like his own they were fire and desire. More than torrid, more than tropical: They two were riding the Equator. They embraced as if with violent holding they could weld the two of them one.

> [from *Pax* by John Harvey (Holland House Press)]

But then I came across an insightful defense of Bad Sex Writing by the estimable Judith Shulevitz, who argued in *The New York Times Book Review* that the sneers of the Bad Sex Writing nabobs would lead to the extirpation of something valuable: all experimentation in sexual writing (aside from pornography) in literature nearly a century after the courts had licensed us to read Lawrence, Joyce, and Updike. Writers are still learning. They must, Ms. Shulevitz says, unlearn Lawrence and relearn Joyce.

Still, my belief is that even the putative superiority of Molly Bloom's soliloquy is undermined by the fact that it is entirely a male writer's attempt at least at a woman's inner voice ventriloquized into describing what it's like to surrender to love and sex simultaneously. A woman's voice makes it much different, even in, say, Edith Wharton's "Beatrice Palmato." Do you know it?

It was my American Studies professor at Yale, R. W. B. Lewis, who became Wharton's biographer and found the porn—a typescript overlooked before—in a trove of her papers. Those who think of Wharton as a purely delicate artist of refinement will be shocked at "Beatrice Palmato," a long short-story-length piece of frank though uninspired pornographic prose, with what turns out to be a father-daughter relationship as its center (there had been much speculation among Wharton scholars about the nature of her real-life attachment to her actual father). There are some Wharton-esque euphemisms for sexual organs, and it climaxes, yes, in a stylized description of coitus. Lewis reprinted it as an appendix to his massive biography; it has since been accepted with some embarrassment into the Wharton canon as genuine.

Still, it was not a clumsy male description from the outside of a woman's body. Not the grim silent (mostly male) and mainly self-congratulatory exterior descriptions and contorted analogies from animal nature (many sleek seals) that constitute most Bad Sex Writing.

All of which raises the question of the existence of Good Sex Writing and the even more difficult question: Is there such a thing as explicitly erotic Good Writing About Love (Not Just Sex)? The self-satisfaction of Bloom's (Joyce's) fantasy, which few men are willing to point out: It was Bloom as Molly or Joyce as Bloom as Molly. There was no Molly there but male conceptions of Molly's orgasm, her love.

I believe it took cinema at last to give us at least a half-convincing glimpse of erotic love (as opposed to porn) where words fail. But first I want to raise what I feel certain will be a controversial question: Has "good" sex become too good?

Has sex itself become a subtle but powerful enemy of love? Has sex become too good for its own good? This thought crossed my mind when I read the fascinating, I think deliberately provocative, not necessarily ironic aforementioned statement about oral sex from the controversial literary novelist Sheila Heti.

Recall what she said: "We live in an age of really great blow-job artists. Every era has its art form. The nineteenth century, I know was tops for the novel." That last sentence suggests irony, that she was saying this tongue in cheek, so to speak. It could be that she wasn't making the remark at the expense of other arts and artists, literary, cinematic, musical, and visual. She was just saying that none of them brought something new, a new kind of artistry, to the party recently; none of them exemplified the zeitgeist the way oral sex did in its privileging of pure pleasure.

Even if it's satiric hyperbole calling it an art, one could make a case for it. As someone whose adult life has been nearly coterminous with the evolution of what I've proposed to call "The Age of Oral Sex," one could become aware of what might be called a "learning curve" on the part of all genders. And if one were otherwise at a loss, one could make the comparison between the inscriptions made by the nib of an artist's pen—think Japanese calligraphy paintings, or Pollock's frenzied jazz adagios in paint, or the exquisitely erotic improvisatory licks of tenor sax virtuosi, and—you can see where I'm going here—the delicate tracery of a tongue on a "canvas" of nerve and skin. If not art, it's at least artisanal. No longer just an act, but an exquisitely evocative performance art.

Indeed, the quality of the act depends not merely on physical technique but on the actor—on the successful impersonation of sincerity and enthusiasm, that may be key to it. It's more than a matter of nerve endings. It's the simulacrum of sincerity. Faking sincerity is to the Age of Great Blowjob Artists what faking orgasms was to the previous age. Virtuoso acting: Perhaps the greatest art of all.

Love has to be very hot and strong to compete with a readily available arsenal of such exquisite artisanal arousal. It is my impression that in the early years of the Age of Oral Sex, monogamous or married love often didn't survive the competition with next-level sex. Certainly, it would be a better world if it always did, but it often doesn't. Or you could say, it really wasn't love.

And it's true (I'm told) that there has been a quantum leap in the art involved and an exponential increase in the pleasure derived. What was once an act that derived its excitement from its transgressiveness and the controversy that erupted over *Portnoy's Complaint* now has transcended transgressiveness to some realm of the senses many had not imagined before. A whole "other nature," as Sir Philip Sidney might say.

And the fact that it's available, even if not easily available, makes genuine love and fidelity more vulnerable to challenge. Others would argue that it could take love to new levels as well. The powerful sincerity of the genuine loving gaze is hard to deny.

Crimes of Passion

When I say I've written about love before, yes, I've written about love *in* Shakespeare and I've written a five-hundred-page book, *The Shakespeare Wars,* about the love *of* Shakespeare one finds in the most impassioned scholars, actors, and directors, and their clashes. And I've devoted close study to "The Phoenix and the Turtle," perhaps Shakespeare's most mystical, metaphysical love poem of all ("Turtle" is short for turtledove—not the slimy mud crawler). Which a book such as this shouldn't hurry by. Few know "Phoenix," fewer can figure it out. Centuries of scholars and readers have sought to understand its enigmatic recondite mystical language. One quatrain at its heart in particular:

So they lov'd, as love in twain
Had the essence but in one;
Two distincts, division none:
Number there in love was slain.

Mind-bending, is it not? But worth thinking about. Particularly "Number there in love was slain," which I came to believe means that love as two ("twain")—even love as a oneness—could not express the intense magnitude of this love. No oneness, no twoness; number itself was "slain" by the attempt to express what love at its peak, this love, was about.

I've written about love in the Metaphysical poets, in Donne

and in George Herbert—"Love (III)"!—and love in Sappho, in Philip Larkin and other poets. And I've written about love in country music. Surprisingly often, in fact: When I look back on it, I've spent a lot of time talking about love and love songs with four of the best C&W singer-songwriters, Emmylou Harris, Willie Nelson, Rosanne Cash, Rodney Crowell. (They are the true savants; they are *our* Metaphysical poets.) I believe that country music may be the last redoubt in art of unashamed demonstrative love in our culture (well, there is Rihanna's "We Found Love").

And I've written about love in the lives of others. Though when I think back about it now, most of these stories have ended (or begun) in murder, madness, suicide, or overdose. Love as a curse. Love as a crime of passion.

I've written about Angela Davis, the brilliant Marxist political theorist, and her involvement with charismatic convicted murderer George Jackson, a prisoner in San Quentin's "Adjustment Center" (I visited that hellhole) and the alleged kidnap/murder conspiracy that ended in her acquittal on all charges. I've written about the murder of blueblood painter Mary Pinchot Meyer, whose affair with President Kennedy unleashed a raft of conspiracy theories which my reporting did not bear out although the affair involved a cast of CIA characters, including her close friend, master counterspy James Jesus Angleton. Ms. Meyer had been called "the Lady Ottoline of Camelot." She'd been dragged off the C&O canal jogging path and shot a year after JFK was killed in Dallas. No connection beyond lost love.

Then there was "the most beautiful woman in the world," which is what *Vogue* once called British actress Sarah Miles. And her stalkerish journalist consort, David Whiting, the Fitzgerald wannabe found dead in Ms. Miles's motel room under mysterious circumstances in the bleak desert outpost called Gila Bend, Arizona. "He thought I was his personal cunt," was the tender way Sarah Miles described his love to me.

And there was the strange double death of the identical twin gynecologists—"Dead Ringers," I called it (before David Cronenberg's film of that name)—which I saw as a kind of love story, too. Oh, right: Nancy Spungen, the girlfriend of the Sex Pistols' Sid Vicious, found dead in the Chelsea Hotel. I was on it, investigating the role of the great love of Sid's life, a woman known to jealous rivals in Sex Pistols circles as "Nauseating Nancy." (It was true love, vicious and nauseating as it sounds. Or, alternatively, a mutual addiction to fame, love, and heroin.)

I spent considerable time investigating the death of a crack-murder nabob in the ravaged neighborhoods around Bed-Stuy in eighties Brooklyn. Yes, some of these might seem tabloid-ish, but I sought not to treat them that way. I sought to find the novelistic noir "double indemnity" nature of the love that lay beneath the crimes.

That's what tabloid stories (not celebrity "famous for being famous" stories) do. Take you to places inside the human heart where no cardiologist can go. Almost all the Greek myths were tabloidish, were they not? Adultery, cheating, rape, apparently occupying most of the time on Mount Olympus where, as the tabloid headlines might put it, VENUS NETTED IN NAKED LOVE TRAP BY LAME HUBBY. And the *Iliad* opens with AGAMEMNON AND ACHILLES IN SEX-SLAVE SMACK-DOWN. Without adultery there would be no novel, no tabloids, no Homer and Aeschylus, either.

And even though I debunked the most salacious, conspiracy-theory versions of their relationship in my book *Explaining Hitler*, I nonetheless felt it necessary to investigate the pecu-liar obsession of Adolf Hitler with his nineteen-year-old half-niece Geli Raubal, who was found shot through the heart in her bedroom in Hitler's Munich apartment in 1930. I felt a need to debunk the murder and perversion rumors in favor of suicide. Though he could have driven her to take her life (wasn't Hitler bad enough?). Yes, it raises difficult questions about the limits of what we talk about when we talk about love. Can we conceive of a Hitler in love? Is this the final forbidden obscenity?

Or a subject worthy of Socratic dialogue: It's not just what it might tell us about Hitler, it's what it might tell us about love. Does it truly conquer all? The fateful, cruel indiscriminateness in all these stories that is the other side of the soaring euphoria. Love itself the enemy of love. "Amor vincit omnia," as the Wife of Bath's locket proclaimed.

Thinking about it, I suppose that is why I've focused on crimes of passion more than others. I suppose I've come to believe one knows more of another human being from knowing what they'll do for love in extremis. One knows more about oneself. "I love therefore I am" may be truer than Descartes's formula. And I should mention, I suppose, I have been in love myself. I am in love as I write this. Perhaps that is one reason why I've sought to write a defense of love. But there is more to the story of why.

CHAPTER 2

Why?

W HY SHOULD I CARE about the growing cultural phenomenon that attempts the reduction of mysteries such
as art and love—even Evil—to numbers and algorithms? I think
you might want to know the answer to the question *Why*? Why
am I so concerned about this particular devaluation of our culture? Of our very consciousness? Of our humanity—as little
more than solutions to complex equations?

And I'd like to offer an account of the evolution, the origin
story of my concern.

It's something I only realized in retrospect, but, more than
anything, I think it goes back to a struggle, a decade-long literary battle over a seventeenth-century poem called "A Funeral
Elegy," which, for a benighted decade, was falsely attributed to
Shakespeare with the crucial assistance of a crude Big Data digital database that its inventor called SHAXICON.

My defense of love from the reductionists can be traced back
to my defense of Shakespeare from SHAXICON.

I won't devote much time to ridiculing the ludicrous bad sci-fi
nomenclature of "SHAXICON." But I have much reason to ridicule the *use* of SHAXICON and why it helped convince virtually the entire Shakespeare scholar establishment in the United

States (and much of the anglophone world) of the validity of the misbegotten attribution of that "funeral elegy" to Shakespeare. I've chronicled the affair in my Shakespeare book but have more to say about what it tells us about the flawed and false reverence for the Big Data number crunching that has eaten up the intellects of individuals and institutions devoted to the humanities, to the quantification and digitization of Mystery. Of poetic beauty, of evil as well as death and love. It is here we find a clue to the origin of my anger, my alarm at the consequences for the culture at large.

To begin at the beginning, there was that poem, that "Funeral Elegy," dated 1612, four years before Shakespeare's death, written by an author who identified himself with nothing but the initials "W.S." It was at a time when Shakespeare had largely absented himself from the public stage for bucolic retirement in his hometown village of Stratford-upon-Avon. All the more easily subject to impersonation in the chaotic book and pamphlet sellers' markets of St. Paul's Churchyard in London.

If the author had been hoping by use of those initials to seduce readers into believing it was *that* W.S., he had failed: The poem had been largely ignored by the public and gathered dust on the shelves of Oxford's renowned Bodleian Library for four centuries.

Until the fateful moment at the end of the twentieth century when a Vassar professor took it under his wing and tenderly fed it into the jaws of SHAXICON, his custom-crafted Big Data base that atomized all the words of Shakespeare's known works in an obscure fashion he never disclosed and, he claimed, proved in some esoteric, misguided way that the "Funeral Elegy"'s words aligned it indisputably with the works of Shakespeare.

Voilà! A "new" work by Shakespeare, one in what were supposedly his own words or voice (not those of a dramatic character), six hundred lines of his voice, pure Shakespearean meditation, his final thoughts on the great mystery of Death.

There had been, and still are, long-running debates among Shakespeareans about the possible provenance of such sketchy stage-plays as *Arden of Faversham* and *A Yorkshire Tragedy* and the well-named *Double Falsehood* (all boldly ushered into the canon by the New Oxford Shakespeare with greater and lesser acceptance).

The debates were most worthy in their focus on just how to define that numinous, indefinable phenomenon of "the Shakespearean." What makes a work "Shakespearean" in ways others lack? Controversies similar to debates over what qualities qualify an emotion as Love—is it a numinous feeling or a chemical equation? (Yes, I am attracted to the concept of the "numinous," one I first gleaned from Kant's distinction between "noumena" and "phenomena" in *The Critique of Pure Reason*. "Phenomena" he defined with some certainty as those qualities discernible by Reason and the Senses; the former, the noumena, everything else, invisible, undefinable, ungraspable by Reason and the Senses— the dark matter of consciousness, that which can be conceived but not precisely perceived. Like Love.)

But the SHAXICON "discovery" added a new level to the quest to define "the Shakespearean." Sound the PR siren, as the professor did, thinking he had inserted himself into literary history (along with SHAXICON, who always makes me think of "Robby the Robot" from the sci-fi film *Forbidden Planet* where, according to a somewhat overhyped film poster, he was "The Science Monster That Would Destroy the World").

The professor baited the hook—"new" Shakespeare poem— and all levels of culture, literary to pop to tabloid, swallowed it whole. The white-hot glare of celebrity spotlit him as he was 'coptered down from the quiet Vassar campus in the Hudson River town of Poughkeepsie to the breathlessly waiting broadcast studios of a major network morning show where he preened as a featured guest.

What followed was an even more disturbing scandal at the very heart of the Shakespeare scholarship establishment: All three respected Collected Works editions of Shakespeare raced to stop the presses so they could jam the six hundred lines of the "Elegy" and some compliant publicity-hungry profs' hosannas into their forthcoming new editions of Shakespeare.

Oh, the glamour of Big Data meeting Big Poet! ("We have the 'new' Shakespeare!") Shakespeare meditating about the mystery of Death so close to his own! And there was almost complete silence and complicity from the entire remainder of the Shakespeare establishment disgracefully intimidated by the digital claims of this Big Data atrocity.

At least that's what I called it as, almost alone, I dissented and denied the attribution whole cloth as a fake or a forgery or just a Big Dumb Big Data mistake in a series of essays in the *New York Observer*.

It was shocking to me, the silence and compliance of serious academics in the face of Big Data's dictum, when I believed, as an unaffiliated human being who had immersed himself in a lifetime's study of the words and works of Shakespeare, that I was witnessing the academic world I left take the attribution seriously, making fools of themselves.

And I think that shock alerted me to similar instances emblematic of what was happening not merely to Shakespeare, with this knee-jerk obeisance to Big Data, but to more and more aspects of culture, to poetry, to death, and to Love.

To all the other Mysteries that were victims of the number-crunching appetites of the Big Data manipulators. I saw it happen on my Shakespeare scholars LISTSERV, where weeks would be taken up with rival algorithmic distillations of what was or wasn't "Shakespearean" based on pseudoscientific concepts like "word adjacency."

Perhaps I should give you at least a brief sample of the sad botch of the "Elegy" SHAXICON called "Shakespearean." I don't want you to think my antagonism was mere nostalgia for the good old days of the humanities, but rather an indictment of the reckless foolishness of a disturbing aspect of contemporary culture. Not a rejection of modernity as a whole.

Anyway, here's a sample of the terrible twisted verse that the Professor and his pal SHAXICON claimed was "Shakespearean":

"A Funeral Elegy"

Since time, and his predestinated end,
Abridged the circuit of his hopeful days,
Whiles both his youth and virtue did intend
The good endeavors of deserving praise,
What memorable monument can last
Whereon to build his never-blemished name
But his own worth, wherein his life was graced...
Sith as that ever he maintained the same?
Oblivion in the darkest day to come,
When sin shall tread on merit in the dust,
Cannot rase out the lamentable tomb
Of his short-lived deserts; but still they must,
Even in the hearts and memories of men,
Claim fit respect, that they, in every limb
Remembering what he was, with comfort then
May pattern out one truly good, by him.

For he was truly good, if honest care
Of harmless conversation may commend
A life free from such stains as follies are
Ill recompensed only in his end.
Nor can the tongue of him who loved him least
(If there can be minority of love
To one superlative above the rest
Of many men in steady faith) reprove
His constant temper

That's only the first 5 percent of this incomprehensible verbiage. Congratulations to whomever read that through with mind left intact. But you have 575 more lines of this sedulous bilge left to go. Think of a real Shakespearean funeral elegy: Mark Antony's for Caesar, by comparison.

At the heart of my objection was something I had taken away from a discussion with the great British Shakespeare scholar Frank Kermode, who wrote an impassioned essay about why it was important to allow that Shakespeare could write badly at times—if we wished to give him credit for the far larger number of moments of transcendent greatness.

Yes, I said in my essays on the wretched "Elegy," Shakespeare *was* capable of writing badly, but when it came to the six-hundred-line "Funeral Elegy," not *that* badly, not at such great unvaried awful length.

To make a long story short, after years of contention, mostly me against the approbation or complicit silence of the academic Shakespearean establishment, I was finally vindicated when UK Shakespeare savant Sir Brian Vickers and a French scholar were able to discover the identity of the actual author of the awful poem beyond doubt, even extracting a grudging concession from the Vassar professor.

It was recalling this struggle against the digitizing reductionists who claimed to be able to define numerically a numinous quality such as the "Shakespearean" that made me more acutely conscious of what Big Data and its cohorts might be doing to an even more numinous ungraspable quality such as Love.

Love, I believe, is still a mystery, but I thought it worth examining those scientists and pseudoscientists who felt they had solved it. And as I thought more on the subject, some of my other related investigations were recalled to me: the "Elegy" controversy was not the first time I had defended a fundamental mystery against those who believed they had a simpleminded solution to it.

In my book *Explaining Hitler*, to cite one example, I spent time examining "solutions" to the mystery of Evil as embodied in Hitler. There were, for instance, the dueling psychoanalysts (at a time when Freudians still posed as "scientists"). Alice Miller, celebrated Swiss Freudian who claimed she had solved the mystery of Hitler's evil by tracing it to the alleged "fact" that his father, Alois Hitler, had beaten young Adolf, perhaps because Alois feared his son had inherited "Jewish blood" on his mother's side. (Not true, just stupid on Alois's and Alice's part.)

On the other hand, there was the German (later American) psychoanalyst Erich Fromm, who denied Hitler's father's culpability for the mystery of Hitler's evil—Fromm's Alois was a gentle beekeeper—and instead Fromm claimed it was Hitler's *mother*, meek Klara, who overprotected young Adolf and developed in him a syndrome Fromm made up out of whole cloth (later to be woefully overused), one he called "malignant narcissism."

Both couldn't be right. Sure, put a scientific-sounding official *DSM* name to Hitler's evil and we can feel it's been taken care of, that once "explained" there's less to fear. (Or more to fear that that explanation will lead to exculpation—"to understand all is to forgive all.") Thus, shrinks of all varieties sought to validate their own theoretical frameworks by demonstrating that they alone could pull the sword from the stone of Hitler.

Eventually, after submitting a paper on the simpleminded hubristic pseudoscience of evil to the Cambridge University Fellowship I'd been admitted to, I published an essay called "Rescuing Evil" (from the reductionists). Just as I now feel defending love requires a book-length rescue of love.

I can't help but mention perhaps the most emblematic reductionist solution to the mystery of Hitler's evil—the mosquito bite theory. The one that traced it all to his infection by a tiny insect bite from a mosquito that transmitted the epileptic encephalitis endemic in the Great War trenches. A syndrome of increasing psychopathy that a peer-reviewed paper I dug up, published in the late 1920s, claimed were "late sequelae"—years later—of an infected mosquito bite. Sequelae that included psychopathic symptoms Hitler evinced as he came closer and closer to power. All the evil to come, generated from a tiny mosquito bite? Science says yes. Well, *some* science.

But even before that, I discovered a fallacious use of what was once science—at least to the Nazi "scientists" in Germany—the pseudoscience of eugenics, which had spread from an origin in the United States to Europe and eventually wormed its serpentine way back to the United States, into the elevated precincts of the most elite Ivy League colleges in the form of the "nude posture photo" that reduced every human to a three-digit number.

I could go on: One of my favorite examples of the numerological conversion of the noumenal was—still is—the almost universal acceptance of Elisabeth Kübler-Ross's pseudoscientific "Five Stages" of death and/or dying and grief, which had nothing but a sketchy anecdotal basis for its original use by hospice and ICU nurses to quiet dying patients down so they *would* "go gentle into that good night" (rather than follow Dylan Thomas's preference to defy that mandate and "rage, rage against the dying of the light"). And yet the aura of scientific validity has made the progress to quiet acceptance a kind of moral imperative.

But what about the "why" question? Why did I take it so personally? Yes, I'm still angry—why hide it?

I felt irritation, even outrage, when I became aware of the numerological neuroscience reductionist fallacies, when I saw them surfacing in the pop science, the pop pseudoscience of love. Unlike the postural ratios or the temperament of Hitler's father, I took the digitization of love personally, as I did my lifelong love of Shakespeare.

And I have felt *offended* by the sheer foolishness, the category mistake, the arrogance, the hubris of the pretenders to science who assert the ability to divine the nature of one's most intimate feelings, feelings that define the self as something more than chemistry sets. Perhaps because of their pretense that they could solve the mystery of myself, which for a lifetime had eluded me. Especially when these theories sought to reduce something as numinous as love, something as close to my heart.

Still, the so-called science of love could at least provide—as you'll see—almost endless laughable entertainment value on close examination. Helen Fisher's "trait constellations," for instance, the latest "scientific" model from the single most famous popularizer of "love science" in America.

Yes, when it came down to love, yes, there was something personal about my reaction. I took it personally when hubristic savants of the various persuasions I will unfold here tried to tell me that what I was feeling could be reduced to equations and electron paths and brain chemical conjunctions. It was akin to what I felt when another love of mine, the love of Shakespeare, came under attack by pseudoscience.

I took it personally and I resented it not merely because the "explanations" of love, the attempts to reformulate emotional states into theoretical frameworks, procrustean beds, were so often misguided, but because they were all making claims about my inner being, my emotional life, what made me who I was, what I felt, all without a search warrant beyond an fMRI slide. An invasion of privacy that seemed somehow an obscene voyeuristic intrusion. Obscene because it involved another human being—the person I was in love with—who had become intimately inextricable from who I was.

Love was something I had firsthand experience of—of the beauties and the trials and the tenuous contingencies, the strengths and the fragilities. I didn't want elephantine theorists trampling upon and crushing those things that were so precious and personal to me.

The "Why" question. Why am I so concerned about number crunchers devouring works of mystery and beauty, in particular love? I wrote this book because I have questions, not answers. And I resent those who claim baselessly that they have answers.

Well, I have one answer, as my past investigations of numinous mysteries attest: Love is not an algorithm. Lovers are not walking equations.

But the other question, the haunting question, remains: If not that, then what? If "what will survive of us is love," as Larkin concludes, what is the what?

Through the ages, poets, philosophers, songwriters have

sought to capture the bright elusive butterfly of love, as the cringe-making song has it. But speaking of butterflies, I cannot neglect the strange enigmatic quest Vladimir Nabokov engaged in. A quest more obscure, esoteric, and recondite than the nymphet novel he is famous for, a bitterly controversial and, I think, misunderstood book. (Most readers have ignored the signals he implanted that he was *aware* of the horror of child rape beneath the jeweled prose. And that it was that very contradiction he was anatomizing: the sinister mask of beautiful prose. The flaw may have been that he was content to make the signals—the "analysis" of Dr. John Ray, for instance—*too* ambiguous.)

But Nabokov collected more than nymphets, the scientific term for newly fledged butterflies. More than the nymphets of his fiction (a few too many unfledged young girls for comfort, as Martin Amis, a once fervid admirer, admitted a few years ago after he counted ten out of seventeen Nabokov novels infested with nymphets, as I recall).

Nabokov also collected something more specific to his butterfly obsession, the netted, collected, and dissected results of which could once, but no longer, be seen in the so-called Genitalia Cabinet in Harvard's Museum of Natural History. Permit me a digression here about the contents of the cabinet and their possible significance in regard to love.

It was a cabinet where one could find, preserved and meticulously labeled, hundreds of butterfly phalluses for… I don't know exactly why. Perhaps for Nabokov's "why" question. Another mystery recently described thusly. Nabokov, famed in the world of lepidopterology, the scientific study of butterflies,

focused his classification theory on one specific point: the study of male butterfly genitalia. Invisible to our bare eyes, the butterflies' privates were described by Nabokov as "minuscule sculptural hooks, teeth, spurs, etc.... visible only under a microscope." These specimens would be taken away from each specimen, placed in little vials or on glass plates, and labeled. By doing so, Nabokov could observe new physiognomic differences between identical-looking butterflies and reevaluate their belonging to one species or another. Each specimen was indexed and placed in a small wooden cabinet.

The scientific purpose of these minuscule studies, we're told, was that Nabokov was seeking clues to evolutionary distinctions and differentiations in butterfly species, particularly his favorites, later officially named "Nabokov Blues" by genetic lepidopterists, who ultimately affirmed the validity of the taxonomy behind this singular task.

But one can't help thinking that the long exacting hours Nabokov spent microscopically categorizing the extricated organs were—in some obscure way, like the labor over the minutiae of his efflorescent prose—a labor of love. He might well have been speculating about the mystery of love, its inexplicably "infinite variety," as Shakespeare said of Cleopatra's charms, and its relationship to nature and evolution.

One could even call the genesis of *Lolita* a product of his butterfly genitalia studies and the sinister variations of male desire that floridly disguise lust as love in humans.

He must at some point have asked himself the question "why?" I suspect that the answer is that in all those hours, months, years of gazing at the microscopic characteristics of Lepidoptera genitalia, Nabokov was doing more than making a contribution to science; it was his way of meditating on the mystery of love.

Was Nabokov foolish, a fool for love, if that's what was really going on in the subterranean corridors of his labyrinthine brain?

And am I unwise for spending so much of my time, of my life, cumulatively thinking about the mystery of love? The hours, weeks, months, years, devoted to it. To looking for love, to finding love, to mourning the loss of love, to wondering what this transformative emotion is that I am so easily possessed and obsessed by, to wondering where it's gone when it goes, and to resuming the endless cycle again.

When I study literature as I have, almost as much as love—I believe my superpower is close reading, a skill developed in the Yale English department—I feel I am getting somewhere, I am getting deeper, learning more, discovering new vistas. And yet with love, after an equal or greater amount of close study, I'm not sure I have really made similar progress, but I don't regret a moment. At least I am able to discern the flaws in the theories of those who think they have figured it out. That is what I feel, why I've written this book, to defend love from pseudoscience and sophistry.

The why question. Why have I spent so much of my life on . . . what, exactly? On this elusive enigmatic feeling, on acquiring it and mourning its loss. Why do some ignite its flame and others, indeed often the same ones, trigger it and then tamp it out? Why has love as opposed to merely lust meant so much to me? If I were smarter, I could have put that time into curing cancer or solving the problem of inequality. Or building a phallically shaped rocket ship. Maybe not that.

And yet I will defend all that time as, if not necessarily a noble, an inherently human pursuit, what makes us human rather than Robby the Robots. And so, in subsequent chapters, I will seek to define and defend Love from its enemies. To defend what is human from the anti-human deformations of love.

Is that enough of a why for you? You will certainly find more disclosed in subsequent chapters. Beginning with one of the deepest questions of all: that of consciousness and how it relates to the consciousness of love.

CHAPTER 3

The Hard Problem of Love

"I Was Adored Once"

One thing I think the assault on love by the reductionists does is force those who want to reject the attacks to answer the question: If love cannot be defined or reduced to a molecular or electron-level phenomenon, if it is not the product of chemical or other determinisms, just what is it? What is that "other nature" Sir Philip Sidney would claim for it? And, as I've sought to show in the previous chapter, why do I care? But it's not just me. Just about every song on the Billboard 200 is a love song. I could name hundreds, but I think it's enough to say that almost every single Beatles song is about love in one form or another. B. B. King's "Live at the Regal" changed my life. And then there are rom-com books and movies. And all without exception ask that question: What is it?

In this regard I suppose I should confess that in addition to having written about love, in addition to having studied love in literature, in the lab, and in the lives of others, I have been in love. And, perhaps more important, I have been loved. Or so I've been told. (And married once, since you asked.)

And though it may seem a bit melancholic to admit this,

nonetheless, of all Shakespeare's lovers, I identify most closely with Sir Andrew Aguecheek. You may recall Sir Andrew from *Twelfth Night*, a relatively minor character of the sort that, so often in Shakespeare, utters lines with major resonance.

Yes, Sir Andrew, the knight of the woeful countenance who is duped into thinking that Countess Olivia might favor his lovesick suit. After he learns he's been gulled, and that he never had a chance, there's a moment when we find him left alone on the stage—clearly Shakespeare wanted to spotlight this moment—and he utters a single sentence, four words that disclose worlds. Sir Andrew cries out from his forlorn plight by exclaiming, "I was *adored* once!"

A tragic, comic moment, but when a skilled actor utters that lament, milking the line, usually stretching out "adored" to something between a soft howl and a hymn suspended in the air, it comes off, not as a laugh line (although it often gets a laugh), but as a line endowed with profound pathos and the throbbing ache of loss, the loss of hope, the hell of hopelessness—and yet, a touch of amazement. It's long gone, but it's still there. It's amazing but still thrilling to him that he was adored once.

And in the desperate attempt to maintain dignity in the face of mockery, he finds solace in his memory, in his amazement. I can relate ... I think the amazement I still feel that I ever was adored, each time it's happened, never lessens or fades. There's some of that there in that line, which of course heightens the sense of Love's true tragedy: Who can ever know whether, once adored, one will ever be adored again? Or at the same level. Is diminished adoration worse than not having had it at all? Who can ever know whether one was truly adored in the first place? All the more reason to cherish desperately the memory—or the delusion—one was once.

It's a rare moment of this sort of tenderness in Shakespeare, where love is usually wholly won or wholly lost but here less lost than held, still shimmering, wavering in lovesick memory. Both the possession and the loss embraced simultaneously. A case can be made that love is felt most acutely as an absence of love. Not the comic mockery of love at first sight in *A Midsummer Night's Dream*, not the savage self-laceration and misogyny of the Sonnets, still treasured, no need to denigrate them.

Keats captured that romantic sadness in "La Belle Dame sans Merci," which—it suddenly occurred to me—might well have been inspired by "I was adored once": the famous line, "Oh what can ail thee knight at arms / Alone and palely loitering?" might well be addressed to Sir Andrew. La Belle Dame: not the lost lover of the moment, but beautiful and sometimes merciless Love itself.

I dwell on "I was adored once" because it's an expression of the complexity and depths of feeling that love evokes, of which love is composed. But also as an indicator of just how impossible it is to reduce the experience to the on/off synaptic switch of an fMRI. Love is not binary but forever both on and off.

I dwell on "I was adored once" not because I've always been a loser in love. And anyway, it's an open question about whether there are winners and losers: Frankly I increasingly cherish that feeling of wistful loss sometimes punctuated by a stab of pain. Better than the remorse of not loving or being loved in some way. It happened this morning: I thought of a day in London some twenty years ago when—don't laugh—I refused to go to the National Portrait Gallery with my wonderful girlfriend at the time who is now no longer with us. Just out of some fake anti-Anglophile obstinacy.

I can never have that chance again! I can never forgive myself. The "sharp tender shock," as Larkin would have it, of grief, somehow more real than the day before in Paris, which she pronounced the best day of her life. Why do I not dwell more on that? Of course, neither registered as much or as profoundly as the week after with her, on the shabby gaudy pier at Brighton when the organist was playing "When I Grow Too Old to Dream."

My Objectivity

In certain ways, remorse then is a more sure sign of love than love. You only know love through the lens of loss. Loss is a constant cost, a recurrent curse that cannot be exorcised. And despite the cost, I've proceeded to sentence myself to a lifetime of loss and remorse by believing in love—which is perhaps one reason I'm disposed to defend its existence, its ineluctable, undeconstructable existence, from its enemies, the doubters, the determinists, and the reductionists. Don't try to tell me it was never real, I wasn't duped by some crack-littered dopamine neural pathway. More than real! An "other nature." It was that or it was nothing. If it wasn't that, it was not love. So if you detect a hint of anger in my approach to the love deniers, you would probably be correct.

The only thing more intense than love is lost love. Lost love proves the existence of love like nothing else.

"Dost thou understand what thou hast done for me, and is it not a somewhat fearful thought that a few slight circumstances might have prevented us from meeting?" That was Nathaniel Hawthorne in a letter to Sophia Peabody, dated October 1840.

Yes, "a somewhat fearful thought," indeed.

Love in the Time of the MRI

Lost love is one thing. But what about unrequited love, never requited love, love that is sent out into the ether and escapes Earth's gravity and dissipates in the vast emptiness of space (as I sometimes like to think of it). There is no true taxonomy proceeding from the unrequited to requited and then the unrequited-yet-again spectrum of love. The difference between unrequited love and love that morphs into "requitedness" before becoming unrequited again may be even more tragic than if never requited the first time. Or never, but nearly requited? (My father used to sing aloud from *South Pacific* a song that still tears me up: "This Nearly Was Mine.") Maybe that's the problem: Although I was adored once, twice, etc., I feel I missed or lost so many chances ("If I Loved You"—another of my father's favorites that destabilizes me still). Fortunately I've come to believe in the multiverse theory of the universe, which means that in some alternate realities I took up those chances I now miss. But at least I took one last chance. And how much love can one have in a lifetime? How many different serious loves, ones that last three or more years, say, and involve a lease.

I dwell on these matters because they suggest the complexities and depths of a subject that resists reductionism to an fMRI numerical singularity. Did I tell you how they measure lost love in the *Journal of Neurophysiology*? It's in volume 104, in case you missed that issue. "Reward, Addiction, and Emotion Regulation Systems Associated with Rejection in Love" is the title of the peer-reviewed paper. Really my Exhibit A against the neuroscientific attempt to make pronouncements about love after a few shoddy experiments. To colonize love for their white-jacketed straitjacketed scientism. And yet so influential, I'll need to devote an entire chapter to debunking it.

But just this one juicy tidbit now I can't resist to explain my anger. An instance not only of the hubris of neuroscience in its assumption that it can quantify and map love in the brain, but also the cruelty of applying MRI human experimentation methods to romantic love.

Consider this: for the "Rejection in Love" neuro study they rounded up a couple dozen unsuspecting subjects. All they had to do to qualify was be willing to state they had experienced rejection by a lover. Apparently any reason would do, any degree of sexual intimacy, didn't matter. How long the supposed lost relationship lasted? Didn't matter. Was it ever reciprocated? Didn't matter. There is so much left unspecified with these *Journal of Neurophysiology* studies just from the statistical science standpoint, not merely the philosophical ignorance and failure of common sense they display.

They reach new frontiers in human experimentation cruelty—"enhanced emotional interrogation," you might call it. Romantic waterboarding.

They stuck these poor souls in an MRI capsule that was equipped with a kind of rearview mirror that forced the subjects to gaze out on projections of "a photograph of the rejecting beloved" alternating with that of a neutral, control figure. "The Rejecting Beloved" sounds like a Molière farce (you almost wish that one of the subjects fell in love with the "control figure").

They were asked to stare at the person who had deeply hurt them, while the neurologist's fMRI recorded blood flow to various regions of the brain. (You know, of course, all a magnetic resonance imager does is respond to the iron in blood—thus more magnetically responding sectors indicate greater quantity of blood flow in a particular area.) Quantity, not quality, the degree of excitation but no measure of the nature of the feeling.

But, undeterred by the incompleteness of their methodology,

the scientists got their conclusion about the poor souls in the fMRI capsules: "Their responses while looking at their rejecter included love, despair, good and bad memories and wondering *why this happened*" (my italics).

"Their rejecter." "The rejecting beloved." "The rejecter's image." These are now scientific terms. Seriously. Stop the presses. People are unhappy when viewing their "rejecters." Science proves it. Then they told us the scene(s) of the crime in the brain: "activation specific to the image of the beloved occurred in areas associated with… the ventral tegmental area (VTA) bilaterally, ventral striatum, medial and lateral orbitofrontal/prefrontal cortex and cingulate gyrus."

They really should have specified the areas *not* responding to the "rejecter's image."

And locating these regions tells us nothing about love. Unless they are prepping to do mini-emotional lobotomies as in that film about erasing the memory of love—*Eternal Sunshine of the Spotless Mind*.

But think about what they're doing to the rejectees. Think of the suffering inflicted on the unsuspecting subjects now "wondering why this happened." Just when they should be trying to forget. They made them feel horrible and measured it. Thanks, science. Human experimentation of this sort might well be reported to the International Criminal Court for violations of the Geneva Conventions (hyperbole).

In truth, the only thing one can learn while being in love is how little one knows about love from being in love. If love doesn't introduce you to uncertainty, it's not love. Even so, I've been on the case. I've been in love a lot. I've been thrown out of love a lot, so in the crime lab of my heart I've done a lot of forensics. I had a "good enough" childhood—no abuse—so was my ventral tegmental area just genetically or epigenetically "expressed" more intensely, setting me up to be a Love Addict, as it used to be called?

But I can't remember a time I have not been in love, or just out of love, or looking for love. Ever since my first-grade crush (her name was Julie and she had braids—I still remember). All that time! My whole life in love or loss. There has been a long discourse in women's (and men's) magazines about The Number. And always it's been about The Number of one's sexual partners, regardless of the duration and the meaning—shaming or triumphal—attached to said sexual number.

But the real Number, it seems to me, or anyway a very, very different number, is not the number of sexual encounters but the number of times one has been in love, the number of times that love has been reciprocated. Of course, one must then figure in the length of time the reciprocity has been sustained, at what point the axes of intensity diverge. No algorithm for that. Love will not yield, however besieged, to the quants. With this number as well, there is nothing to boast of or be ashamed of. Life-long monogamous love versus serial monogamy? Who can judge (except that when one describes oneself—as I do—as a serial monogamist, one is vulnerable to jests about serial killers)?

Still, it's interesting to calculate how much of one's life has been taken up with it, whatever it is. Love, not sex. I know: not easy to separate at all times. And perhaps it's just me who's more obsessed with love than sex, although I don't think I'm alone being a love junkie rather than a sex addict.

And it's shocking if you start to monitor it: the number of hours spent thinking about love lost, love that never was but might have been. It's ridiculous if you think too much about how much you think about it. Insane how much mental space in one's life is occupied by the thousands of love songs one obsesses over, weeps over, unsuccessfully attempts to extirpate from the mind. The sheer number of hours. That's a Number worth respecting—or blanching at. How did I write six books while thus distracted?

Love songs. Mostly love laments. "I was adored once" laments. I do not believe evolutionary psychology can explain it on selfish gene grounds. Nobody reads love poetry anymore (except me and a few ex–English majors—academics read love poetry Theory). Once, when poetry was at the center of culture, love was virtually the only subject. That and death. Oh, and the weather, too. The ultimate mysteries. My contention: Love still is a mystery worth investigation no matter how many millions of lines of verse have been devoted to it. And I have been an investigative reporter. What better to investigate?

If love isn't what the reductionists reduce it to, just what is it? There it is, I said it. I dread it. But that's the Big Question. That's really the task I've set for myself if I'm declaring war on reductionism.

If love is resistant to reductionism, then what is that "other nature" it seems to inhabit? Does that mean it exists independently of earthbound causality? Is it Shakespeare's "uncaused cause / that alters not when it alteration finds"? Or is that just mysticism? Is it when you see a stranger across a crowded room and "suddenly" you know? What is it you know?

It's an important issue: Are we truly getting closer to proving that love as depicted and explained in five millennia of Western literature (and as many of the East) was always a delusion, an artificially induced, predictable madness mediated by the dopamine pathway? It's an important issue, the way—from every angle, scientific to literary—love is being defined out of existence. Or at the very least being ghettoized in the Harlequin, rom-com spectrum. Or for men in the espionage genre where betrayal is the essence of love, else nothing worth betraying—Graham Greene and le Carré, it could be said, wrote rom-coms for men.

But I should tell you about the other more specific inciting incident that has driven me to writing about love. Not just the generalized need to defend it, but the need to define it in some other appropriate way. After a lifetime of love, of adoring and being adored—and finally being thrown out the door and astonishingly finding someone who would allow me back in—I was trying to understand (wondering like that poor MRI "rejecter" study guy who was "wondering why this happened"), What had all this been about?

I'd trace my current obsession with love to that Philip Larkin poem "An Arundel Tomb," and its last line: "What will survive of us is love." At the most basic level, what exactly is it that survives?

"An Arundel Tomb" is a poem in which the speaker (not necessarily Larkin), wandering through Chichester Cathedral graveyard, comes upon a stone carving on the casket of the 14th Earl of Arundel and his wife. I urge you to Google a photo of the stark, bleached-out, prone stone figures. An image that Larkin, perhaps the greatest anti-sentimentalist in anglophone poetry, comes close to sentimentalizing in a thrilling kind of way.

In the poem, Larkin's speaker is suddenly struck by a detail in the worn stone figurations of the couple: The long-dead Earl and his long-dead wife are depicted holding hands. This despite the fact that the Earl is otherwise encased in full battle armor, including mailed iron gloves. Well, as Larkin's speaker suddenly notices, on looking more closely, not quite. The Earl has apparently withdrawn his hand from one of those heavy mailed gloves, which is carved hanging empty from his hand. This "bare" hand is shown—in stone—having reached out to clasp the stone-carved flesh of his wife's bare hand. Flesh on flesh, yes, I know, stone on stone, but it comes as a kind of surprise to the speaker: "One sees with a sharp tender shock / His hand withdrawn, holding her hand" [withdrawn from the glove].

That line about "a sharp tender shock" can come as a kind of shock to a reader, at least it always does to this reader. Those three words in particular: the "sharp tender shock." What a perfectly expressed compression of love at first sight (and often second, third, and so on). The flesh-piercing physicality of the image, the flesh-piercing meta-physicality, love as a wound, the wound that never heals. Immemorially depicted as the wound of a sharpened arrow. Not always called tender.

The rest of this poem could be seen as the speaker's not quite successful attempt to recover from this shock, in a way to talk himself out of it, or what it implies, by meditating on the conflicting possibilities it raises.

How do we know the Earl made a special point of telling the sculptor to fashion this "effigy" of devoted love? How do we know that distinctive hand-holding gesture was there because he wished it, wished his love to live on beyond the life of the lovers? Or was it just "faithfulness in effigy," perhaps a convention of memorial sculpture? Or even something the sculptor dreamed up himself for a dramatic touch with no input from the Earl and his wife at all, nothing to do with whatever love ever existed between the two? Larkin wonders.

The final stanza, then, raises the stakes of these questions. Does the survival of this image and the unmistakable effect it creates—however false to the facts of the matter—ironically validate the idea that love survives death? That "what will survive of us is love"—even if the Earl and his wife didn't mean it? That it was not the conscious intention of lovers or sculptor? Larkin concludes:

> Time has transfigured them into Untruth.
> The stone finality.
> The hardly meant has come to be
> Their final blazon, and to prove
> Our almost-instinct almost true:
> What will survive of us is love.

The sculpted image has weathered the centuries and—whether intended or not—the gravamen of the engraved image has triumphed over the incertitude of the reality. He goes from "Untruth" to "almost true" in the space of four lines.

But perhaps because it proves something we know or think we know is truth—

> "Our almost-instinct almost true:
> What will survive of us is love."

It's that final line, which, ironically, like the Arundel tomb sculpture, has undergone a similar fate. It's hard to tell from the poem itself whether we should believe the last line or not. Yet it has been taken up as if we must. Or whether the last line really is an untruth despite our "almost instinct" to believe it. Larkin's hesitation, his later embarrassment at the open affirmation, can't help but bring up another great twentieth-century poet's very similar embarrassment at the open expression of love: The two instances suggest the need for a defense of love from an ironic age.

W. H. Auden, you might remember, originally ended his famous poem "September 1, 1939" (the opening date of the Second World War, written, we are told, "in a dive on 52nd Street"), with the final line: "We must love one another or die." The world loved that line. All except for Auden, who seemed rather rapidly to feel mortified by it, probably because of its all too greeting card–ready sentiment. So upset was he that he refused to grant rights to publish any version of the poem that included that line, even struck off the verse it was in for good. Love was an embarrassment as it was to Larkin, the open poetic declaration of it. Embarrassment about love was endemic to some poets. The great critic Christopher Ricks even wrote a book called *Keats and Embarrassment* because of the effect of the open assertion of love on sophisticated poets and their audiences as well. Today was not the first time love was in trouble, or that love needed defense.

Well, what *will* survive of us if not love?

Just on the most literal level, the poem begs you to ask: How will love survive and what exactly is it that will survive? Age has already "blurred" the faces of the stone figures, and ultimately will erase or decompose the entire image, so what exactly is it that "will survive"? Some immaterial ethereal spiritual force? A vaporous distillation, as the alchemists might call it? Orgone radiation, as the semi-crackpot Freudian/Marxist mystic Wilhelm Reich called it? Something like the Force in *Star Wars*?

Or none of the above. But something of the sort Sir Philip Sidney called "an other nature." Martin Amis, Larkin's soulmate, who has read his letters, told me that in Larkin's letters (which should not be decisive—I resist biographical criticism) Larkin seems torn about whether he has gone too far in affirmation with the line. He questions himself almost like Auden did. We question him.

These questions so persistent, ancient, even—somehow they've become new again. But as Houellebecq, doyenne of the international avant-garde, suggests when he tells us that all he cares about in his novels now are the questions of love and the materialism that seeks to make it "disappear," these questions are back with us. Like "the question of the existence of God in Dostoyevsky," he says they have never gone away.

Defending love requires more than debunking determinism, scientism, and reductionism, although it's a necessary pleasure. I want to explore the question that comes after the debunking. The question that amounts to: If it ain't all that, what is it? It's a question that will lead us to what neuro-philosophers call "The Hard Problem of Consciousness"—which I believe is not dissimilar, asking the same difficult questions as what I call "The Hard Problem of Love."

Two Hard Problems

I'm not sure how familiar readers might be with "The Hard Problem of Consciousness," which has that slightly weird, donnish phrasing that questions in the realm of the Philosophy of Mind tend to have.

And yet it remains the great unanswered question. The question at the very borderline between science and philosophy. How does the brain, a six-pound lump of meat in a shell, produce the mind, the king of infinite space, capable of being—or at least appreciating—Mozart and Dostoyevsky?

The hardness of The Hard Problem of Consciousness inheres in its maddening obscurity. I found it intriguing when I read a puzzled theater critic report a jest from Tom Stoppard. Stoppard had let slip word that the title of his forthcoming play would be *The Hard Problem*. To which he added, "The only thing else I'll say is that it's not about ED."

A kind of in-joke for those (unlike the baffled theater critic) who recognized—it being Stoppard—that it must be about "The Hard Problem of Consciousness," something that has preoccupied his work.

So it might be worth quoting a definitional paragraph from the actual inventor of the phrase "Hard Problem of Consciousness," Oxford philosopher David Chalmers. When reading this description of Chalmers's argument, try this experiment: Substitute the word "love" or "being in love" every time you come upon the word "consciousness" or "being conscious" to see what I'm getting at.

> Several questions about consciousness [love] must be resolved in order to acquire a full understanding of it ... whether being conscious [in love] could be wholly described in physical terms, such as the aggregation of neural processes in the brain. If consciousness [love] cannot be explained exclusively by physical events, it must transcend the capabilities of physical systems and require an explanation of nonphysical means. For philosophers who assert that consciousness [love] is nonphysical in nature, there remains a question about what outside of physical theory is required to explain consciousness [love].

As my favorite line from the White Stripes has it: I'll "say it once again 'cause it bears repeating" to emphasize the rather stunning implications:

> If consciousness [love] cannot be explained exclusively by physical events, it must transcend the capabilities of physical systems and require an explanation of nonphysical means. For philosophers who assert that consciousness [love] is nonphysical in nature, there remains a ques-

tion about what "outside of physical theory is required to explain consciousness [love]."

So the hardness of "The Hard Problem of Love" consists of what "outside" of physical theory is required to explain love. Is there what Sir Philip Sidney calls "an other nature"?

Or to encapsulate it: If The Hard Problem of Consciousness is how to explain how the brain "generates" the mind, The Hard Problem of Love is how to explain how the heart (physical being) engenders love as a transphysical phenomenon, another nature "outside physical theory."

This is the Hard Problem we must face after we tear down the edifice of the "science of love" and attempt to defend love from the reductionists.

"The Hard Problem of Love." It's the question Shakespeare poses in *A Midsummer Night's Dream:* Is "love" just an arbitrary chemical consequence of artificial intoxication of one sort or another, such as the aphrodisiac juice of the flower "love in idleness" that Puck drops in the various sets of sleeping eyes in the *Dream*? Thus "love at first sight" (ESIRL—Early-Stage Intense Romantic Love—as the love scientists call it) is really a kind of joke, an illusion of transcendence that arises from a chemically induced, almost psychedelic prank. Or, on the other hand, could artificially enhanced transcendence reveal one's authentic self?

"Is consciousness [is love?]" some kind of emanation from the brain beyond the known electromagnetic spectrum? The love that "survives" for Larkin: Is it the effect it has on a succession of beings who experience the Arundel Tomb's "sharp tender shock"—or read of it in the poem that keeps it alive? Which would make it up to us to keep love alive, like clapping for Tinker Bell.

And if it's not the fragile succession—and consonance—of beings that support the survival of love, as a matter of faith, is it then the totality of Being? Is love a ground of being we are embedded in, suspended in, an ever-full reservoir we can call upon—or that calls upon us? Never absent, if not always consciously noticed?

Here I would like to call upon philosopher of mind Thomas Nagel, whose statement of the hard problem seems irrefutable to me: "Conscious subjects and their mental lives are inescapable components of reality *not* describable by the *physical sciences*" (italics mine).

Thus conscious subjects like love are not merely fantasies partaken of and then exhaled somehow back to its origin, to its Cloud, to use a digital metaphor. Conscious subjects like love are real, as real as can be, but not physical, electrical, or chemical. Are they partaken of in greater or lesser quantities and intensities during life and given back to the universe upon death? Does love operate like the Holy Ghost, a spirit that possesses and causes the possessed to speak in tongues?

The Hard Problem of Fucking

This doesn't begin to exhaust the possibilities. Does love have, for instance, the spirituality that David Foster Wallace imputed to human sexual desire here (in an essay for Dave Eggers's long defunct magazine, *Might*):

The human will to fuck? Any animal can fuck. But only humans can experience sexual passion, something wholly different from the biological urge to mate. And sexual passion's endured for millennia as a vital psychic force in human life not despite impediments but because of them. Plain old coitus becomes erotically charged and spiritually potent at just those points where impediments, conflicts, taboos, and consequences lend it a double-edged character. And meaningful sex is both an overcoming and a succumbing, a transcendence and a transgression, triumphant and terrible and ecstatic and sad. Turtles and gnats can mate, but only the human will can defy, transgress, overcome, love: choose.

There it is, amidst all that fucking: *love.*

"The Hard Problem of Fucking." An intriguing way of looking at things. (And I particularly like the emphasis on "impediments." "Let us not to the marriage of true minds / Admit impediments," Shakespeare's Sonnet 116 tells us. Yet in fact, in practice, whether we admit them or not, "the marriage of true minds," or at least their fleshly embodiment, may need impediments.) But more to the point, this passage from Wallace raises some of the same questions as The Hard Problem of Consciousness and The Hard Problem of Love. When he speaks of "a vital psychic force," "spiritually potent" eros, and "transcendence"—these are all "outside physical theory" that scientists use to describe a phenomenon. They all "require an explanation of nonphysical means," as David Chalmers and Thomas Nagel assert.

Wallace seems to have been a dualist like Chalmers, or an anti-materialist anyway. He believes in a nondeterminist non-mechanistic "spirit." I know he's no longer fashionable, but he's onto something (or on something—or both). It's more than just hand waving here. But what is this "psychic force," this "spiritually potent" force? What kind of spiritual transcendence does it imply? Is it the same as the love that survives in the claim that "what survives of us is love"? Invisible yet powerful.

He seems to be making an implicit distinction between "sexual passion" and love, he seems to think that something more than sexual passion is wanted: "meaningful" sexual passion. And yes, at the close, he slides in "love." As an act of defiance, transgression, choice. All in all, a powerful reproof to the reductionists and materialists from a philosophical thinker and novelist.

In fact, I prefer DFW the philosopher to the novelist. His book on the dizzying realm of the "larger" mathematical infinities, *Everything and More,* can be seen from the title on to be a key to his best fiction, *Infinite Jest,* which demonstrated that he shared a fascination with infinity with that other philosophic soul, Hamlet, putative "king of infinite space." (This might seem a bit of a digression but I'm fond of Rebecca Solnit's long lovely digressive essay "In Praise of the Meander," in which she argues *apparent* digressions can shed reflected light on what they appear to depart from—Google it.) And love, love the infinite, as in unquantifiable, emotion. Everything and more. He deserves to be remembered for his willingness to reopen and explore these questions. A reproof to those quants who think that infinite emotions have been reduced to mere numbers. (As we shall see, infinity arises again in the next chapter in Tolstoy's wife's "mirror novel.") And I really must mention a recent book by Katherine Rundell about John Donne's love poetry whose title is *Super-Infinite.*

What stands out in DFW's defense of love as "spiritually potent" is that it doesn't seem to be spiritual in a religious sense. In a pantheistic sense? But that seems to imply some kind of theism. Where does it come from? In what model of the universe does this spiritual aspect of Being exist? What created it?

And can we definitively rule out a physicalist source for love, some unexplored aspects of quantum cosmology? The universe, as the Harvard cosmologist Lisa Randall once painstakingly explained to me, is composed of 70 percent "Dark Matter" and 21 percent "Dark Energy." And these mysterious phenomena, we're told, are required by quantum cosmology to keep the universe from flying apart or collapsing. But we don't have the slightest knowledge of what they are composed of. We know them only from speculative equations, cosmological theory, rather than observation or detection. It still strikes me as astonishing that the entire edifice of cosmology is based on the sketchy observation (by my reckoning) of only 9 percent of the cosmos. Which you might think would give materialists some pause in their claims made for that sliver of existence they reason from. For all we know, love might be the "dark matter." Love often is a dark matter.

Is there a Venn diagram where Larkin's surviving love and Wallace's "spiritual transcendence" intersect? Are they talking about essentially the same thing? Wallace emphasizing the sexual, Larkin not ignoring the centrality of flesh on flesh but emphasizing love qua love. The Wallace passage is another example—like Houellebecq—of the way contemporary artists and thinkers have been returning to the most primal of all questions—the questions about the relation between body and soul, matter and spirit, the existence of a soul that the reductionists either fail to understand or seek to explain away. The nature of love. It's exciting to love and to think about love.

Alas we no longer live in sixteenth- and seventeenth-century England when the Metaphysical poets were able to envision some mediating "spirits" that conceived of soul and body, matter and spirit somehow unified or linked. Recent scholarship on the cosmology—and culture—of the Metaphysical poets has made a persuasive case that humans then had internalized a fairly well-defined hierarchical vision of the soul that partook of elements of both worlds, matter and spirit. A link between the earthly anatomical and the ethereal realm of the spiritual.

"The smoke of the soul," as John Donne called it in a characteristically memorable image for the "spirits" that transported love from the earthly to the celestial. I like that phrase, which is the title of a recent book about Donne called *The Smoke of the Soul: Science, Religion, and the Invention of the Self* by Richard Sugg, after a line in a 1619 work. The smoke of the soul, the incense of the senses. A seductive image of the workings of love: "the soul and spirits as habitual and organic facts vibrating down the nerves and arteries, pulsing in the blood, occasionally throbbing out to the tips of one's fingers, the fiery light of the eyes, the ends of the hair," as Sugg put it. He calls John Donne's 1619 description of the realm of love: "a kind of middle nature between soul and body those spirits are able to unite the faculties of the soul to the organs of the body."

"A middle nature" like Sidney's "other nature"? Well, no one wants to believe any seventeenth-century fantasies, now, do they (I do), but clearly they were aware of The Hard Problem of Love, even then, in devising these metaphors.

Is the "Mysterian" Solution a Solution at All?

Can The Hard Problem of Love ever be solved? Or is it a matter of faith? Or a matter for the Mysterians?

The Mysterians? Yes, The Hard Problem of Consciousness in this schema is usually associated with either "dualism": The world is made up of two kinds of phenomena—matter in all its materiality, and consciousness in all its ethereality, its Cartesian invisible essence.

Consciousness is a substance of some kind but not substantial. We can't put it in a specimen jar. The materialists believe that—theoretically anyway—everything in the brain could be predicted if one knew enough about every molecule in every neuron. Everything there happens through a chain of causality, in which input can predict output and determinism reigns. Not so with consciousness, one of the defining characteristics of which is, in humans, its unpredictability, its ability to choose free from the shackles of mechanistic causality. Free will, in other words.

And by the way, don't talk to me about "quantum unpredictability." The recent attempts to find a physical basis for free will (and thus autonomous consciousness) in quantum-level unpredictability escaping determinism have so far not resulted in any way to link unpredictability in the subatomic realm to coherent conscious choices in the macro Mind. Sorry, Sir Roger Penrose.

And if we're talking quantum physics metaphors, I have a better one, I think: the newly resurgent doctrine of "entanglement," quantum entanglement, based on new evidence for "Bell's Theorem." A theorem that Einstein once rejected but later embraced. A theorem that is based on observation.

A *New York Times* story in late 2014 reported new experimental support for Bell's Theorem, which suggests that some kind of faster-than-light, indeed, instantaneous, constant entanglement or awareness can subsist between two particles that have started out spinning together but flown apart. Or one that has split. Entanglement, thus far observed, concerns the behavior of tiny particles, such as electrons, that have interacted in the past and then moved apart. "Tickle one particle here," the *Times* story says, "by measuring one of its properties—its position, momentum or 'spin'—and its 'partner' should dance, instantaneously, no matter how far away the second particle has traveled." The key word is "instantaneously." "The entangled particles could be separated across the galaxy, and somehow, according to quantum entanglement theory, [making] measurements on one particle should affect the characteristics of the far-off twin faster than light (or information) could have traveled between them."

I know physics metaphors are dicey, but this notion of constant instantaneous "entanglement" between particles is hard to resist as a metaphor for love. At first, Einstein dismissed as impossible Bell's Theorem that entanglement meant instantaneous communication between separated particles, but then he changed his mind, as have a number of top quantum physicists who seem to believe in some inexplicable magic-like communicativeness, an awareness between particles that were once together yet maintain contact with each other. It sounds so unscientific, but then so does love.

Do you see why I'm going on about this? Love is a kind of entanglement between two consciousnesses. What is distinctive about love is that it can give one the feeling of instantaneous awareness of the other. A simultaneous awareness of something shared.

For another thing, although entanglement is the very latest in hypermodern quantum physics, it couldn't help but remind me of an analogue to an ancient metaphoric version of this. To be found in Aristophanes's exordium on the mythic origin of love in Plato's *Symposium*. Aristophanes, the fifth-century BC playwright, expounds on an elaborate myth about human beings: initially, upon creation by the gods, beings shaped like eggs. Both sexes contained in one body. And then, because of some tinkering by then inhabitants of Mount Olympus, they were split into two beings, and scattered across the Earth. Each half, each fragment, then lost track of the other. And—because of the embedded memory of previous entanglement—they have been forever searching for the one with which they were originally entangled. The one who will complete them. The only one. That drive to restore intimate physical and metaphysical entanglement is what is called love, said Aristophanes. And love is the kind of radar that (under ideal circumstances) allows them to relocate each other and...entangle again. (It takes two to entangle.)

I'm not betting there will be scientific proof of love entanglement, that two beings whose subatomic particles are entangled therefore fall in love and forever seek each other. But it rings true metaphorically. It captures the feeling of fatedness, the long ridiculed but long persistent belief that some people are made for each other, complete each other, and are meant to find love together. Even though tragically they often don't.

The Aristophanes–Bell's Theorem model does offer a respite from the constant hectoring of those who say one must "work" at a relationship that never was meant to be. One of the most exhilarating contemporary books by a woman on love is Laura Kipnis's *Against Love* (she's emphatically for it; the title is mostly ironic). In her book, Kipnis hilariously riffs on the emotional labor these "work" scolds condemn couples to, couples who probably weren't meant to be entangled in the first place. It's a theory, it's a fragment of the truth we shore up against our ruin—that the right one is still out there, looking for us, and once found no laborious "work."

Three thousand years and this debate between dualism and monism/materialism has been going on, and despite the hubris of neurosciences, even convinced materialists such as Daniel Dennett now argue that free will—not the illusion of free will—is somehow compatible with determinism.

But few are satisfied that Dennett has ended the debate. Enter the Mysterians. Actually they've been around since the nineties, but neither the dualists nor the materialists have been willing to abandon their own certainty for the near Terminal Uncertainty the Mysterians offer.

I first came upon the Mysterian position in the writings of the controversial philosopher Colin McGinn, who made a persuasive argument that consciousness may not yet—and may never—achieve the ability to explain consciousness. Consciousness may be beyond the grasp of consciousness.

Mysterian? There was an early proto-punk Tex-Mex band called ? and the Mysterians. (Copyeditor note: they used the ? mark, not the words "question mark," in their band name.) A one-hit-wonder band whose mainstream hit was "96 Tears," a song that mostly consisted of them chanting in a strange echoey monotone: "Cry, cry, cry 96 tears." A love song, in other words.

Nonetheless, when it came time for the small group of well-regarded philosophers who doubted the explicability of consciousness to give their group a name, they demonstrated a sense of humor and pop culture awareness that academic philosophers are not widely known for and called their tendency "Mysterian." And after all, it was a kind of punk stance, disruptive, we'd say now, to champion an ineradicable, inarticulate question mark sign that suggested that all those who claimed to have the answer to "The Hard Problems" were wrong.

At least the Mysterians have humility, which of course has led to their being attacked by both sides in the dualist-versus-materialist war.

Can we be satisfied with a Mysterian solution to The Hard Problem of Love? Can love be grasped by those who have been in love? To be in it after all implies that one can't "explain" it until one is out of it, and then all is fleeting and beyond the grasp of rational discourse. It is still a mystery.

Nothing recent I've seen in the consciousness debate has indicated to me that the dualists or the materialists have refuted the Mysterian position. Indeed one way of reading the important philosopher Thomas Nagel on the nature of Mind is to say that he was a Mysterian avant la lettre. Nagel's brilliantly compressed summation: "Conscious subjects and their mental lives are inescapable components of reality *not describable by the physical sciences*" (italics mine). Real but an ineluctable mystery.

Do I take the Mysterian position on The Hard Problem of Love? I will leave that a mystery for the moment. I have one matter I need to deal with before resuming the defense of Love: the question of permission. What gives a straight white Western cis-male the right to ask these questions and mediate among the answers? Or why should Others listen? I felt there should be at least one woman, preferably a respected feminist, who might entertain my conflicted thoughts on these matters. To imagine my views might have some useful place in the discourse.

Fortunately, I found someone who was asking for such views.

Where Are the Men?

"Where are the men?"

In an essay I happened on long ago in the September 2012 edition of *BBC Magazine*, entitled "Where Are the Men?," Sarah Dunant, well known in the U.K. as a novelist and feminist, asked that provocative question. In the context of what seemed at the time like a torrent of torrid novels, memoirs, and essays by women on sexuality (it was the season that saw publication of both Naomi Wolf's *Vagina: A New Biography* and *Fifty Shades of Grey*).

Yes, she contended, women were speaking out about their desires, their sexual experiences, their fantasies, their special preferences, their attitude toward love, lust, eros, desire. Women were speaking out both fictionally and nonfictionally, setting off sparks and controversies. There was this glorious efflorescence of estrogenic wit and wisdom—and yet, Sarah Dunant argued in her essay, there was something missing.

"That, I suppose, is what worries me," she wrote. "Where are the heavyweight male voices debating contemporary sexuality?

"We accept that in the aftermath of feminism, growing up male can be hard: but where are the big public conversations.... The impact of pornography. How far has our desire changed theirs? Is their line between what is and is not acceptably different from ours?"

"How far has our desire changed theirs?" One of many excellent questions. And by sex and sexuality—by "desire"—I'm assuming she's including the touchy question of love as well. Can it be analyzed by science? And the difference its presence or absence makes to sexuality.

Speaking of which, let me go no further before making a preemptive apology to any of those readers who find any aspect of my exploratory observations and speculations offensive in what can be territory land-mined with controversy. Let me assure you that I don't have an agenda or an ideology, just a number of questions and observations, and a desire to defend love as an irreducible ontological entity, not an algorithm; my observations are personal, not programmatic, and in the face of continuing questions raised by love's mysteries I have ever more questions than answers.

Note, though, that she asked, "Where are the heavyweight male voices?" Good question! Would a humble middleweight voice do in a pinch? How about, since we're using boxing metaphors, a welterweight male voice, a category I've never fully understood but which, I think, lies between middleweight and light heavyweight (and I've always liked the word "welter" anyway—one of the translations of the Aramaic phrase in Genesis for the wasteland that existed before the Creation is "Tohu bohu," "welter and waste").

I'd ask you, then, to accept a welterweight voice, punching above his weight perhaps—a deplorable phrase, by the way, "punching above his weight," that men use to put down other men who, they believe, are paired with women who are, to use another sports metaphor, "out of their league." Another analogue: "overmatched." I've heard it, believe me. Really, Sarah Dunant, if you only knew how crass men were in judging each other. Something I'm sure women don't do. (This is meant ironically.) There are so many things I fear that "if women only knew," it would confirm their worst suspicions. (I will be your welterweight spy in the house of love.) Nor am I exempting myself. And, by the way, I don't proclaim myself a male feminist. Yes, I'm male (cis-hetero) and, yes, I've supported feminism ever since my early years in New York when I lived with and learned from a member of the Redstockings Collective, which was of the Shulamith Firestone and Ellen Willis's tendency in the Second Wave movement. But I would concede my feminism partakes as much as anything from a dystopian view of men, cis-men, anyway.

Frankly, no matter how badly you think of men, Sarah Dunant, I would suggest you think worse. I know many women have a justifiably low opinion of men, but in my experience it's not low enough. Men should be ashamed of themselves, most of them. Not just because of sexual assault, sexual discrimination, the disrespect of women in all fundamentalist patriarchal religions, but a planet infested with male-initiated wars and cruel—male—tyrannies founded on theories and ideologies devised and implemented by men (Mao, Alito). Men *should* be ashamed of themselves.

It's true there's a certain kind of non-sleazy male I'd call "the uxorious type." The exception proves the rule. But the rule is sleazy. On the other hand, I don't want to give the impression that shame is necessarily an entirely bad thing. No, shame is the way, shame is a path to the truth. In Yeats's poem "The Circus Animals' Desertion," one must "lie down where all the ladders start / In the foul rag and bone shop of the heart" to learn the truth about men.

But note that this is the place where "ladders start." Implying an upward ascent. (Although down further is still an option.) And implying the existence of a heart, however rotten.

Shame is the way up. "Shame is a revolutionary emotion." Guess who said that? Karl Marx. I believe love can only be defended if we acknowledge just how shameful men are.

The Brodkey-Mailer Heavyweight Orgasm Epics

Just look at how often the "heavyweight" male voices make fools of themselves when it comes to sex and love. I'm thinking of Norman Mailer, self-described "Prisoner of Sex," not the earlier "Armies of the Night" Mailer so much as Norman Mailer at his worst in the very early endless short story "The Time of Her Time." That story about the labor-intensive attempts of the existentialist/hipster Mailer-esque narrator (the one he called "Sergius O'Shaughnessy") to bring his bohemian girlfriend to her first orgasm (with him, anyway). Endless existential thrusting did not do the job. Finally he accomplished it with anal penetration and a hard slap in the face. Tender.

And you, too, Harold Brodkey. Remember him? The late wunderkind of the labor-intensive overwrought prose that preened at its own difficulty, mistaking sophistry for profundity? Remember Brodkey's once-celebrated, now incredibly embarrassing, 1971 story "Innocence." The one about his sexual triumph at the end of an interminable, overly minute description of another Everest-like Journey to Orgasm. Here with his Harvard-educated but (according to him) sexually oblivious girlfriend, the one his narrator modestly describes as "the most heart-stoppingly beautiful girl at Radcliffe" and—in a once-famous phrase (well, famous on the Upper West Side): "To see her in sunlight was to see Marxism die." (On the other hand, to read Brodkey was to see Capitalism cringe—to see the entire structure of privilege that enabled his celebrity collapse.)

For these guys, in these stories, all that laborious thrusting accompanied by Wagnerian purple prose essentially blamed women for their difficulties. Women were like defective sex toys. Oh, well.

For now, this way to the foul rag and bone shop—to be found somewhat surprisingly in the revealing last novellas of Tolstoy, which require a defense of love.

CHAPTER 4

Tolstoy's Complaint

Could Tolstoy Be an Enemy of Love?

Deep in a Russian forest, in a well-concealed hermit's cave, the lone occupant, who hadn't spoken to another human being for seven years, a hermit named Sergius who had renounced the world, is forced to resist the wiles of a worldly woman who has come to seduce him and almost succeeds had he not, Tolstoy tells us, forfended her intentions by taking an axe and chopping off one of his fingers "below the second joint."

While, in a contemporaneous Tolstoy novella, a wealthy rural landowner, Evgeny, alone in his study, tries to contain his obsession with the vision of a serving girl with "dark eyes," and, failing to do so, takes out his pistol and contemplates a choice: whether to murder the serving girl whose laughing eyes have him transfixed, or to put a bullet through his brain to preserve his "honor."

And elsewhere, in a third novella, out on the frozen steppes, the passengers in the crowded compartment of a long-distance train find themselves at the mercy of Pozdnyshev, a confessed wife-murderer, who, Tolstoy tells us, has only just been released on grounds of insanity but insists on taking up the long rail journey by offering his extremely long-winded "explanation" for slashing his wife to death with his saber.

What do these three scenes have in common? Each is the dark center of one of Lev Tolstoy's trilogy of late novellas whose venomous animus against love, sex, and human reproduction leads to what is his most shocking argument of all: that all of mankind would be better off if it were to die out, exterminate itself by ceasing "swinish" sexual reproduction and abandoning the love that all too often led to it. Exterminate itself. Seriously.

Three different stories of murder, insanity, and self-mutilation in the very different, very bitter, seldom-read trilogy of late Tolstoy novellas—*Father Sergius, The Devil,* and the exterminationist *The Kreutzer Sonata*—all three written late in Tolstoy's life (somewhere between 1880 and his death in 1910) and unfamiliar to most of those readers who have been entranced by the two massive earlier novels, *War and Peace* and *Anna Karenina* (1869 and 1877, respectively).

Should you wonder why Tolstoy belongs in a book called *In Defense of Love,* think of Tolstoy as a not-well-recognized enemy of love. A new perception to me prompted by the startling surfacing in 2010 of an "answer novel" to Lev's *Kreutzer Sonata* by Tolstoy's wife, Sofiya. Her novella, called *Whose Fault?,* put a spotlight on the animus to women, sex, love, marriage, and human reproduction Lev portrayed in *The Kreutzer Sonata.* Such a critique of Lev's dark, hate-filled final works had rarely been on the cultural radar, which has tended to exalt Tolstoy's saintly "wisdom" uncritically.

Sofiya's long-unpublished, untranslated manuscript, hidden for a century in the Moscow State Library Tolstoy Collection, apparently at the insistence of the Tolstoy estate for its exposure of the view of the "other" Tolstoy, Tolstoy's wife. Her novella is a portrait of a marriage and a love affair that implicitly depicts Lev Tolstoy's denial of love's existence or worth. Her fictionalized account of the trial of a marriage like hers is both heartbreaking and well written.

Her "answer novel" or "mirror novel," as she sometimes called it, is a work that took arms against her husband's grand ambition for the extinction of the human race—and his petty animosity toward love. When translated into English by scholar Michael R. Katz and published by Yale University Press in 2014 (in an anthology called *The Kreutzer Sonata Variations*), it gave a newness to a neglected aspect of Tolstoy's work—his hostility toward humanity in his largely overlooked late work. New to those who hadn't read the late trilogy of his novellas and their poisonous attitude toward sexual reproduction and love. They will shock many for whom Lev Tolstoy was a near-prophetic giver of wisdom to the world.

What the three novellas—*Father Sergius, The Devil,* and *The Kreutzer Sonata*—have in common is a bleak, dark vision of love and sex that made late Tolstoy seem almost a different person from the celebrated genius and sage whose peerless worldwide reputation for sanctity and sagacity was unequaled in the nineteenth century and sustained long beyond it. I believe, however, that it is important to let us have the whole of Tolstoy, not just the genius/sage of Russian romanticism.

And that is why Tolstoy's wife's novel seems significant to me: It offers a vision of love not as an enemy but as a possibility. Tolstoy's wife's "answer novel" is a kind of defense of love, in a way, like Sir Philip Sidney's "apology for poetry." A defense of a different kind of love than the "swinish" interaction late Tolstoy came to envision eros as.

All this drama—especially his *Kreutzer* novella and her "answer" to it, to his vicious view of love—made me want to dig deeper into that dark trilogy and look anew at the source of Tolstoy's rage. What made him an enemy of love?

Although scholars have not definitively posited a sequence in which Tolstoy wrote the three works and he might have been composing them simultaneously, I see in them a continuum of escalating malice in which *Father Sergius* comes first (and offers a skeleton key to the psychology of the others), followed in murderous succession by *The Devil*, which is particularly tricky since Tolstoy wrote an even more extreme alternative murderous end that he hid from his wife and the world and was only discovered posthumously. And finally, *Kreutzer,* which takes us to the edge of madness, and indeed over the edge. It was *Kreutzer* that drove his wife to answer its sick rage, his turn toward extermination of the human race.

Yes, I said it, extermination of the human race. Not the way Hitler's genocide proceeded, with all the apparatus of death camps, gas chambers, and the like. More passive but more vast an extermination. A demand for a total cessation of "swinish" sexual congress and a condemnation of love as a dangerous adjunct that could—horrors—lead to reproduction. He advocated, in all seriousness, a slow dying out of what had been human life from total anti-sexual chastity. No fucking at all. Somehow readers have not seen this as the terminal development of a deep theme of his work. Perhaps other more aggressive genocides have overshadowed the peaceful extermination Tolstoy envisioned.

I doubt he had an actual belief that this would happen. It was his belief that it should happen. It was Tolstoy's dream.

What happened to Tolstoy?

Did he lose his mind over love or hatred of love?

It's the "hard problem of love," redux. Before dealing with

"the enemies of love," a definition of love would be desirable, but would it be possible? I believe the hard problem of love is harder than "The Hard Problem of Consciousness." It may be the hardest problem of all. And at the heart of the hardest problem is the problem of the qualia.

At least we know consciousness when it's happening to us. It's certainly different from unconsciousness. You might think of Love as a flavor of consciousness. But does that help? One of the most difficult if not impossible things the human mind fails at is describing flavor and other sensual qualities abstracted from the objects in which they inhere. Yes, a red apple, but what is red, and, yes, a smoky garlic-flavored rib, but define garlic flavor. You can identify (name) the color or flavor but not the intrinsic properties—how it feels to you. Your unique subjectivity.

Philosophers call it "the problem of the qualia," qualia being those pesky attributes—those qualities, hence the Latinate term—whose nature challenges coherent definition. In what sense is red my red and not your blue? In what sense is love love and not sex, eros, or affection, or close friendship or some combination of elements? One can grasp at it but never quite capture it.

I love the term "qualia." It can't help summoning up images of the feathered quail so determinedly but often futilely hunted. The philosophers like a pack of hunting dogs on the gallop in attempting to sniff out and track down a way of expressing or analyzing whether one's qualia correspond to another's, indeed to anyone but oneself. And how could we know?

We can know the effects of love, yes. Usually after its departure. I've said I am addicted to sad country music, contemporary poetry of loss at its finest. Country singer-songwriters are our Metaphysical poets. (One of my proudest reportorial achievements was getting Willie Nelson to disclose the hidden heartbreaking verse of "Angel Flying Too Close to the Ground." That title, a wrenchingly sad, lovely metaphysical phrase in itself involving the unity of the realms of earth and sky.)

Did Tolstoy's qualia—or lack of them—explain his change of heart in his later work? Qualia can't be reduced to mathematics or digitized fMRI traces. Qualia are everything that fMRI machines can't measure with brain scans that light up under certain stimuli, but do your fMRI voltage equivalences tell us how to describe the subjective feeling it is supposed to represent other than its quantitative magnitude? Or how deeply we feel, much less how Tolstoy felt? Did Tolstoy lack or lose the qualia of love by the time he wrote the *Kreutzer* trilogy? Not only can we not define or articulate what flavors taste like or even, more difficult, whether they taste the same to everyone. It's an ancient problem of philosophy: How do I know that the taste I get from chocolate is the same as the taste you get from chocolate; or, maybe your chocolate might be raspberry to me, and vice versa. It's dizzying. Like love.

Neuroscience can identify correlations between nerve endings sharing an identical electron pattern in two different people, but it cannot tell us if two identical maps of sensation in the brain indicate that the same feeling in the heart is evoked by that sensation. That was Philip Larkin's point—one of them—in "An Arundel Tomb": How can we know what feeling, if any, inspired the stone handclasp on the sarcophagus? There may be an intensity scale in some lab, but there isn't in most hearts. A scale of feeling, a metric of emotion. But is "what will survive of us," that aspect of love, the same for all of us?

At what point can we say we've passed over from one realm, one magisterium, to another, from sex to love, say, and do we leave one behind or just add another? How does one define the difference between love and sex? Is the latter so deeply embedded in the former that it's a hopeless task, like trying to separate a swirl of crème fraîche from the soup it's in? The foam from the latte?

Can we learn anything from the radical change in Tolstoy that scholars locate taking place between 1878 and 1883? Some kind of spiritual crisis, but what?

Love Is the Great Disrupter

In Sofiya Tolstoy's novel, with its thinly disguised, indirect portrait of the Tolstoy marriage, we witness a husband's inability to feel the way centuries of poets felt about love, the difference between his and their qualia. Tolstoy taking on Love as an enemy is why the final bitter trilogy deserves our attention—for what it says about Tolstoy, for what it says about love, its nature or its absence. The absence of tenderness or the disappearance of the tenderness briefly glimpsed in the final scene between Natasha and the dying Prince Andrei in *War and Peace*.

This elusive, evanescent thing called love: Do we even know when it's happening to us? When we cross over, so to speak, from lust, infatuation, all those adjacencies? Can we define what makes it different—if anything—from affectionate sex? Where is the borderline between the two, if there is one? Let us say a word (or more) for tenderness. It's so ephemeral. Is it different for men, for women, for nonbinary people? How exactly? As I reread the three sinister novellas, beginning with *Father Sergius*, it struck me, the matter of tenderness, so notable by its absence. Tolstoy, a writer of such prodigious gifts, is rarely able to conjure up tenderness in any convincing manner in his late trilogy. Once he did, perhaps: Another source of his rage in the final trilogy may be that he's lost it, whatever ability he once had to capture it. All that's left is sex and jealousy.

Which suggests that the lord of the manor has no real experience of love anymore beyond preying on serving maids, or he's banished it through an act of will. Knows lust, can recite the word "love," but usually portrays it as a sham, a trap baited for fools. We are back where we started, back to the legendary Raymond Carver question, "What do we talk about when we talk about love?"

Maybe we've gone about it the wrong way, seeking a coherent abstract theory that will cover it (in both senses of "cover"). Maybe we can only approach an answer experientially, not theoretically. By experientially, I mean that love cannot necessarily be pinned to a point on a map with GPS coordinates, but is rather a journey, a narrative, a story on which that point lies. Love is a cumulative narrative of the awakening of that feeling, a narrative, not a definition. A journey rendered most memorably and revealingly in the arts, visual and literary, painting and poetry. In fourteen-line sonnets. In Sir Philip Sidney's hundred-sonnet sequences. In Sappho's outcries. In the ungloved hand in Larkin's "An Arundel Tomb" and his meditation on the unknowability of the gesture's meaning—what the onetime flesh-and-blood people behind the stone effigies felt. In Austen's *Persuasion,* her deepest work. Nor should the accounts of survivors and victims be neglected, particularly the ones to whose loss of love we bear witness. These are evidence, testifying to the existence of something real, lost, or incommunicable.

So let us talk about how and why so many people get Tolstoy wrong. Because (to oversimplify) there are two Tolstoys. We have a Schrödinger's Tolstoy situation. This is one of the things we are reminded of in Sofiya Tolstoy's long-buried "answer novel."

There is the Tolstoy who exemplified Russian romanticism in his two great novels—1869's *War and Peace* and 1877's *Anna Karenina*. Dashing troikas in pillowy snow, dashing gentlemen and ladies in love, beautiful women in expensive furs, fateful Onegin-like emotions, Natasha and the death of Prince Andrei, wonder at the great mysteries of things, death as a spiritual experience in *The Death of Ivan Ilych*. What it is to be lost in the vast currents of history. Tolstoy was (once) open to such metaphysical speculations as opposed to extreme (and punitive) biblical literalism. And then there is this, the other Tolstoy, capable of having his character utter this (in *The Kreutzer Sonata*): " 'What is filthy above all,' he began, 'is that it's supposed in theory that love is something ideal, lofty, but in practice love is something loathsome, swinish… but here… people pretend that the loathsome and shameful is beautiful and lofty.' " Yes, a character, but an utterance identical to that of his nonfiction self in his addendum to *The Kreutzer Sonata*.

I don't want to say everybody gets Tolstoy wrong, but it's hard to get him completely right. Because of those two incompatible Tolstoys. There is the Tolstoy who could stir the heart and soul, that gave Tolstoy a reputation as more than a novelist but a sage, a white-robed guru of spiritual enlightenment who casts his spell on the dilemmas of being human.

And then there is the Tolstoy of the last thirty years of his life, 1880–1910, when he became a tiresome scold, the Russian Polonius lecturing humanity about its flaws and boasting of the depth of his tedious self-reflection, climaxing it all with that shocking trilogy of rebarbative anti-sexual, antihuman novellas whose final work, *The Kreutzer Sonata*, is an argument for the extermination of the human species. It may be that, having written a book—*Explaining Hitler*—that examined the source of the exterminations, and then the fact that my mother's family is said to have come from the Russian-Polish city of Lvov (now Ukrainian Lviv), whose Jews were murdered early in the war, I refuse to take advocacy of extermination of any kind lightly.

Oddly perhaps, I think of Henry Kissinger when reading late Tolstoy's advocacy of extermination. Henry was fascinated by the possibility of nuclear extinction, or what he called in one of his first books "the death of consciousness." Yes, "the death of consciousness" after nuclear extermination. That is a hard problem. Think about that—no one to be conscious of the absence of consciousness. Contemplating it can be quite scary. What time is it without us? Is it ever any time? It has a je ne sais quoi mind-bending quality to it, does it not? Nobody around to notice that there's nobody around. No one to sin or to love. Tolstoy's dream.

Shame

Few people know or talk about that Tolstoy. Self-reflection became the obsession of the Tolstoy of the last thirty years of his life when he became a tiresome, spiritual scold and worse. The final trilogy of novellas are self-revelations of shame. Not only of his protagonists but of his own shame, of his preoccupation with the theme of shame. Shame is the key to understanding the deep source of his rage. Of his derangement and actual advocacy of the extermination of the human species because of what he called "the pigsty" of sex and love.

What happened to Tolstoy? It was while reading *Father Sergius* that I began to focus on a dynamic, a dialectic that involved the words "shame" and "honor." I think the word "shame" and its counterpoint, "honor," if looked at closely, take us a long way.

Consider what we learn in the opening pages of *Father Sergius*. Young Stepan (only later "Sergius"), a "cadet" from a good but not noble family, has just been promoted to the inner circle of the Tsar's court, one step away from being elevated to aide-de-camp to the Tsar.

But all is not well in his mind. There is a two-step dialectic. He feels proud at his elevation and the honor that accompanies it, but then almost immediately feels shame at his pride, pride being one of the deadly sins. He cannot escape the vicious cycle.

It is very much the same with the Tolstoyan landowner in what I regard as the "next" of the trilogy, *The Devil:* desire to honor his wife by being faithful but shame that he cannot stop thinking of putting his hands on the serving girls, particularly the one with the laughing dark eyes. Of course, Tolstoy's idea of honoring women requires that they measure up to his requirements of them. Today, we would rightfully call Tolstoy's deranged view of women, well, just that—deranged. Here are his fervidly argued prohibitions for the female sex as extracted from the rantings of Pozdnyshev on the train journey in *The Kreutzer Sonata*.

—no education allowed
—mandatory breast-feeding of children. (Other methods allow, encourage women to engage in "coquetry," a door beyond which they must never go for fear of entirely disrupting society.) Love the great disrupter.
—no tolerance for any behavior that could arouse jealousy, which puts them and their suspected lovers in constant jeopardy of legalized murder
—no abortion for any reason
—no use of contraception of any kind: It turns women into "prostitutes"

—no love for children (yes, seriously), which "puts parents into a perpetual state of panic on their behalf" that interferes with adult preoccupations ·

Of course, these iron rules then extend their anti-woman emanations to the social behavior of the entire gender, which must be submissive in every respect to men. And the men, the rules were very different for the men.

Let me begin with *Father Sergius*—although it doesn't go much beyond soft-core porn and bloody self-mutilation, to murder like the other two, it gives us clues to Tolstoy's deadly direction. There's a thematic clue in *Father Sergius* that could be seen as a key to the more overt rages in the subsequent two novellas. And it involves love depicted in a less-than-celebratory way. In fact, more self-love than outwardly directed love.

It's true there are those two brief moments in *War and Peace* as Prince Andrei is dying and in his delirium conjures up some abstract eternal love which offers immortality—"the new principle of eternal love revealed to him, the more he unconsciously detached himself from earthly life. To love everything and everybody and always to sacrifice oneself for love meant not to love anyone." But a generalized, ground-of-being type love. Not the love of two hearts.

It could be seen as a kind of answer to Larkin's assertion that "What will survive of us is love"—a return to non-personal universality.

" 'Everything is, everything exists, only because I love,' Andrei says. 'Everything is united by it alone. Love is God, and to die means that I, a particle of love, shall return to the general and eternal source.' " (What will survive of us!)

But Tolstoy and Andrei are clear this abstract love forbids

his earthly love for Natasha, which would mean irredeemable death because it does not dissolve into generality. That numinous abstract love is the closest to—and furthest from—deep love between two humans. And it is only a step off that precipice to the abysmal pigsty carnival of carnal love that was not Love. "The foul rag and bone shop of the heart."

"Inside him," Tolstoy writes of Stepan, "complex and intense work was going on... in appearance, [it was] most varied, but in essence... [it consisted] in attaining perfection and success in every task that came his way, earning people's praise and astonishment." Ultimately, though, he rejects pride in his pride. In fact he becomes so ashamed of his pride that he makes successive attempts to extirpate it root and branch.

It doesn't really make complete sense, but this is Tolstoy for whom pride and honor would supposedly be forbidden fruit for a man who thought of himself as peerless, beyond a mortal pride, a man among men, unequaled, unexampled. Who amongst us makes total sense to ourselves?

"[Stepan] always set himself some sort of goal," Tolstoy writes, "and, however insignificant it was, he gave himself to it entirely... until he achieved it. But as soon as he achieved the appointed goal, another at once emerged in his consciousness and replaced the previous one. This striving to distinguish himself... filled his life."

Is this Tolstoy speaking about himself here? It must have been a burden, then, to say the least, being the revered Lev Tolstoy. The burden of reverence. We watch as Stepan decides he wishes to belong to the highest circles of court society, and that marriage would win him the place his middling social background would not. And so he falls in love—or acts as if he has, strategically, a chess move—with one of the Tsar's favorites, the maid of honor.

It is here that we find a rare and significant early mention of "Love" in Tolstoy's final anti-sex trilogy. And one that, significantly, depicts it as little more than a ploy. Nothing that compares in intensity with the later obsessions, which have more to do with lust. One can find love mentioned elsewhere but here, never much more than "he fell in love," a flat assertion of an achievement as in "he passed the SATs." And here it seems love is clearly utilitarian. Not an emotion but a step up the ladder.

One hesitates to say there is no love in Tolstoy because it's clear Tolstoy thinks there is love in Tolstoy, and who are we to argue with him? But take the pair of lovers in *Anna Karenina*. There is barely any sex, much less love, or none depicted or even barely implied in the novel's single sex scene. As novelist Elif Batuman, a Slavic language doctorate, and author of a brilliant nonfiction book about Tolstoy obsessives (*The Possessed*), took pains to point out to me: "We see the two of them rush to their room of assignation. And then . . . nothing!" The next glimpse Tolstoy gives us is the proud Count Vronsky standing over Anna's prone, still undressed, body like a hunter over the carcass of a slain deer. He's finishing getting dressed before leaving.

Nothing much sensual, much less sexual or romantic. Not even a farewell kiss goodbye, each encased in their own sealed compartment of shame. Sex? It happened, certainly, but we never get to glimpse it. Unless we watch the Keira Knightley film of *Anna Karenina* in which we are treated to a sequence of erotic writhing and mimicking of real ecstasy with a barely clothed, heavily breathing Anna, who eventually has what looks like an extra-heavy-breathing, audibly moaning, orgasm.

A major mistake, it seems to me, because one of the mysteries of *Anna* that makes it such an enigmatic love story is the absence of any certainty of what the sex was like, even by implication—whether it was transformed to love or whether the love they supposedly felt disguised mere desire. How did the emotional dynamic between the characters change because of it? Was it, in fact, the reason for Anna's continued attachment to Vronsky, despite what seems like his relative postcoital indifference to her for the rest of the novel? Tolstoy makes her pay the emotional cost of transgressing the societal rules of the road. Where is the love she thought she was owed in return for daring to break those rules?

Some women (I'm told) are moved to momentary feelings of love by orgasm that are nonetheless transitory. For some it lasts longer; for others it doesn't have the same potency or longevity. The film adaptation imposes a shallow, all-too-obvious orgasmic theory on the mystery Tolstoy created and may not have wanted to be solved so superficially.

And so, absent a Tolstoyan description of the sex, we are left to project our wonder and our fantasies on that absence, that aporia, as they say—and see whether it adds up to more than transitory, or not transcendent, love. Does it at the very least account for Anna spending the rest of the novel obsessed about her honor, nagging Vronsky to act as if he loved her until she lets a steam engine get the final word as she jumps to her death on the track in its path? Tolstoy's metaphor for male libidinal desire is, of course, the pressure rising on a steam boiler. (It's regrettable that a more censorious age and culture denied us Tolstoy's more explicit verbal evocation of sex. Although it's debatable whether he would have deigned to mar his prose with such "pigsty" behavior.)

Some would say it's better that way, we wouldn't want Tolstoy to end up in the *Literary Review*'s "bad sex writing" finals. Still, what was it like, between Anna and Vronsky in bed? Did it involve more than sex, but the even more risky word, "love"? Was there tenderness or brutality?

In fact, Vronsky only visibly displays love when he's cuddling his new racehorse in the stable before he rides her to her death in her first steeplechase outing by breaking her leg when he forces her to leap a water hazard beyond her capability, causing her to be shot shortly after. (A fairly clear foreshadowing of Anna's own tragic fate. Ah, love!) An allegory, I'd say, of the tragic repercussions of a leap too far beyond the bounds of propriety.

Is there love in Tolstoy? Well, high school teachers are given to tediously recounting the blazing affair (irony) of the second couple in *Anna*—Levin and Kitty, whom we see and hear all too much of (if you ask me) as they murmur sweet nothings to each other in the wheat fields when Levin has a moment to put down his scythe and stop baling his hay, or whatever farmers do. This is not full-blooded love but, from the little we're told, a gluten-free, mild, watered-down, agricultural sort of affection. But one finds none of that even in that final trilogy.

I think this would be a good moment to cite an amazing offhand remark by one of America's leading Tolstoy scholars, Caryl Emerson, emeritus professor of Slavic languages at Princeton. Something I came across in an essay she wrote in the February 7, 2020, issue of the *TLS*, surveying the problems of Tolstoy biographers.

"Writing biographies of Tolstoy has always been difficult," she asserted, "because his life was devoid of the familiar needy markers of interpersonal love."

What a remarkable, shocking, and enlightening remark. It goes a long way to explain why Tolstoy ended up an enemy of love. He had never experienced it! Yes, she says, he was a habitué of brothels and took sexual pleasure from "serfs and servants" but no "interpersonal love." No love qualia.

Of course, he's not alone among great or celebrated writers. One is almost tempted to say that monogamy is an impossible demand even for the most profound manifestations of love, not just in the nineteenth-century novel. Consider Philip Roth, who, on the subject of monogamy and love, could be considered a counterpart to Tolstoy. Hating love for the impossible demands of monogamy it imposes. I'm thinking of the moment when Roth breaks out into his most impassioned cri de coeur against monogamy. His declaration of the impossibility of its demands. I'm thinking of this line from Roth's summa of love-hatred, *Sabbath's Theater:* when he, well, his Rothian, debased character, Mickey Sabbath, tells his wife that "there is no punishment too extreme for the crazy bastard who came up with the idea of fidelity."

Polyamorists might disagree; they point to certain varieties of chimps, usually the bonobos, who have "open marriages," so to speak, and thus supposedly something we should emulate because—according to the social anthropologists' chimp mind reading—there is no sexual jealousy. An argument that makes me feel less archaic believing in monogamy, as a prerequisite, a goal, for the deepest kind of love, a monogamy based on equality, which feminism has made more defensible, if not more possible.

Anyway, Tolstoy is contemptuous of Stepan, poor fellow, who we're told "fell in love" in order to advance his place in the Tsar's court.

What a dunce, it turns out. Answered prayers and all that. In Stepan's case, enthralled by his prospective bride, he doesn't suspect the closeness of the Tsar to the woman he now wants, wants for his wife, or that her closeness to the Tsar might have something more to it than her ability to take dictation (or other secretarial tasks): her beauty, sexuality, noble family class superiority, and the consequent sexual relationship with the ruler of all Russia.

Tolstoy rarely describes with any explicitness his own secret life, or that of his characters, blithely assuming that his wife will disregard the hidden life with almost inevitably diseased prostitutes that the men claim is the double life they need to lead in order to—get this—preserve their health by letting off the "pneumatic pressure" of their steam engine boiler–driven sexuality. Not that we'd want Tolstoy to be D. H. Lawrence. Indeed, D. H. Lawrence was not D. H. Lawrence—not the sex guru of legend.

Elif Batuman pointed out to me Doris Lessing's report: that Lawrence told his sexual partners that they must lie still and flat beneath him and not enjoy any touching by hand (apparently Lawrence did not get that memo about the clitoris). As Elif concluded from Lessing's account of Lawrence, "there's a man who has been lied to all his life" (by the women who faked orgasm for him). One is tempted to speculate that Tolstoy was himself similarly dictatorial in his sexual encounters with subservient lower-class women. And similarly deceived.

But Tolstoy was seriously convinced of a pseudoscientific theory he embraces with the foolish certitude of "science." That male libido is like a steam boiler. And so, he claims, after marriage to their stainless brides, men will abandon their uxorious purity if the steam engine boiler pressure of lust calls again for further release for "health" through the "gasket" of the phallus.

As I was writing this chapter, I was occasionally watching a remake of *Howards End*, the E. M. Forster depiction of late Victorian Britain, in which the imperious Mr. Wilcox makes a premarital confession of sexual profligacy and treats it and his intended bride with disregard for what her feelings might be. He doesn't care whether, in fact, she might not want to know about his sneaky philandering. Yes, she ultimately forgives him and accepts it largely—let's not fool ourselves—because of his wealth and class. But leaves us to wonder, as does the novel, with several relationships whether love, actual love, is involved. Still, compared with *Howards End* and its piquant ambiguities, *Father Sergius* is in many ways a more unambiguous work. Especially when it reaches the bloody climax.

Was Stepan "in love," as for centuries, even millennia, poets have understood it? I don't think so. John Donne, for instance, understood. He knew love was as much about farewell as anything (cf. "A Valediction: Forbidding Mourning"). Bob Dylan understood, incessantly writing heartbreaking love songs about loss. ("If You See Her, Say Hello," by far the most wrenching. If you ask me.) Dylan virtually owns romantic regret. Evidence of Dylan's efficacy as a love song writer can be found in the hundreds (thousands, it seems) of male and female children named "Dylan," often because they were conceived while Dylan songs were playing.

My favorite form of love poetry (since you asked) is the so-called aubade, which, from the time of Chaucer, at least, has been a plea for more time, more covering darkness when lovers see the first light of dawn come creeping into their room of assignation. They essentially vocalize poetic pleas that call for the sun to "hold back the dawn" or for the dawn to hold itself back and give them a brief moment, a respite from parting, a brief hour more to enjoy each other's erotic pleasures. Although Shakespeare did not seem to believe in love at first sight lasting much beyond that first sight, he did believe, or believe lovers could believe, in love at first night, or banishing first light.

There is little more beautiful in Shakespeare than the aubade between Romeo and Juliet in which she boldly seeks to banish oncoming dawn so the night can continue and he, the lunkhead, decides to argue about it. I will quote only one aubade exchange:

JULIET

Wilt thou be gone? It is not yet near day.
It was the nightingale, and not the lark,
That pierced the fearful hollow of thine ear.
Nightly she sings on yon pomegranate tree.
Believe me, love, it was the nightingale.

ROMEO

It was the lark, the herald of the morn,
No nightingale. Look, love, what envious streaks
Do lace the severing clouds in yonder east.
Night's candles are burnt out, and jocund day
Stands tiptoe on the misty mountain tops.

Almost Vronsky-like in his indifference to her plea. Or is he teasing her? The best love poems are about parting's sweet sorrow.

Stepan was "in love" as the enemies of love have laughingly understood it. Tolstoy doesn't seem to take it seriously in the late novellas, seeming dismissive of love while paying great respect to the primal power of sex, however much he claimed he loathed it. Love in *Father Sergius* is framed as a canny career move expedited by beauty, but rarely more than skin deep.

"[Stepan] . . . did not notice what almost everyone in town knew, that a year ago his fiancée had been Nikolai Pavlovich's [the Tsar's] mistress." Tolstoy believes some people can be deeply in love. But usually only naïve oblivious fools. Tolstoy's contempt for "love" sees it as a mutually oblivious transaction in which each party to the deal agrees to pretend there is something deeper, something "deep" in their attachment that transcends material, social, or sexual advantage.

Look at the marriage of convenience from the point of view of the countess whom Stepan was to marry. When she chose to reveal all to him. Specifically her sexual submission to the Tsar.

In Stepan's mind, when she confesses, he cannot admit he is capable of sullying his perfection with someone so flawed.

Stepan, whose life has been about perfection, is shattered. He suddenly sees their relationship not as love but as one of cynical social convenience.

"He jumped up and, pale as death, with twitching cheekbones, stood before her.... When summer was over, he did not return to Petersburg, but went to a monastery and entered it as a monk."

Tolstoy's Letter to *Penthouse*

What Stepan, now Sergius, discovered at the monastery was that he escaped—only for a brief moment—the temptations of the flesh but it was only to find himself in another arena that called for competition and sociability and tested his ability to achieve perfection. Tested the limits of his pride. "[Stepan] found joy in the monastery in attaining to the greatest outer as well as inner perfection... so as a monk he strove to be perfect: always hardworking, abstemious, humble, meek, pure not only in deed but in thought, and obedient.... Any possibility of doubting anything at all was removed by the same obedience to the elder."

By becoming a monk, he was showing his scorn for all those material and social and sensual things that had seemed so important to others, and had seemed so important to him.

Seven years of avoiding carnal temptation served him well

in moderating this aspect of his soul. However, "Generally, in the seventh year of his life in the monastery, Sergius became bored. . . . There was a lady known for her bad behavior who began to ingratiate herself with Sergius." He can't escape the superficial charm with which he attracts outsiders and finally realizes he must retreat even farther from the world and from women and love in particular if he seeks perfection.

Thus it was in desperation that he decides he must abandon the monastery to become a wordless hermit. He finds a cave outside the city and reduces his life to chopping wood and drawing water and incessant prayer for forgiveness for sins he had yet to commit.

Aside from Sergius's "sense of awareness of his superiority over others, which [he] experienced in the monastery," nothing was what it seemed. One senses Tolstoy has pitilessly x-rayed his own psyche—his Being—and found nothing but the bones he would end as. But perfect in their grave.

Everywhere he looks, Sergius finds the sad spectacle of the awfulness of men. I don't want to contest the judgment of awfulness; it seems obvious. Who starts wars that use rape as a weapon? Who cages toddlers in filth? Not women. But why men? I don't believe men do these things because they're mustache-twirling Snidely Whiplash evil villains.

Then why? Does Tolstoy offer an answer in the late trilogy that includes *Sergius, The Devil,* and *Kreutzer*? The dates of composition are not set in stone for these last three novellas. It was almost as if Tolstoy was in a frenzy juggling three anti-love novellas at once.

I can only say the first one I read was *Father Sergius,* with its unforgettable scene of soft-core porn and self-mutilation. That soft-core porn scene is unlike anything I'd read in Tolstoy before. Almost like one of those "Letters to *Penthouse*" from fake "ordinary guys" whose fake letters to the onetime sleazier rival to *Playboy* told soft-core stories of how alleged readers somehow get seduced by hot, sexy young women.

And it is here that Tolstoy's prose takes an unaccustomed turn, an unmistakably soft-core twist, and Sergius faces his greatest test. Here's the "Letters to *Penthouse*" part. These missives would begin with an accidental encounter. "Dear *Penthouse*, You can imagine my surprise when I was hanging out in my hermit's cave and a sexy divorcée paid me a visit, etc...."

Or as Tolstoy writes it in *Father Sergius:*

"A merry company of rich people, men and women, from the neighboring town, after pancakes and drink, went for a troika ride" past Sergius's cave, which allows them to gawk at the purlieu of a man who has chosen such a divergent lifestyle.

Night is coming but they merrily say they can spend the night in Sergius's cave. It starts to snow, and all but one decides they'd be better off taking shelter at the next settlement. The one who wants to be let off to see the cave happens to be a vivacious young woman who thinks it a lark—or more—to spend the night with a chaste wordless monk. And perhaps test his famous chastity.

Sergius sees her coming and feels a mixture of "doubt and fleshly lust." By the time she arrives at the cave she is soaked to the skin from the snow, and he is frenziedly reciting psalms to forestall temptation.

At first the prayers seem to work as he communicates with her only unseen from behind the curtained-off back of the cave.

Then she ups the ante, makes it clear she has a carnal agenda, if he had any doubt.

She begs him to let her come into the front section of the cave and dry off. He tormentedly consents, gives her some robes to dry off with and put on, and retires back behind the curtain. But their encounter isn't over. She falls ill or falls on the bed feigning illness and calls out to Sergius for help.

"She heard him whispering something—he was evidently praying. . . . But he heard everything. He heard how she rustled the silk fabric, taking off her dress, how she stepped barefoot across the floor; he heard her rub her feet with her hand. He felt that he was weak and might perish at any moment, and therefore he prayed without ceasing."

Asking for help, she "unbuttoned her dress, exposed her breast, and threw back her arms." It's those little signals.

He thinks of some church story of a holy father in such a situation who "laid one hand on the harlot and put the other into a brazier." To distract the sensual messages to his brain.

Sergius, seeking to emulate this act of fire piety, puts his hand in a lamp flame.

She calls out, "For God's sake . . . I'm dying!"

He calls back, "I'll come to you at once."

And what does he do after that moment? "Not looking at her, he went past her to the door of the front hall, [and outside] where he usually chopped wood, felt for the block on which he chopped wood, and for the axe leaning against the wall."

And "taking the axe in his right hand, he put the index finger of his left hand on the block, swung the axe, and struck it below the second joint. The finger bounced off more easily than a stick of the same thickness, spun in the air, and plopped onto the edge of the block and then onto the floor."

A grotesque scene that will horrify and please Freudian readers who imagine a different chop to a different body part.

He stops to experience the pain, then turns and goes back into the main space of the cave, looks at the woman, and asks, "What is it you want?" as if that were not already rather clear.

She stammers at the sight of blood. He begs her to leave. She begs for his blessing. He gives it. She gets back into the sledge and a year later she takes holy vows. A year later after that "she was a tonsured nun."

Well, the reader wants to say, Tolstoy! The axe, the finger. Few would doubt you've won this round. Some men are crazed—not by sex but by the attempt to suppress it.

And after that climax, the story peters out, you might say. There is even an immortal line in which Tolstoy writes (in one translation), "he raised the wrinkled stub of the cut-off finger and kissed it." Not one of those lines that will be sewn into pillows.

Some might find this a moving piece of prose, others not so much. Tolstoy seems unable to find a satisfactory way of concluding the story. In the end, years later Sergius becomes a pathetic drinker and the temptress in the cave, now a nun, finds him and comforts him. The End.

What a story. Who could have predicted that finger chop? I suppose one could say they find a kind of love in the end. But given the opportunity, Tolstoy refrains from using the word. No wonder no one promotes it to the first rank of his work for its literary grace. It is more an illustration of just how difficult it is for even the greatest of writers to bring the elements of sex and spirituality into some kind of harmony, much less love.

But it was something—the apparent impossibility of convincingly rendering that harmony—of rendering Love—that tempts Tolstoy again and finds him writing a story arguably more dramatic although of equally bizarre conclusions, this time with two endings and two gunshots and one question: Which of the two protagonists is The Devil?

In *Father Sergius* the protagonist was a bright star of the rising nobility revered for his mental and physical perfection. In *The Devil* (Version Two) our protagonist is The Devil. Or perhaps Tolstoy's a bit unfair to his protagonist. I think in the vast majority of cases men are not demonically, knowingly evil but commit evil acts nonetheless.

Here I think Tolstoy is at the stage where his protagonist does not explicitly hate sex or despise Love, he hates himself for succumbing to its temptation and the stain on his honor the shame such submission represents.

Who Is the Devil?

The Devil takes us a large escalatory step up the ladder from self-mutilation to suicide and murder.

We haven't spoken much yet about *The Devil;* it's one of Tolstoy's more obscure works, but whenever, in what order it was written, it likely represented the final lines from Tolstoy uncovered so far. His last words on love and sex discovered (posthumously), anyway. I'm not sure why, but I think of the revised ending of *The Devil*—the one that he had hidden under an ottoman cushion (my fanciful speculation about the hiding place) shortly before his death—as his final words. Not hidden well enough for it to stay hidden; in fact, in its reversal, or rather its alternative ending of the first version, it was almost begging to be found. Because the posthumous ending radically revises the identity of the Devil in the story.

Needless to say, it was anti-love, anti-women from the start, far more than the conventional misogyny of his previous work. It is not an accident that the epigraph of *The Devil* is perhaps the most famous—or notorious—citation from the New Testament on sex. The one from Matthew, chapter 5, verses 28–30. The one that sticks a shiv into the amour propre of every self-satisfied happily married man on the planet. The one that deals with "lust in the heart." The one that goes, "Whosoever looketh on a woman to lust after her hath committed adultery already with her in his heart."

Everybody laughed at Jimmy Carter—for a variety of reasons—for bringing up the rather stringent standard he posed in a *Playboy* interview during a presidential campaign (1976) by conceding that even he, though long married, had "lust in his heart" at times. Yes, likely a political ploy to defuse the Holy Joe preacher aura he gave off, the aura constantly being exposed in other preacher types who were shamed for lechery and hypocrisy despite marriage vows.

Busted! All the preachers and parishioners living a good life married to good women throwing it all away—like Jimmy Swaggart, with a sex worker he was "counseling." It was fodder for Late Night jokes and yet... and yet, is there not some truth to the fact that even the most pure and self-satisfied minister might find himself a victim of impure thoughts? Do we write it off as just "human nature" or does it make all our pretensions to virtue seem like jokes?

It is in *The Devil* that we find again that remarkable, profound source of the antipathy between Tolstoy and love: shame. One that was implicit in *Father Sergius* but explicit in *The Devil*—in both versions. I think shame—which I've argued *can* have salutary manifestations—is often elided as a powerful source of misogynistic hatred in Tolstoy, particularly in this last trilogy. Especially if we consider one consistent element of the patriarchal zeitgeist in Tolstoy, in all masculinist literature of the sort that sustains his work. Shame at the loss of self-control perhaps more wounding, destabilizing than that of control itself (there's a difference—one is controlling others; the other is controlling oneself, self-control always subject to that great disrupter, Love).

It is the old story of the male need not only to dominate the world, to dominate women, but to dominate one's own impulses, to control the female's straying away from the male's control, a shameful weakness only permitted by male loss of self-control often because of love.

The heart of the hatred is the fear of shame. The weak link in the armor, the wild card: love.

I believe it is a key to the culture of misogyny that prevailed then and prevails now. I believe that love with its recalcitrant unpredictability and uncontrollability—like quantum unpredictability, the quarks that are not necessarily subject to the stringent rules of determinism—love and love's disruptive unpredictability lie at the heart of the shame dialectic; thus love must be conquered, obliterated, made to obey. Perhaps this is why so much of literature is about love escaping control and determinism.

And at the heart of this shame is loss of control. A patriarchal society sets up a hierarchy of behavior in which the allegedly "honorable" is of highest regard and yet, as the wealthy Tolstoyesque landowner in *The Devil* learns, the hierarchy, the hegemony, is vulnerable. Regardless of all the established rules, he has no control over his sexual/romantic impulse. Nor over the way it drives him to dishonorable behavior.

Evgeny, our protagonist, marries a beautiful, accomplished, wise woman whose only flaw is less a flaw than the wariness her attractiveness provokes, the male susceptibility to jealousy. Evgeny is your typical Tolstoyan landowner, which doesn't make it autobiographical but doesn't rule an element of that out, either.

He is Evgeny Irtenev, youthful middle age, lives in a large manor house, runs a bountiful estate. We learn he has "made arrangements" with women in the local village, but nothing "serious" (to him): He has "never lost his head" over any one of them. Translation: He has not done anything foolish or inconvenient such as "fall in love" or otherwise embarrass his wife.

But then one day he's entering his house and feels an unusual lack of resistance when he pushes in the swinging door. It turns out a young woman is opening it from within.

"He stepped aside to let her pass, she also stepped aside." The door between them becomes a metaphor, as does the unexpected ease of opening.

As does also the fact that she—a freed serf serving girl who works in the granary—had pulled up her long skirt to carry something with more ease in its folds, baring her legs and her bare feet.

But this factor was not decisive. He had seen bare legs before. It turns out that the feature that struck him powerfully was her eyes.

"Smiling with her eyes, [she] glanced at him gaily. And, straightening her skirt, she went out the door."

The encounter shouldn't in itself have been life altering, though such encounters rarely seem to be from the outside. But inside Evgeny was thunderstruck: "'What's this nonsense? . . . What is it? . . . It can't be,' Evgeny said, scowling and waving his hand as at a fly, displeased that he had noticed her... and yet he could not tear his eyes from her body, swayed by the strong, agile gait of her bare feet.

"'What am I staring at?' he said to himself, lowering his eyes so as not to see her. 'Yes, anyhow I've got to go in and take another pair of boots.'" But something else soon happens. "He glanced around again, so as to see her one more time. She was turning the corner and at that moment also glanced back at him."

It seems like it was more than a casual "glance." "'Ah, what am I doing?' he cried in his soul. 'She might think something. It's even certain she already does.'"

I quote this passage as evidence that Tolstoy, at least part of him, had not yet become a madman but could still replicate a merry momentary flirtatious interaction. But almost immediately Evgeny shifts to another register. The register of Love—and dread. "'My God! What am I thinking, what am I doing!' He seized the boots and ran with them to the front hall." He meets his wife on the terrace of the house and is already stricken with guilt and shame.

"'My God, if she, thinking me so honest, pure, innocent, if she knew!' he thought."

Obviously, the trivial encounter at the door to the house has had a more profound effect on Evgeny than such a matter might ordinarily call for. His wife greets him radiantly. But he refuses to see it. He thought "she looked especially pale and yellow, long and weak."

What an awful transformation. He is already looking at life through the lens of his door frame encounter. Through the lens of Love. On the other hand—considering the casual proprietary assumption of sexual possession landowners of Tolstoy's class indulged themselves in, why the seismic effect of an encounter with a woman who was virtually a piece of his property even after serfs had been nominally freed? If it was purely an unusually strong sexual attraction, why her? Why more than that? What was it that made it so disruptive?

Or is that what love is? It would be unlikely he'd have a problem acting on it and she clearly seems willing? Or is love that which transcends the calculus of class stratification and power relationships, giving her the upper hand?

From this point on things spiral into madness and murder.

"He feared her attractiveness . . . passionate lust seared him, clutching his heart like a hand."

Elided here, of course, is the power relations of the barely post-serf state: It was his choice whether he assaulted her or not. There would be no legal consequences, no repercussions between him and the state. Only between him and his spouse if she found out.

Evgeny, trying to put his plight in perspective, just happens to recall the very same story Sergius did, about the holy man who put his hand in a fire [here "a brazier"] and burned his fingers seeking to distract himself from the object of his lust. Those hot braziers—sounds like somebody could have made a fortune selling them at a discount to guilt-ridden Russian noblemen.

Then at some point his wife takes a mild fall in the meadow and in her strange meta-recursive memory she exclaims inexplicably, cloudily, " 'Yes, I remember very well how your horses drove me straight under a train.' " The fictional wife, Liza, cries out to Evgeny weirdly using references to previous Tolstoy texts—a strange meta-textual reference to Vronsky's steeplechase horses and Anna's suicide under a train in *Anna Karenina,* which we must assume is a fiction Evgeny's fictional wife has read. Strange, the very texture of reality is being disrupted.

Meanwhile Evgeny fools himself that he is well, but, on the way back from a successful provincial election, he is unable to shake the thought of the serving girl with the black eyes, Stepanida.

" 'It was she who took me, took me and wouldn't let me go. I thought I was free, but I wasn't free.... Once I came together with her, I experienced a new feeling, the real feeling of a husband. Yes, I should have lived with her ... the other life is right here. To take her from her husband, give him money, forget the shame and disgrace, and live with her.... I'm a deceiver, a scoundrel. No, that's too terrible. That can't be done.' " (Note how he slips in a reference to how he "came together" with Stepanida, a sexual incident, which could be said to have a large effect on the outcome and leaves us wondering how much of his unalterable attraction is sexual, and how much is something more and whether and why Tolstoy seems to have neglected to mention it explicitly.)

He wonders: "'It might happen that Liza falls sick and dies.'" Death has already entered the picture, in his sordid wish-fulfillment fantasy about his wife.

"'Oh, villain!'" he justly calls himself. Though it must be noted that affairs between landowner and serf girl were a dime a dozen. What made this different? Once again, the question of what we talk about when we talk about love is raised.

He then proceeds to weigh whether to murder his wife or the granary girl Stepanida.

Shame and disgrace lead him to this soliloquy:

"'Yes, that's how men poison or murder their wives or mistresses. Take a revolver, go and call her out, and, instead of embraces—in the breast. Finished.'" Whew. Honor saved.

And suddenly the ending of *The Devil* becomes Tolstoy's film noir, a matter of dark choices. And at last a previously unspoken of, unspeakable, invisible character enters the story: the Devil.

"'She's a devil. An outright devil. She's taken possession of me against my will,'" Evgeny says of the temptress granary girl. "'Kill? yes. Only two ways out: kill my wife or her. Because to live like this is impossible.'" He stops to think a little longer. "'Ah, yes, there's a third way: [kill] myself,' he said aloud, in a low voice, and a chill suddenly ran over him. 'Yes, myself, then there's no need to kill them.' He became frightened precisely because he felt that this was the only possible way out."

But just as he's decided whom to kill there is a chance meeting with Stepanida, who works in the barn that houses the threshing machine. She's picking up kernels from the chaff. She flashes those most alluring laughing black eyes. Laughing eyes that tell him she knows exactly what he's thinking about, what they could be doing. Worse, laughing at him for pretending everybody doesn't know as well as she what a fool he is.

One accidental encounter with her and the image of her "dark eyes and red kerchief" returns to him.

But the gravamen of the story is not the unique sexual attractiveness and availability, indeed eagerness, of Stepanida, but the humiliating fact that in the power relations of the great Russian state this peasant serving girl, this dairy barn queen, holds more power than a wealthy landowner, essentially her owner, emblem of the patriarchal power structure. She can manipulate him. He is putty in her hands. He has no control over the situation. But he should! It's maddening! Is it love?

Tolstoy devotes microscopic attention to Evgeny's examination of his dilemma in this story. He can't discover a way to shield himself from her alluring enchantments; she has made him powerless over himself. He is her prisoner. Like Sergius, he sees himself as a man of honor above all or almost all, but she has penetrated his mask the way he has penetrated her. They have exchanged selves or at least genders.

Let us then look at the two endings of *The Devil* in that light. In the original published, publishable ending—the one Tolstoy didn't hide—Evgeny the confident landowner feels he has overcome his obsession. Now father of a family and master of his estate, he returns from that provincial election in which he has been accorded the position of leadership he sought.

As they settle themselves in, Tolstoy makes a point of telling us Evgeny's wife, newly a mother, will not be breastfeeding her child. Cue ominous music. We know one of Tolstoy's ironclad rules—against the leisure-class practice of handing a newborn to a peasant woman to breastfeed it because (Tolstoy believes) even this freedom of wives leads to "coquetry" and he (Tolstoy's character) in *The Devil* seems in many ways convinced that this is "science," this allegedly profound peasant knowledge of female physiology and psychology that frees such women to flirt—and more!—with men, since she is not bound with her breasts to her child. Yes, not much more than a century ago. We are told, though, that he is "completely free now of the tortures of his former allurement." But he is told that the seductive Stepanida has separated from her husband in all but name and has become something of a woman-about-town.

"Evgeny looked at [Stepanida], recognized her, and felt with joy that he remained perfectly calm." Not quite Evgeny, as we follow him strolling around his estate looking over a new threshing machine.

But when he strolled among the peasant women, he tried not to pay any attention to them… "a couple of times he noticed the dark eyes and red kerchief of Stepanida…. A couple of times he glanced sidelong at her."

What's fascinating about *The Devil* is Tolstoy's egregious omission of this erotic aporia. The barely mentioned sex. He never tells us anything more about Stepanida than her "dark eyes" and "hips swaying," yet are these the sole properties of Stepanida that distinguish her among the other female servants? Not the fact that they "made love"? Almost hidden, barely referred to, only suggested.

That's what is rewarding and denying about a story like *The Devil*. An encounter in the granary that leads to thoughts of murder opens up fundamental unanswered questions about the nature of love's bond.

Or is it a more earthly matter: Does she know a certain practice that the other granary girls (or his wife) don't know or won't perform (oral sex?)? Does he fear the loss of that exquisite pleasure? There's something more to this magnetism that turns Evgeny murderous. Is that what love is, an instant grip that cannot be unsealcd except by death?

An astute observer once suggested that the attraction here— less than love, more than sex—reminded him of the magnetic force of attraction one finds unspoken of explicitly in film noir and novels such as James M. Cain's *Double Indemnity* or *The Postman Always Rings Twice:* Cain's portrait of a sudden erotic bond that is not rationally explicable but indubitably real.

Must we conclude that they are in some fashion in love in extremis without love ever being said? It is this invisible quality, unseen but all powerful, of the sort that may have irked, irritated, enraged Tolstoy to a near-murderous degree, a mystery Tolstoy found irresolvable, damnable, unfathomable.

Tolstoy must have felt yet could not speak of that kind of hyper-attraction (because of his own wife?). Yet for all his lordly reign over language and human nature, he can't pronounce love when love means Love more than a casual sexual exchange. If powerful magnetic attraction he must have, as we will see, for this story to make any sense, there's more to those eyes than laughter. And more to Evgeny's response than fond appraisal.

Perhaps only with the withering of censorship could writers articulate what has been a fact of human nature for millennia. (Even writers of pornography seem to have failed to find the key to the erotic realm between hard-core and a special realm of esthetic sexuality that Evgeny seems lost in.)

"A couple of times" when their eyes met after one of those surreptitious glances, Evgeny felt that "there was again something," though he wasn't sure what it was. Neither are we, or maybe we are but don't have a name for it. Words fail us. Perhaps that's the point: It's beyond capturing by language. T. S. Eliot described poetic language as "a raid on the inarticulate." In Elif Batuman's new novel *Either/Or,* her main character remarks, "I never had been into transcendental states that defied the limits of language, or anything else that defied the limits of language." Love that defies the limits of language can be frightening.

Yes, we find ourselves in total bewilderment, as does Evgeny, as does, we suspect, Tolstoy. It's a simple story disrupted into mystery by the question of whether or what kind of love is involved.

Whatever it was, Evgeny was unable to take his eyes off the young woman's familiar appealing figure; he knew that "he was lost, completely, irretrievably lost. Again those torments, again all that horror and fear. And no salvation."

Evgeny seems to be in a genuine struggle to preserve his honor out of love for his wife. And so this superficially horrid story is a story about the difficult road of virtue. But we haven't come to the murders yet.

Evgeny may have failed miserably, in his attempt to be uxorious, but the attempt, however difficult, near-impossible, painfully self-denying, is worth it, the story suggests, even if impossible for him, especially considering the murderous alternatives. So rules the lordly Tolstoy who speaks for abstractions, like honor rather than the wayward satisfactions of the flesh. Or maybe he's giving no satisfactory answers, the way the great fiction writers often avoid doing, particularly in their short stories and novellas. Chekhov often offers stories that refuse to inculcate a single "meaning." You do the work, reader. You find the meaning, if any.

In any case, once exposed to those dark eyes even in the slightest encounter, Evgeny was penetrated to the very heart of his being. Tolstoy's *Devil* prompts reflection on love and love's fury. Its fatal madness. Tolstoy apparently didn't think abstinence was sustainable, and from the horrified description of Evgeny's feelings it certainly seemed like he wasn't dreaming this up. Tolstoy is so microscopically detailed in his account of Evgeny's tormented wavering, we can't help feeling *he* knew this suffering, he knew the failure he lived with. And made eros an enemy for it.

And so we come to the climax, the first version, that is. Evgeny leaves his civilized drawing room and is metamorphosed into a beast in the jungle slinking through the veldt.

He told himself he was just taking a walk in the garden and thinking things over, whereas in actual fact he wasn't thinking anything over at all; instead,

> he was insanely, groundlessly waiting for her, waiting for
> her to understand, by some miracle, how he desired her
> to come there or somewhere where no one could see, or at
> night, when there would be no moon, and no one, not even
> herself, would see, on such a night she would come and he
> would touch her body… [a lot covered by the darkness, the
> eclipse of that ellipsis].

He tempts himself, visits the threshing room of the barn where she is gathering up scattered kernels of grain. This time he has gone there with a revolver; he wants to prove or die trying that he can control himself in the face of those dark eyes who know him all too well.

Needless to say she deploys them, those eyes; they're part of her earnestly lovable nature. His heart sinks; she has proven him wrong again. Without further adieu he goes back to his study, takes out his revolver, puts the muzzle of his revolver to his temple, and then hesitates.

Who knew Tolstoy could do suspense so devilishly well? He shudders with horror. "'No, better this.' And he pulled the trigger." Putting a fatal bullet through his brain, killing himself. The story (the originally published version) ends with these short chilling lines:

He is adjudged mentally ill, we are told. "And indeed, if Evgeny Irtenev was mentally ill, then all people are just as mentally ill, and the most mentally ill are undoubtedly those who see signs of madness in others that they do not see in themselves," Tolstoy concludes.

What an amazing statement that amounts to a kind of self-exculpation, doesn't it, we're all crazy, all subject to—subjects of—love's disruption of our consciousness; none of us have control of the power to resist. Love is the great disrupter we—our rational souls—are defenseless against. Universal madness because of a pair of dark eyes. Love has made us all mad in one way or another. That's the beauty of it, some might say.

But the madness of *The Devil* does not stop there. The alternative ending, the one Tolstoy apparently hid from his wife, the ending that can be found appended to most editions of the three grim final stories, takes up from the moment on the threshing floor of the barn.

"She was there. He saw her at once. She was raking up the ears and, seeing him, laughing with her eyes.... Evgeny did not want to look at her, but could not help it. He came to his senses only when she went out of his sight."

She reappeared next to him at the threshing machine and "seared him with her laughing gaze."

With every mention of those eyes one can feel Tolstoy's "hero" losing his reason, the self-control—the "honor"—he's prayed for.

"'Can I really not control myself?' he said to himself. 'Can I really be lost? Lord! But there isn't any God. There is the Devil. And it's she. The Devil has possessed me. And I don't want it, I don't want it. The Devil, yes, the Devil.'"

"He went up close to her, took the revolver from his pocket, and shot her once, twice, three times in the back." Now, he has control.

"She ran and fell onto the heap."

Who is the Devil?

Control, control, control with each gunshot.

And so we have two contradictory—or are they?—versions of *The Devil*. In the first one—though do we know which is the one Tolstoy wrote first, or which is the one he preferred as most truthful? We can spend years in this particular guessing game. It was the suicide version he found publishable, or is it possible—or even likely—that he wrote the murder of Stepanida version, and then didn't have the courage to publish it and then wrote the suicide of Evgeny? Or perhaps he wanted them both to exist simultaneously, entangling each other.

Either way, they are tales of shame and control, or loss of control.

And remember, too, that the ascription of mental illness to all humanity is the same in each ending. The Devil is in us all.

Kreutzer

And so we now approach, with some trepidation, Tolstoy's ultimate wife-murder novella, *The Kreutzer Sonata*.

I will spare you a recounting of the hundred-page-long exterminationist train ride rant—a rant that would take dozens of pages to compress—against newly liberated women, that is the bulk of *The Kreutzer Sonata*.

The subsequent banning of the poisonous novella by the Russian Orthodox Church is most notable, not for its condemnation of the sexual content but for the Church's horror at the novella's own even more stringent condemnation of sexuality than that of the Church.

Tolstoy's novella and its nonfiction, contractually appended "postface," thematically proposes the elimination of *any* sexual reproduction, even when sanctified by a church marriage ceremony. Ironically, no sex at all was condemned as worse than too much sex since the Church had an interest in the perpetuation of the species. And the survival of sex, at least in a properly sanctified context. Love was not an issue; only love of Jesus counted.

When it comes to love, despite its conspicuous absence from the novella, the cause célèbre *Kreutzer* provoked nonetheless offers one undeniable act of love. It is to be found in the unusual saga of the way in which *Kreutzer* made its way into the world, an act that struck me as something that can only be called an act of love.

By this I mean Sofiya Tolstoy, Lev's wife, abandoning pride and even self-respect to save her husband's hateful-to-her last major work, *Kreutzer,* from being consigned to oblivion.

That is how I would interpret her desperate actions when the Church had banned publication of the novella, which, we later learn, she regarded not only as an attack on sex, love, and marriage, but also as a thinly disguised attack on her marriage and on her.

Knowing this, having read the Church-banned novella manuscript, she nonetheless took dramatic action in which she raced by troika and train to the Tsar's court, where she begged the mighty ruler to overrule the equally mighty church establishment's ban on her husband's hard work.

Why would she seek to rescue a novella that left all literate Russians gossiping about her as a wicked woman whose very femininity drove her revered husband to madness?

To my mind it must have been love. A love of her husband

and his literary genius that transcended his misogynist madness because it was *his* and she, despite all, loved him.

Some may see it—what she did, begging (or more) from the Tsar—as a kind of debasement, and it would be hard to argue that there was not an element of it. But it would also be hard to argue that love cannot impel at times either or both partners to make sacrifices of their dignity, their self-respect, for the sake of their beloved.

Love is never, at every moment, a story of perfect equity.

So the fact that the novella that weaponized Tolstoy's animus against love, sex, and human survival could only make its way into print through an act of love is a kind of cosmic literary irony.

Thus *Kreutzer* slowly saw the light and ignited a cause célèbre. At first in a semi-obscured way—according to the compromise Sofiya reached with the Tsar—it was initially buried, deep and unheralded, in a large collection of Tolstoy's shorter prose, still prohibited from stand-alone publication, though available soon in multiple English editions with—as we'll see—Tolstoy's prose "Postface" with his explicit case for extermination accompanying it.

Why think of Sofiya's act as other than love? Yes, there was a brewing dispute over the ownership of Tolstoy's invaluable copyrights. Just as likely, Sofiya wanted the world to know just what she had been dealing with in their long marriage (which produced fourteen living children) amid the domestic autocracy that belied the widespread image of the gentle spiritual sage.

But more than all that, I think she had a plan, an ambition to "answer" the depiction of love, sex, and marriage in *Kreutzer*. A novel she would write on her own as reproof, a rebuke to his venomous vision of love. And assert her own contrary vision.

She wanted the world to know, and perhaps somehow forfend, her husband's exterminationist madness. Save him from the deep end of the pool. Let the world see how far gone he was. Let him see. Offer an alternative vision of love and sex than the "pigsty" Lev denigrated them as. Indeed, Tolstoy was so enraged by the tendency of the Moscow-Petersburg chattering class of literati to construe *Kreutzer* as ironic—that he was mocking his protagonist Pozdnyshev's fanaticism—that he demanded that further publications of *Kreutzer* be accompanied by a "Postface" that followed the text and explicitly denied he was anything but deadly serious in his alignment of his own views of love and sex with that of *Kreutzer*'s extremist narrator. He was that far gone an enemy of love, sex, and sexual reproduction; he had come to the end of that road, as his nonfiction "Postface" proved in its contractually demanded assertion of his exterminationism.

But this did not stop Sofiya. She was hard at work on her "answer novel."

Must we accede to Tolstoy's demand for extermination? Is it possible he was being ironic, mocking Pozdnyshev's fanaticism? There were some, he knew, who had sought to rescue Tolstoy from himself by arguing for an ironic reading.

Tolstoy's seriousness about it can be seen in his reply to those who objected to the implication of his attack on sexual reproduction—their assertion that human life would die out. Yes, said Tolstoy in that "Postface," but science tells us that eventually, billions of years from now, the sun will cool, and human life will die out anyway. We will be spared billions of years of shame.

Glass half full.

One can only say that irony is in the eye of the beholder. Despite his protestations and his "Postface," which insist on a take-no-prisoners exterminationist chastity, could Tolstoy ever-so-subtly be distancing himself from the addled monstrousness of his main character in *Kreutzer*? He is a madman murderer, after all. Consider the way even the "Postface" might be a Kinbotean gesture clumsily—and unreliably—telling you how to read what you've read? (Kinbote, for those who have not read Nabokov's wonderful "bolt from the blue" novel *Pale Fire,* is the awkward but inadvertently charming and pedantic "commentator" on the poem in *Pale Fire,* who at least in part is a parody of the type of writer who needs comic/absurdist prefaces and postfaces to underline his distance from the main text. You could trace it back to the wonderful graphic devices in Laurence Sterne's *Tristram Shandy.*)

It's similar to the way Nabokov distances himself from the superficially charming monstrousness of his main character, Humbert, in *Lolita,* with the obviously bogus psychiatric report of "Dr. John Ray" as his foreword (a device suggested to him by Tolstoy's "Postface"? I believe it's possible).

But first I want to foreground the conjunction that has been lost in translation, so to speak, buried in the depths of *The Kreutzer Sonata.* The link Tolstoy sees between the subtle hideousness music is capable of evoking and that of love. And its subtly sinister capacity for inflaming jealousy into murder.

Most of the story will be familiar to those who have read the other two novellas in the exterminationist trilogy, *Father Sergius* and *The Devil.* (I'm sorry if you feel I've gone too far in the use of the word "exterminationist," but I'm a little sensitive on the subject, especially when Tolstoy feebly attempts to walk back his belief that reproductive sex should cease along with—eventually after a generation or so—the human race. In his "Postface" he says this—the extinction of the human species is "just an ideal," one he believes set forth in Christ's teaching. The Holocaust was "just an ideal" for Hitler—at first.) Also one can catch him in an act of biblical bad faith when he quotes the "lust in the heart" passage from Matthew in the New Testament, wherein it is said that glancing at a woman is equivalent to full-blown adultery.

Tolstoy claimed that Matthew, too, wants to extinguish life through no-sex chastity, but in fact the New Testament endorses marital sex (thus perpetuation of the species) when it says, "It is better to marry than to burn" (Paul).

In *Kreutzer* the murder is announced first or fairly early, a few pages in: The main character, Pozdnyshev, has already murdered his wife in a fit of jealousy. Later we get the details: he finds she has been practicing a duet of the Beethoven violin and piano sonata with her music teacher while he is away on business. He's tormented by jealousy during the long journey home; he arrives early, not expecting them to be dining and rehearsing alone together. He cannot stop himself from creeping up on them. Losing all control, he throttles his wife and, when she fights for her life, slashes her with a saber until she bleeds to death. Love.

Pozdnyshev has already been tried and acquitted of murder—though there's no doubt he did it—on grounds of insanity when he boards the train for the journey he will fill with his noxious rants about women, marriage, and sex. The gravamen is that his murderous jealous insanity is the inevitable consequence of love and the nature of women, to be specific. And music.

The train journey that constitutes almost the entirety of the plot before the reminiscence of the murder is devoted to his sick self-justification on the grounds of piety and the wicked wiles of women.

But buried late in this account are the several pages that justify the title and suggest that in describing in such meticulous detail the oft-malign spell that music—this piece of music in particular—has on his main character, Tolstoy is allowing us a window into his own malign consciousness and the way music affects him.

That sonata is "'a fearful thing,'" Pozdnyshev tells his fellow train passengers. "'Precisely that part,'" he adds, referring to the madly complicated opening presto movement. "What is music? What does it do?" he asks rhetorically.

He explains: "They say music has an elevating effect on the soul—nonsense, lies! It affects one, affects one fearfully. . . . It affects the soul neither in an elevating nor in an abasing way, but in a provoking way."

Then he goes into a strange riff: "'Music, at once, transports me directly into the inner state of the one who wrote the music. I merge with him in my soul and, together with him, am transported from one state to another, but why I do that I don't know.'" He enters what Sir Philip Sidney would call "another nature."

"'Take, for instance, this sonata,'" Pozdnyshev claims, justifying his deranged, jealous murder. "'The first presto. How can that presto be played in a drawing room among ladies in décolleté?'" Pozdnyshev asks. "'On me, at least, this thing had a terrible effect; it seemed to me as if completely new feelings, new possibilities, which I hadn't known until then, were revealed to me.'" (You know, insanity and murder.) He is describing a hallucinatory, music-induced nervous breakdown. The symptoms much like those of a psilocybin mushroom trip. Tolstoy's region of Russia was known for its psychedelic mushrooms. I think it's as good an explanation as any.

Shakespeare wrote, "If music be the food of love, play on." Tolstoy hated Shakespeare (talk about jealousy): There are many theories why, but I think it's just because he could not read him in English. What makes Shakespeare "Shakespeare" is nigh unto untranslatable. But here we have, "If music be the food of love, trip on it." Still, one can see, or one can read, commonalities between music and love. From the way it's produced—the friction of the bow on the catgut strings of the violin suggests erotic friction—to the friction on the nerves that, according to Tolstoy, can cause, or bring to the surface, murderous agitation.

A note of background here: Evidence that the Kreutzer Sonata, in particular, can arouse some kind of agitation may be found in a strange story—a kind of love story—about the debut duet of the sonata in front of the noble and crowned heads of Europe. It was such a fantastic success that Beethoven (at the piano) became so excited that he jumped up and joyfully embraced his violinist in the duet, George Bridgetower, for incarnating his music so perfectly. And then demanded that he do it again, a command with which Bridgetower complied with equal success.

However, the backstory of this triumph suggests that it was a prelude to agitation. It was an unusually early morning concert and Beethoven had only finished the fiendishly difficult sonata at roughly 4:00 A.M. when he handed his scrawls to Bridgetower. Bridgetower, however, was a whiz at sight reading and played the violin part he'd never seen before by looking over Beethoven's shoulder at the debut. Everyone was amazed at the music and at his skill.

But after the concert was over, the story goes that Beethoven and Bridgetower were having a drink and Bridgetower made an off-color remark about a woman Beethoven was involved with.

The result: Beethoven broke off all relations with Bridgetower, who died in obscurity and left, at the time of his burial, a note pleading for credit for his part in making the sonata famous. Beethoven, meanwhile, gave the work a different name *(Kreutzer)*—he had originally dedicated it to Bridgetower—but now, after an otherwise obscure musician he never met (Kreutzer) and who has been quoted as saying he never liked it. All we have left of Bridgetower is a beautiful poem about him by Pulitzer Prize–winning poet Rita Dove.

Music plus love equals agitation.

. . .

Anyone who has suffered the pangs of jealousy could attest to the way music—like love—can amplify agitation. Tolstoy's portrait of the hours before Pozdnyshev arrives home, which he devoted to tormenting himself with fantasies of his wife and the music teacher, will be, if not appreciated, then recognized by those who stand in awe of Tolstoy's art in his account of every micro-nano step in the detailed progress of the horror of jealousy growing in Poz's head. It's Tolstoy at his finest, if you consider portraits of self-degradation fine. This is one of the best in fiction I've read. Hyperrealism. It's the old Tolstoy who is painting a portrait newly imbued or indoctrinated with anti-love ideology.

Music is like love in so many aspects. Whether it is to be good depends on complete synchronization—of instruments resonating against each other. Of sensibilities, emotions inflaming each other. Music, like love, can—must—cast a spell to fulfill its dharma. On the other hand, as in *Kreutzer,* it seems their juxtapositions in Tolstoy's mind could exacerbate murderous tendencies.

Love and music. It would be easy to say Tolstoy hated them both. But it might be more accurate to say he came to fear them in equal measure and together. Feared their seductive power that would put him in a state where "'I feel what, in fact, I do not feel, that I understand what I do not understand, that I can do what I cannot do,'" as Pozdnyshev puts it (e.g., murder his wife).

Music and love, they both arouse fear in the post-1880 Tolstoy. And there's another passage late in *The Kreutzer Sonata* that bears closer inspection. The setting was a reception where his wife played duets with the smarmy music teacher who P. is convinced is out to cuckold him—a moment that sends P. into a mystical revery. He says she looks transformed from wifey:

"Those shining eyes, that severity and significance of expression while she played, and that complete melting away, the weak, pathetic, and blissful smile after they finished." That melting-away quality! Frightening destabilization of the integral self!

P. wonders if his wife had felt the same destabilization from the music as he did—or was it love? Presumably, the music teacher with whom she's playing a duet alone in the house experienced it. P. fears they were "melting" together. Experiencing "another nature" together.

P. imagines that "'she was experiencing the same things as I, and that to her, as to me, new, never experienced feelings had been revealed.'" Or old, but still erotically inflammatory. The music may have tripped him into an alternate universe of love and jealous dread. A dark spiritual "other nature."

But the key word for me, in that passage—and I believe it comes from deep inside the author—is that word about the effect of music: "melting." The slow dissolution of the integral self—of once again, as in *The Devil*, loss of control, or self-control, either alone or in an erotic combination with another. If you substitute "Love" for "music" in *Kreutzer* (the novella), you will see that the depersonalized state music puts him into—and it is described with great particularity—is the same state poets often speak of when they speak of love. Keats's "Odes" (the waking dream) and Shakespeare's Sonnets, for instance. The lack of self-control late Tolstoy calls "swinish." And it frightens him immensely to lose himself to it. Some people are just unable to go with the melting flow. Not when there is no certainty they will return to their comforting integral solidity. There is the threat of losing and never again finding one's old self. "I'm melting!" Remember the words of the dying Wicked Witch of the West in *The Wizard of Oz*. Melting, not dying. Waving, not drowning. Melting can mean love or death.

For Tolstoy and his insufferably bourgeois character on the train, it is death (for his wife rather than him). But melting to convergence of flesh, heart, bodies, selves—love—can be beautiful to others. To P., it is either "agitation" at the least or aural poison at the worst. ("Aural poison" plays a key role in one of literature's signature, unconventional murders: Hamlet's father, I recall, was poisoned with a liquid dose poured into his ear.)

It can be beautiful but all the more deadly.

Tolstoy may or may not have been a conscious enemy of love, but he seems unable to flee from the belief that love is an enemy of him. Of his own self, his self-possession, his heart, and soul. It's hard to deny that love needs defense from Tolstoy. Fortunately, one has recently surfaced.

Coda:

A Beautiful "Mirror Novel"

A word about this coda. When I first heard about—and then wrote about—Sofiya's novella (for *Slate* back in 2015), I found myself so exultant about its loveliness that my prose and my praise were unrestrained. I had no notion then that it would fit into a chapter dissecting Tolstoy's final bitter trilogy, which I had yet to read. So, when Sofiya's work became the perfect counterpoint to Lev's bitterness, I sought to recapture that initial rhapsodic response. But I kept producing what I thought of as subpar paraphrases of my initial response, hobbled by attempts to avoid repetition. I felt the only alternative here that would do justice to the kind of response Sofiya's novella evoked (and that I thought it deserved) was my first unmediated written reaction.

I thought *again* of Keats's "On First Looking into Chapman's Homer," his celebration of a sixteenth-century translation of the *Iliad* and the *Odyssey* into English. And the importance to the poem of "firstness," which Keats compares to that of the Spanish explorers' amazement on first glimpsing the vast Pacific Ocean. What would Keats have said if someone had asked him to write about what he felt the *second* time he read Chapman's Homer? Whatever exegetical improvements it might have, it would lose the thrill, the spell of the first time. Which is what I'd like to preserve here in my account of my reaction to the discovery of Sofiya's long-buried marvel.

But before getting deeper into it, I'd like to adduce further testimony beyond my own of how uniquely captivating Sofiya's prose can be. Just as I was going through the final edit of this chapter, I received an email from my longtime friend Errol Morris, the brilliant documentary filmmaker, telling me that his friend (and mentor), the legendary documentary filmmaker Frederick Wiseman, now ninety-three, had a film debuting at the forthcoming Vienna Film Festival based on Sofiya Tolstoy's diaries! In a phone call, Errol reminded me that I had sent him a copy some time ago of my *Slate* essay rhapsodizing about Sofiya's novella and Errol told me of something I had not known: that he, Errol, had forwarded my essay to Fred Wiseman some time ago.

Well, naturally, perhaps unjustifiably, I wanted to believe that my essay had inspired Wiseman to turn the genius of his lens on the words of Sofiya, not the novella but her diaries. But one further tribute, nonetheless, to the kind of spell, a love spell, she transmitted somehow.

Even further (this time incontrovertible) personal evidence for which is the fact that my Sofiya tribute brought me together with the woman I love and have been in love with for the seven years since she read it and got in touch with me because, as she would tell me, it gave her a sense of something important we shared about love.

And so what follows in this coda is an edited version of what you might call my "On First Looking into Sofiya Tolstoy's Lost and Found Novella," a version of which first appeared in *Slate*.

It seemed like sensational news to me. I'm not sure why it hasn't become more of a high-profile issue in literary circles. I found it to be—in the words of Mary McCarthy's awestruck review of Nabokov's *Pale Fire*—"a bolt from the blue."

In *The New York Times* on August 19, 2014, news surfaced of the discovery in the Tolstoy archive section of the Moscow State Library of a long-lost or ignored novella by Sofiya Tolstoy, Lev's wife, one she called an "answer novel" or "a mirror novel." One that answered subtly, indirectly, but heartbreakingly her husband's views on love, sex, and marriage that appeared cumulatively in the final trilogy and especially *The Kreutzer Sonata*. Written from the tormented point of view of a wife like the one murdered in *Kreutzer*. What's more, in Michael R. Katz's translation, it was no mere archival detritus but, I believe, a brilliant literary work on its own.

To my mind, Sofiya's novella deserves a stand-alone edition, and I hope it will be forthcoming since otherwise Sofiya Tolstoy's long-lost or deliberately buried work might be seen merely as one of many other family responses, while none of the others merit the distinctiveness of Sofiya's work.* Why it lay untouched,

---

*Yale University Press has published a collection of Tolstoy family members' memoirs that includes Sofiya's novella, though I found the others not on the same level as literature: *The Kreutzer Sonata Variations,* edited and translated by Michael R. Katz (New Haven: Yale University Press, 2014).

unread for a century in the Tolstoy Collection of the Moscow State Library, is a mystery. Did the Tolstoy family estate know of it but wish to keep it secret because of the unfavorable light it shed on the Tolstoy marriage? Or was the Russian state cultural bureaucracy—which finally allowed a portion to be published in Russian in 1994—unable to decide whether to publish something that cast a less-than-favorable light on the supreme icon of Russian culture? There is no certain answer.

But while reading the Yale University Press version of Sofiya's novella I was swept away by its delicate, evanescent yet powerful animating spirit. And by the surprise that she could write so well, and write about love in a way in which her husband rarely succeeded.

It went beyond the Tolstoy marriage to raise questions about love itself.

I am generally reluctant to engage in biographical criticism (and had only three years of Russian in high school, enough only to allow me to do a crude translation of Pushkin's *Pikovaya Dama*, "The Queen of Spades").

And this is a revelation about the mind of Lev Nikolaevitch Tolstoy. That Tolstoy, conventionally credited with being the greatest illuminator of the human experience in Western literature. The same one who—and fewer readers are aware of this—late in his life turned into a sex-hating, love-loathing crank who (seriously) argued that the extinction of the human species would be a small price to pay for the immediate cessation of all sexual intercourse. Everyone, everywhere. You there, hiding in the shadows: Stop fucking now!

Seriously. Yes, it's shocking, especially from a novelist whose works are known for their superb vitality, bursting with the love of life. And yet, far less well-known is that trilogy of late anti-sexual novellas: *Father Sergius*, *The Devil*, and, most vicious, venomous, and sex-hating of all, the hundred-page-long *Kreutzer Sonata*.

(It's worth reading *The Last Station*, Jay Parini's historically based novel about the last days of Tolstoy's bitter marriage—just to see how emotionally murderous that marriage had become in the decade before he died in 1910.)

None too surprisingly, Tolstoy's wife, Sofiya, took his tale of a wife-murderer personally, especially since it seemed to her it was inspired by the "issues" in her own marriage. Most especially his inability to express love, not merely lust. The *Kreutzer* narrator, Pozdnyshev—a Tolstoy-like landowner—fantasized an adulterous tryst between his wife and the violinist she played duets with. Mad sexual jealousy. And then when he comes home one night and unexpectedly finds the two dining together, he imagines the worst and kills her.

It was fair to say that Sofiya was humiliated and incensed when the novella was published and her marriage to The Great Man became suspect, subject to nationwide speculation.

For a long time, it had been thought that Sofiya kept her dismay to her private diary. But it turns out she wrote an entire novella of her own that has languished unpublished and untranslated in the depths of the archives of the Tolstoy Collection in the State Library in Moscow for more than a century.

And what a novella it is! It has not been established whether Sofiya ever wanted the novella published, or was content to let it remain a silent reproof in her possessions. In any case, evidence of how she felt about her husband's depiction of their marriage in *Kreutzer* can be found in her list of possible titles for her novella:

Is She Guilty?
Murdered

Long Since Murdered
Gradual Murder
How She Was Murdered
How Husbands Murder Their Wives
One More Murdered Woman [or Wife]

Ultimately she chose a somewhat graceless alternative: *Whose Fault?*

So now, more than a century after *Kreutzer*'s 1889 publication, Tolstoy's wife gets to have her say. It will take years to assimilate all the variations in Katz's translation of Tolstoy family responses, but I want to focus on the single most impressive thing I found on my first reading: Sofiya Tolstoy can write! I'm still puzzled by the *Times* story's somewhat cavalier unwillingness to consider her novella's literary merit and even more by the subhead's sexist characterization of her work as nothing but "a scorned wife's rebuttal." So condescending and so oblivious to the novella's own remarkable transcendence of mere scorned-wife revenge novel genre. In fact, I think it's more than just good. It is a superb compact nineteenth-century novel of marriage and fantasied adultery. A Russian *Madame Bovary*. At times one could almost say she's . . . Tolstoyan. And when it comes to love and sex, she shows her fictional husband up for the demented fool he became.

Specifically, Sofiya pulls off a remarkable structural feat in mirroring *Kreutzer*'s wife-murder plot from the point of view of the murdered wife. And she does it with prose that (in English at least) comes across as graceful, emotionally intuitive, and heartbreaking.

Thematically, she counters her husband's rage against sex and love with what is, cumulatively, a deeply affecting defense of love. Akin to Sir Philip Sydney's defense of poetry. A portrait of love from a woman's point of view unlike any you can find (or I have found) in Tolstoy.

Sofiya accomplishes something different in her novella, which, despite its defensive title, offers more than a he-said, she-said document. Instead, Countess Tolstoy counterpoises her husband's mad denunciation of sex with a skillfully evoked account of the evolution of love. Love in all its facets, from the sexual to the familial to the fantasized adulterous. Love, in all its contradictory complexities and unresolvable mysteries, from a woman's point of view. From inside a woman's mind and heart, with a subtlety that makes her husband, Lev Nikolaevitch (at least in his late work), look like a blockhead. I don't take any pleasure in saying this: I found it painful almost to write as I did for *Slate* a dissection of him as portrayed in Sofiya's novella.

In the novella Sofiya gives us a touching portrait of a tender, hopeful young girl, Anna (not an accidentally chosen name), at first finding herself falling under the spell of an older man, an elegant-looking local landowner, a count like the one who became Sofiya's husband. He's not a successful writer, but he does seem to pen boring polemics she can't really respect. He holds strong convictions, especially about sex and marriage. He's very similar to the crank Sofiya's husband became in his dotage—and almost identical in his opinions to the wife-murderer in *Kreutzer*. They are the opinions of an ignorant male presuming to be sophisticated about sex. (Fortunately we no longer have these types around these days!)

Behold sexual ignoramus Tolstoy, sermonizing to us in *Kreutzer* about his hydraulic, pneumatic, steam-engine-gasket theory of male sexuality. "Pressure," he writes, builds up and must seek "relief." ("Relief"—his charming word for the climax of his attentions to his wife, with no regard for her needs. Her relief only comes when he falls asleep.) Unsurprisingly, as its wife-murderer-to-be Pozdnyshev looks on women as nothing but an instrument for man's pressure-gasket release of steam, so to speak, *Kreutzer* offers no sense of the interiority of women. And it sees sexual passion—the sexual pressure cooker—as a terrible demand against which men must struggle to avoid shame and degradation, even when the passion concerns one's lawfully wedded wife.

Anna's narrative in Sofiya's novel offers us something else entirely. The woman in *Whose Fault?* reveals complexity, conflictedness, perplexity. During courtship, when the murderer-to-be first kisses her, "she feels a wave of passion such as she had never experienced run through her body."

And yet for a considerable time after marriage, she refuses to have sex with her husband. She is fearful of the unknown. It doesn't seem logical, but there is an awareness in the character Sofiya draws of the complex entwinement and dissociation of love and sex. She ultimately succumbs, with a briefly mentioned docility, to "relations" with him. But she finds herself almost horrified, in a detached way, by her body's response, and even more repulsed by the brutal, utilitarian nature of her husband's attention. Even after his momentary pressure gasket relief, he is never peacefully sated, or loving, but actually becomes angry and hostile at the way he believes he has degraded himself.

And yet, and yet. She finds love in the family situation, primarily love for her children and, dutifully, some kind of love for her husband. It is enough at first.

Enter Bekhmetev. He's an old friend of the husband, has been out of the country because of illness. Frail, gentle, he likes drawing and conversation. His "chivalrous politeness, propriety, respectful admiration" of Anna allows him to "completely yet imperceptibly enter" her "familial and personal life," without—at first—arousing "the Prince's vicious feelings of jealousy."

A sly dog? Not from Anna's point of view.

It is here, with extraordinary delicacy, that Sofiya begins to evoke the intangible boundary between platonic and romantic love. The love her heroine starts to experience is nothing like the hectic headlong Eros of that other Anna, Karenina.

What Sofiya succeeds in doing in her novel is to counterpoise, to her husband's inability to conjure love, her own utterly different vision. Is it one unique to women? I like Flannery O'Connor's line in this context: "Everything that rises must converge." The beauty of Sofiya's novel is in its moments of convergence or near convergence, when unity between Anna and her consort, the new man in the picture, Bekhmetev, seems imminent, so close. There are recurrent suspenseful moments of near-adulterous physical passion—love as a suspense story.

The high point, the moment of near-to-total convergence between Anna and Bekhmetev, is one of those lovely instances in literature in which conversation can transcend words and merge spirits in an erotic way.

It is the scene in which Anna and Bekhmetev exchange thoughts on the nature of infinity, not as mathematicians but as souls possessed by the same transcendent dream of limitlessness. He discovers she's been reading "a classic author, Lamartine." She says she's taking great pleasure in the work and he asks if he can read aloud to her. (Smooth move.)

He picks a passage, and it's not clear how he knows it, but she says, "That's just where I stopped" (or so she says). The passage from Lamartine's French is about night: how "night is the mysterious book of meditations for lovers and poets. Only they know how to read it, only they possess the key to it. This key is the infinite" (*l'infini*).

At this moment they both realize the implications. They both "possess the key" to the infinite. They both know how to read and translate the Book of Night.

He then says something dramatic that invokes the infinite, something about its wonder and terror: "And the relationship of night to the infinite, to *l'infini*—is astonishingly poetic. If one doesn't believe in this *l'infini*, it's terrifying to die."

The stakes are now higher. The "key" they share is the key to life, to courage in the face of death. To love. Love defined as that which gives courage to those aware of and squarely facing *l'infini*. (John Donne, DFW, Katherine Rundell, and Adam Kirsch would understand.)

(It's fascinating when you think of all the—let's face it—windy, half-baked philosophy of life, death, and history Lev Tolstoy inflicts on us, to the point, I've felt, in *War and Peace*, of obscuring the intensity of human feeling he can achieve, and does achieve, when he stops his incessant lecturing. And fascinating that his wife is able to offer a glimpse of the transcendence his grand formulations rarely deliver.)

To return to Sofiya's novel, it is no accident that, almost immediately after this *infini* moment, Anna's husband senses something and begins his death spiral into murderous jealousy. He senses something but he has no idea what it could be and can only think that his possession is in jeopardy. He becomes tormented with jealousy, with hatred of the woman he wished to possess alone.

She notes with revulsion now his lust for her: "Along with this hatred grew his passion, his unrestrained, animal passion, whose strength he felt, and as a result of which his anger grew even stronger."

It is here on this very page that Sofiya gives away the game, not explicitly, but leaving no doubt of the dynamic going on in her own matrimonial prison: "He didn't know her, he had never made the effort to understand the sort of woman she really was. He knew her shoulders, her lovely eyes, her passionate temperament (he was so happy when he had finally managed to awaken it)."

"He knew her shoulders." In Tolstoy's world of glittering soirees, when he speaks of bare shoulders, it is metonymy for a woman's naked availability. Her shoulders inflame Anna's husband because he knows they will inflame other men. Filtering that through the realization that she is subject to carnal desires too (her "passionate temperament") makes for an explosive mix in the man's increasingly deranged mind.

So things progress. Anna is spending glorious summer days painting with Bekhmetev by the riverside, and at last Bekhmetev hesitantly discloses that he has more than reading to her in mind. His acknowledgment of her desirability is cloaked: "You know that if anyone falls in love with a woman like you, it's dangerous; it's impossible to stop halfway on the road to love; it consumes you entirely."

This is, they both recognize, a transgression. Not merely an observation about "other men," but a dramatic declaration that his own feelings have leaped from platonic spiritual bonds to passionate, potentially carnal love. And we're told "he turns pale and gasps for breath." His health, never good, seems to teeter on the brink of a breakdown.

She tries to be cautious and, in a highly charged moment of implicit Eros, this exchange ensues:

"But such demand of love kills it…"

"How then, Princess, can love survive, that is, live for a long time?"

Forgive me. I couldn't help making an anachronistic connection when I read "How then, Princess, can love survive." Philip

Larkin's great poem on love, "An Arundel Tomb," ends with the line "What will survive of us is love." What is the "love" that will survive of us? It's a question I began this book with. It's a question implicit in what Bekhmetev asks: What sort of substance is this surviving love, mortal or infinite, *l'infini*?

Some spirit, Anna hastily tries to say, shying away from their physical closeness. "Oh, of course, only by a spiritual connection can love endure."

Hesitantly, awkwardly, he ventures, "You think, a spiritual connection exclusively?" (You have to feel a bit sorry for the poor guy.)

"I don't know whether exclusively or not," she says, which admits the possibility that their physical closeness could become closer.

Sofiya is incredibly adroit, suggesting in the subtext the undertow of the words and silences between them. There is an erotic charge to what they leave unsaid. Here, as throughout, in Countess Tolstoy's description of love something rings true to the array, the changeableness, the spectrum of embodiments from physical to metaphysical human love, especially a woman's love, can take.

And then, she tells us, "his glance . . . glowed inside her." Another euphemism, but what a beautiful one, luminous and sexual.

I hesitate to pursue the details to their horrifying conclusion. Ultimately nothing physical is consummated; she's too honorable. Her husband refuses to believe it. He murders her by hurling a heavy paperweight that strikes her forehead. But if her surrogate must die, Sofiya lives on in this astonishingly skillful novella. The final exclamation point to Lev Tolstoy's career.

CHAPTER 5

Love in the Age of Algorithms

Conscious subjects and their mental lives are inescapable components of reality. But *not describable by the physical sciences*. [emphasis mine] —THOMAS NAGEL

Some men say an army of horse
And some men say an army of men on foot...
Is the most beautiful thing...
But I say it is what you love

    —from SAPPHO, FRAGMENT 16, translated by Anne Carson

Love is a chemically induced drive, not an emotion, more like hunger, thirst or cocaine addiction.

    —HELEN FISHER, America's queen of love science

[Algorithms] can be an effective way of solving problems [but] the "crisis moment" comes when the intrinsically neither-good-nor-bad algorithm comes to be applied for the resolution of problems ... in many new domains of human social life, and *jumps the fence* [italics mine] that contained it to now structuring our social life together as a whole. That's when the crisis starts.

    —JUSTIN E. H. SMITH

An Intellectual Horror Story
or
Here Come the Sex Robots

There is a battle going on, a battle for the soul of love. The very identity, the existence, of what we, most of us—and five thousand–plus years of poets, songwriters, storytellers, and love-struck amateurs—thought of as love is now a matter of contention between the poets and the reductionists. The latter of whom claim that love as we have known it is not even an emotion.

Love is under attack particularly by certain brain-scan neuroscientists and their media popularizers who believe love is nothing more than an accidental conjunction of brain chemicals. Reducible to faint traces in the cloud chamber of the cortex. Not an emotion but a drive, no different in essence from cocaine addiction.

Even those who have been left cynical by losing in love—most of them, most of us, at one time or another—believe it is or was a real emotion we were experiencing, not merely a chemical reaction. No, say the neuroscience popularizers, it isn't—wasn't—an emotion at all.

That belief—that love is not a mystery, that it's been "solved" by science, that it is the outcome of a prescribed combination of brain chemicals, a belief popularized by the media and figures like Dr. Helen Fisher, a biological anthropologist, whose theory is that love is not an emotion—has come to be accepted virtually without challenge by the hosts of her many TED talks, lectures, broadcast and cable interviews, periodical features from the pulps to the glossies—the entire apparatus of media hagiography, even *The Wall Street Journal*. All but a relatively outnumbered few known as "neuroskeptics" who look askance at this kind of analysis.

That love is a drive and not an emotion and a cascade of consequences from that conclusion has become the new orthodoxy pur-
portedly based on the advance in brain-scan science made by the
now pervasive fMRI (functional Magnetic Resonance Imaging)
technology. Which, Dr. Fisher insists, has proven that love is nothing more than the product of the dopamine-mediated neurochemical reward signaling system in the brain that imperiously drives
the need to satisfy the demands of hunger, thirst, and—Dr. Fisher
likes to add in her TED Talks and other media appearances, I
think because it makes her seem "edgy"—cocaine addiction. And
love—dating and mating and all that—is there mainly to acceler-
ate the survival of the fittest progeny by helping to find and align
correspondingly compatible chemically based "trait constellations," as she calls them, in other humans male or female. (She
does not, as far as I can tell, consider nonbinary people.)

So the search for love is then not unlike the way coke addicts
search for their ideal dealers. Not something as evanescent and
contingent and unpredictable as an emotion. For one thing,
emotions are not objectively describable like those phenomena
prized by science.

We have been here before. There is a recent misbegotten history to such attempts to "scientize" emotions. The late Elisabeth
Kübler-Ross's alleged "five stages" of grieving, for instance (the
proper "scientific" way to mourn the death of others—and to
experience one's own dying), a moral "progress" of sorts, which
had no actual scientific grounding, just the scientific-sounding
numerical extrapolation from some anecdotal testimony of some
hospice nurses.

I won't dwell on the Kübler-Ross subsequent promotion
of a conman spirit medium who (seriously) persuaded her he
could bring back "entities" from the dead who would supposedly

engage in sex with her acolytes, except to say it challenged her scientific credibility.

Not that my exposé (in *Harper's*) had much of an effect, the five stages have become enshrined as an all-purpose go-to cultural meme.

Why should it matter? In a way such prescriptions of how we should die and who we should love (as we shall see) outsource the actual existential experience of an emotion and a choice to a slide deck. It's a substitute for genuine introspection; it denatures the need for self-awareness. "Oh, it's grieving stage four" or "Oh, we must have poorly matched chemically based 'trait constellations' for love." It insulates the self from the true experience of the self.

It may be too late for love, yes, but I feel someone has to pull the rug out from under love pseudoscience. Although it might be gentler to call it "intrudo-science"—scientific mind and method intruding upon, like a bull in a china shop knocking over the delicacies of romantic emotions. (I might call it "deludo-science" and you might as well, once I have laid out for you the way this "science" has programmed how to act with a potential date or mate with different chemical trait "constellations.")

But although the five stages have become accepted almost universally in pop culture as scientific observation and mapped onto all sorts of human experiences as scientifically derived, they have no foundation in actual science, just subjective observations. No basis for choosing whether to "go gentle into that good night" or to "rage, rage against the dying of the light."

The idea that science calls for one to follow a certain path in dealing with grief, dying, and love has a soft totalitarian vibe. Don't act out or be typed as a "bad mourner" undeserving of empathy.

Now love has been given the scientific staging treatment of the sort Kübler-Ross gave grief and death.

Something similar has gone wrong with "love science" as recently updated by Dr. Fisher—no, no afterlife entities—but an elaboration, an embroidery matrix of the original sketchy science that makes it look more like astrology than science. It sounds ridiculous yet her "trait constellation" systematizing has been accepted credulously—and promoted relentlessly—by no less a venue than *The Wall Street Journal*. And nobody has taken it seriously enough, apparently, to debunk it. I'm sorry, it seems to me it's the peak of reductionist hubris. At the close of this chapter I will present a goodly sample. It will, I believe, speak for itself about something terribly second rate taking over a crucial sector of the culture. The re-astrologizing of love, I'd call it.

And it seems to me that once you claim you have science behind you, you can get away with claiming virtually anything. So, does it matter what we call Love, qualitative emotion or quantitative drive? It doesn't seem to matter to the worshipful hosts of Dr. Fisher's reverent broadcast and cable interviewers, the many awed profile and feature writers in scores of periodicals. They all seem to take for granted that she is the unchallenged, unchallengeable voice of settled science. And Science tells us to forget thinking of love as an emotion. Dr. Fisher's decree is the most prominent voice heard in popular culture on the subject.

Does it matter? I can't help but think it matters when the discourse of an entire culture redefines an essential aspect of our humanity—who we choose to love and why we feel we do. Now we're told it is not a matter of free will, of "agency," as the academics prefer to call it. Rather that we should construe, humanity should construe, human beings as nothing more than algorithmically driven robots—"sex robots" the phrase the poet and essayist Patricia Lockwood used (in her scorching essay on John Updike in the *London Review of Books*) to describe Updike's sexually obsessed, loveless characters.

"Sex robots" programmed by a few brain chemical signals to perform one task—to choose *for* us. Love is thus at best an accelerant, our "choices" only self-deceptively "ours," but instead chemically programmed, although we often think they are our willing choices, however counterproductively they turn out.

The "sex robots" metaphor can't help recall to me the TV series *The Walking Dead*—beings zombified, emptied out of frivolous emotions such as love. Indeed figures from another horror movie come to mind as well: *Invasion of the Body Snatchers,* in which humans become nothing more than soulless "pods," sacks of sentient chemicals, simulacra of selves, nothing more. An intellectual horror show.

I hasten to add that skepticism about the kind of claims Dr. Fisher makes, claims about "love science" in general, are not in any way "anti-science" like the claims of climate deniers, or evangelical anti-evolution devotees. Rather, they reflect a growing civil war *within* science that the media has not caught up to or would rather not complexify their clickbait "what is love?" features with.

It is a war about the encroachment of a dehumanized reductionist science that in more areas than love—in questions of morality, values, "agency," free will, even racism and other evils— sees humans as little more than walking mechanically deterministic algorithms. That is what is at stake. Or as the eminent philosopher of mind Thomas Nagel so succinctly and saliently put it, science is blindly seizing upon human qualities, which are "inescapable components of reality"—things like consciousness and love, "that are real," as real as real can be but "*not* describable by the physical sciences." As the philosopher Justin E. H. Smith put it, the algorithm has "jumped the fence" from hard science to structuring human relations and our social lives.

(To be fair to the other side in this scientific schism I will cite my friend Errol Morris, the filmmaker and philosophical thinker, author of a book on Thomas Kuhn's history of the philosophy of science—the "paradigm shift" and all that—a two-word addendum he likes to mention when I quote Nagel's "not describable by the physical sciences.")

"Not yet," says Errol.

"Not ever," I believe. They are alien categories. No advancement in science will result in knowledge of phenomena that are not amenable to scientific inquiry. Apples and oranges. (Nor do I add this out of some religious conviction—I am an atheist-adjacent agnostic.)

Alas we will likely never observe—and thus be able to make calculations about—the molecules of thought because thought is not composed of molecules. Similarly, we will not see the quarks of love because love is not made up of subatomic particles. (If you think it is, tell us.)

The extreme form of reductionism that argues we could thus reduce love and other aspects of consciousness to itty-bitty material particles (the quarks of the quarks of love) is called "physicalism." Consider a recent essay by Adam Frank, an astrophysicist, no less, at the University of Rochester (no poet he) in the journal *Aeon*—an essay called "The Blind Spot," meaning the blind spot of science. It's an essay that could be seen as an expansion of Thomas Nagel's assertion that "conscious subjects and their mental lives are inescapable components of reality" but are "not describable by the physical sciences," and expands upon "physicalism." Physicalism, Professor Frank argues, is a blind spot of science because it does what Nagel warned against (so far without convincing refutation and I've read all the latest ones, "emergent properties" and the like, all of which devolve unconvincingly into arguing that some tiny, tiny physical bits will turn out to be just a little better—somehow more sentient—than the previous little bits we've known, the quarks and photons. Yes, partisans of physicalism are driven to argue that rocks and stones have some primitive "sentience").

Behind the "Blind Spot," Frank says, "sits the belief that physical reality has absolute primacy in human knowledge"—nothing exists in the universe that is not composed of teeny tiny particles of irreducible matter—"a view that can be called scientific materialism. In philosophical terms, it combines scientific objectivism (science tells us about the real, mind-independent world) and physicalism (science tells us that physical reality is all there is). Elementary particles [the electromagnetic spectrum], moments in time, genes, the brain—all these things are assumed to be fundamentally real. By contrast, experience, awareness, and consciousness are taken to be *secondary* [italics mine]. The scientific task becomes about figuring out how to reduce them to something physical."

In the world of the physicalists things like consciousness and love must be reducible to itty-bitty material particles, particles of love, for instance. The great philosopher Lucretius (c. 100 BC), author of the magnificent creation poem "De Rerum Natura" ("Of the Nature of Things"), believed the universe was created by Love, by the goddess of Love, Aphrodite (or Venus), out of waves of little love particles. The contemporary successor to Lucretius, the mystic quasi-scientist Wilhelm Reich, the early disciple of Freud who attempted to combine Freud and Marx, believed that the "orgone energy" that pervaded the universe was not a massless radiant phenomenon but composed of *particles* he called "orgones." (Reich managed to convince "heavyweight" male literary luminaries like Saul Bellow and Norman Mailer to sit in his "orgone accumulator" boxes to revive their erotic drive.)

It is nigh unto ridiculous when you spell it out, but physicalism is the ideology behind "love science." Love, we're told, like everything in the universe, is composed of quark-like invisible but material bits, the ones that make up chemical molecules and electromagnetic currents in the brain. Even if you want to see it as waves, waves are reducible to photons in the electromagnetic spectrum and photons are material particles made up of quarks.

It's "turtles all the way down," as the jocund among philosophers like to say. (A lady, the story goes, was convinced that the universe rested on the back of a giant turtle. When she was asked what held up the giant turtle, she said it rested on an even bigger turtle and beneath that... "It's turtles all the way down." Thus when it comes to the science of consciousness or love, with physicalism it's particles all the way down.)

So, again, does it matter if love is a drive or an emotion? Or is it just a matter of semantics? It is not the only problem with the so-called science of love, not the only problem but a foundational one. A claim of mathematical, statistical determinism that even more absurd claims are built upon. More than anything the claim that love is measurable, quantifiable, reducible to particles.

Not so, I guess it needs to be said, because love is the province of the qualia. Love is the unknown country, the unquantifiable, indefinable, unmeasurable-by-numbers realm of the feelings, yes, the emotions, for which there is no equation, no algorithm, no definable, definitional basic particle, no unitary definition for all humanity.

Snowflakes, Fingerprints, and Chekhov

To see love as an emotion rather than, as Helen Fisher insists, a drive, is to recognize the efflorescence, the gradations, of differences in what evokes love, a phenomenon captured in the way the Molly Bloom soliloquy in Joyce's *Ulysses* is about the evolution of an emotion and differs from some Pornhub video designed to instantly satisfy a drive. Nor does Dr. Fisher focus on the question of whether love differs between same-sex or nonbinary combinations and the heterosexual dating-site couples that are her primary subjects.

I don't think I have to spell out the implications for love when considered as a drive rather than an emotion. As a drive virtually anyone will do, just as for a coke addict any crack will do, whether it be "Bolivian marching powder" or "Peruvian pink flake," for both of which the key ingredient is identical.

While, on the other hand, like snowflakes and fingerprints, no love story, no love, is emotionally identical to any other, not in life and not in serious literature. In the multiplicity of love stories of Chekhov, one finds the unpredictability of the trajectories therein, just to cite one instance in the vast literature of love. It almost could be said that the works of Chekhov are cumulatively about the irreducibility of love to a singular mathematically predictive drive, or formula, but rather an infinite number of unpredictable emotional shadings, twists, and turns with no road signs. As an emotion almost no one will do, or at least the one will rarely be predictable by one of only four of Helen Fisher's "trait constellation" chemicals.

While reviewing a draft of this chapter I came across a lovely comic celebration (I think) of Chekhov in Elif Batuman's just published novel *Either/Or.* She describes her protagonist, Selin, a young Harvard student wrestling with Chekhov's famous story

"The Lady with the Little Dog," a story about an extended adulterous affair. At first Selin gets angry that the characters don't react to each other *logically,* then she discovers herself charmed by the unpredictability, the irrationality, of human nature it portrays, its Chekhovian nature.

A drive reduces eros to something simplistic the reductionists can comprehend, measure, quantify easily like equations, chemical reactions, and the algorithms of dating sites. (It is little wonder that the chief popularizer of the love-is-a-drive-not-an-emotion meme, Dr. Fisher, is a "science consultant" to the vast dating site match.com, through its corporate affiliate, chemistry .com.) And Fisher discloses in her scientific papers that she often chooses her experimental subjects from dating sites.

The complexity, the ambiguity, the temporality, the contingency of an emotion does not submit itself easily or at all to the metrics, the measurability, the quantifiability of a drive. No wonder the new "love scientists" favor the stubbornly quantifiable unchangeability of a drive, the submission of a drive to mathematical calculation, milliliters of brain chemicals, not subject as emotions notoriously are to constant nonformulaic fluctuation in essential qualities. Drives can be depended on to differ only in quantity, not in quality, not in qualia.

No, emotions must first be reduced to simplistic brain-based drives the love scientists can turn into statistical tables—or, as Dr. Fisher calls them now, "trait constellations." Who is destined to love whom—or who is best suited to love whom—the way astrologers supposedly consult galactic constellations. The neuro tech reductionists stay away from attempting an analysis of emotions that involve the heart, not the brain. (The metaphoric heart, not the lump of meat in the chest, although, it's true, the heart has its primal signaling system in the rapidity of the beat, which unfortunately is never precisely translatable—does it mean hope or fear or a complex, conflicted combination of both?)

But having declared emotions to be irrelevant to the genesis of love, the scientists tend to stay away from them like they are kryptonite. Red kryptonite, the kind that disables even Superman.

What convinced Dr. Fisher of this momentous discovery—love is a drive, not an emotion—her mantra in all the lectures, cable and broadcast appearances, reverent unchallenging periodical profiles with which she's captured the discourse of popular culture about the "science" of love?

I've examined some underlying peer-reviewed papers of hers, and her colleagues' earlier experimental "proofs" of this thesis (in the *Journal of Neurophysiology*), and it's not impressive to me. Rather than calibrate differences in its sample participants— economic, ethnic, educational—and their possible effects, they just throw together a bunch of dating site patrons, the latter being particularly easy to find because Dr. Fisher's match.com consultancy gives her access to the vast sea of lonely hearts shopping to find a compatible "trait constellation." Or at least not a serial killer or stalker.

From this pool Dr. Fisher purported to examine ESIRL or Early-Stage Intense Romantic Love—yes, as I've mentioned, but bears repeating: In the new science love is "staged," just like cancer. But in all its successive stages in successive papers in the *Journal of Neurophysiology,* the default assumption is that love is not an emotion.

In that historic, game-changing, culture-shifting study, Fisher and her colleagues used seventeen—yes, that many—experimental subjects. All of whom claimed to have been deeply in love or lost someone they truly, madly, deeply romantically loved. Astonishingly, she appears to have made no distinction in the interior chemical worlds she was purporting to measure between those who were in love and those who had lost love.

Anyway, she and her colleagues put their subjects' heads into the MRI brain scan devices that use the presence of iron in the blood's hemoglobin component to trace blood-borne neurochemical surges in the brain. She claimed to discover that, when her subjects were shown pictures of alleged current or lost loves, dopamine, a key signaling neurochemical of the drive systems in the brain, surged to (among other places) the "ventral tegmental area" and the "caudate nucleus" (then thought to be the cortical regions sensitive to feelings of love), causing an excitation there.

Eureka! Voilà! Dopamine mediates drives and dopamine surges to the love buttons in the brain so love is a drive. Although, as many neuroskeptics have pointed out, this doesn't distinguish between a cause (of love) and a correlation of love (in which the feeling of love, the emotion of love—the mysterious manifestation of love—may cause the surge rather than the surge causing the love). A chicken-or-egg problem, but a fundamental philosophical difference.

But those were the foundational experiments on which she built her career as the queen of love science, inevitably introduced as the voice of science, even though her subjects were mainly cis-hetero, Western, and middle class (or not distinguished identifiably by economic, ethnic, and educational backgrounds). Her conclusions were universal, she claimed, not just true of American suburbs but "cross-culturally," true indeed for more than one hundred cultures across the world she claimed to have "studied," although we will examine what she actually meant by this cross-cultural "study" that claimed love was the same virtually everywhere in the world.

And now she has gone beyond her staging of love studies to an astonishingly complicated system of "trait constellations" that

(*The Wall Street Journal* tells us) depend on a fifty-six-question questionnaire to divide subjects or gullible clients into four "trait constellations" like the twelve houses of the astrologers, only more simplistic. Surprisingly, she did not revert to the brain mapping of her predecessor "brain science," phrenology, which depended on analyzing the alleged psychological significance of bumps on the head. You might say she found the bumps inside the head with her beloved fMRI brain scans.

To be fair to Helen Fisher, she is not alone in seeking to reduce emotions to numbers and equations, to fit it into the straitjacket of a single theory.

In fact, if you spend some time, as I have, looking into contemporary academic theories of the emotions, you will come upon, for instance, Basic Emotion Theory, which a recent essay in the well-respected philosophical journal *Aeon* tells us is "accepted by most psychologists."

The author, Elitsa Dermendzhiyska, characterizes Basic Emotion Theory as the construct accepted by the majority of psychologists today. "They maintain that there are six or so emotions, most often listed as happiness, sadness, anger, surprise, disgust, and fear." (Note the conspicuous absence of love.) These are said to be universal and hardwired, the hard-won products of long evolution. Other emotions are compounds of the basic ones or are not emotions at all.

We learn, according to the *Aeon* essay, that "Basic Emotion Theory dates back to a study undertaken in the 1960s by the psychologists Paul Ekman and Wallace V. Friesen to test their hypothesis that emotions were universally understood 'in the face.'" The concept Helen Fisher seems to have adopted, as one of her research colleagues, Lucy L. Brown, told me—that every emotion can be identified by a signature facial expression. Precisely six.

Proponents of this theory "chose as their subjects the non-Westernised Fore tribespeople of Papua New Guinea. At first, they simply showed photos of faces posed to express the six basic emotions.… The researchers concluded that emotions were constant across cultures—basic and universal. This idea pervades numerous psychology labs today. As the scholar Ruth Leys points out in *The Ascent of Affect* (2017), the theory is particularly attractive to scientists because it leaves out intentionality—something too variable and messy to measure." Intentionality such as love and choice. There is no signature "love face" and, when you think of it, all too many and varied images come to mind.

Love: "too variable and messy to measure," so throw it out of the lab, out of science entirely.

Thus, while Helen Fisher wants to call that which we call love *merely* an emotion, the psychosociologists deny love even the status of an emotion because it eludes, evades, defeats definitive facial identification and thus quantification. "Too variable and messy." Love defeats science, you might say.

What Are the Stakes?

How will love be regarded in the future? Will the literature of love be reduced to archaic relics of primitive prescientific beliefs? Or reduced to numbers and algorithms in new generations of SHAXICON? When studying Dr. Fisher's studies, I found myself thinking of life-changing moments not just in my own experience of love but in the astonishing literature of love now consigned to be the work of fools who didn't realize they were writing poetry, songs, plays, and novels about emotions that were essentially irrelevant and trivial, if not nonexistent, autonomous drives. I thought of the Terminator movies where the machine registers a complex set of numbers, based upon which it announces, "target acquired." We are all sex robots.

Thinking about what a vast gulf there is between those who spend their time measuring dopamine levels in the brain as their approach to the wildly varying experiences of love, those attempting to straitjacket love into numerical categories or Helen Fisher's brand-new "trait constellations" as opposed to those who approach it through reading and writing about the experience of love. Through *having* the experience of love, experience that can't be reduced to an algorithm. Will the future of love, the future of love study, be algorithmic or experiential?

While making my way through *Journal of Neurophysiology* papers, I found fragmentary memories of love literature—of love—surfacing amid the sterile abstractions of "love science."

I think one deep emotional impetus for writing this book has been thinking about the literature of love I've loved and the people I've loved and the way this "science" makes the poets, writers, and songwriters, their beautifully expressed emotions, and those affected by them seem like fools taking foolish things seriously when the reverse is true. The scientists are the fools.

Just to name a few of the alleged fools who thought love was an emotion, I'd begin with Homer and his heartbreakingly beautiful portrait of Penelope at her loom in the *Odyssey*—which is not often recognized as a love story, just an adventure tale of manly men. But it is a beautiful epic love story about the long terrifying delay—ten years—that separates Odysseus from returning to his beloved Penelope.

Is there anything more heartbreaking than Penelope daily weaving a beautiful tapestry almost but never complete, promising the predatory suitors who have descended on the Isle of Ithaca that she will give up hoping for Odysseus's return and choose a marriage partner as soon as her tapestry is completed?

And then nightly, painstakingly, unthreading what she's done on the loom in order to put off the suitors, claiming she's still waiting for the return of her wandering beloved Odysseus, whose eyes the tapestry was meant for. A beautiful image of love. Of the making and unmaking of art. Of the making and unmaking of the heart. No, say the neuroscience popularizers, Penelope was merely obeying a drive mediated by her dopamine-addled brain, a drive for clingy romantic attachment. What a fool she was. What a fool Homer was.

Nor does dopamine explain the anguished cries that echo centuries later in the few fragments we have of Sappho that leave it unclear if they are cries of triumph or despair or both but have moved readers for centuries. An ambiguity that defeats attempts to reduce it to a singular drive.

"What fools these mortals be," as Puck says in *A Midsummer Night's Dream* when he discovers the mixed-up pairs of lovers awakening in the dew outside Athens, after having responded to the elixir Puck dropped in their eyes made from the flower with the strange name—"love in idleness"—although probably dopamine, right?

Fools, Penelope and Homer and Sappho, for believing in such emotions. Fools, the lovers in Shakespeare's *Dream*.

And speaking of love and the *Dream*, I know my life was changed forever, emotionally, when I was lucky enough to be wandering the English Midlands as a youth and stopped at Shakespeare's birthplace in Stratford-upon-Avon the night, the very night, Peter Brook's legendary production of the *Dream* debuted and changed how Shakespeare was played ever after (as Nicholas Hytner, one of today's great Shakespearean directors, once confided to me). Even though the play could be seen as a mockery of love at first sight, it could also be seen as a mockery of the idea of a chemical genesis of love. Puck's eye drops caused whoever had been dosed with their psychedelic power to fall in love with the first human (or creature, in the case of Titania and Bottom) they saw.

The cumulative effect of the astonishing stripped-down brilliance of Peter Brook's actors speaking Shakespeare's lines as if they just came into their head, inspired by love, and Brook's innovative rehearsal techniques (which I've written about in *The Shakespeare Wars*), the cumulative love of the play, the playwright, his language, of the power of artistic metamorphosis, it's hard to explain but it all ignited a conflagration of love that night, in all those of us there. One that in my case turned out to be love at first sight (and last night) with a woman I met in the interlude, with whom I ended up taking a romantic stroll down to the river Avon and watching the swans tuck their necks into their back feathers and drift sleepily away downstream. (I'd never seen swans fall asleep that way before.) After which we politely said good night, I never saw her again, but will never forget her and the "sharp tender shock" when our eyes met.

Nor will I ever forget the play and the night I saw it again on Broadway when the theater literally caught on fire from the candlelit wedding banquet. The *Dream* convinced me there is such a thing as collective love that kindles individual love in us like a candle flame. Fools, of course, all of us mistaking a simplistic drive for a complex emotion. Love is a drive incapable of such beautifully transformative power, right?

But let us not forget that long before the formal birth of love lyrics in the works of Sappho and even the prior vanished oeuvre of the mysterious Archilochus, there were erotic cave paintings, there were love letters and poems inscribed on wax or wet clay.

Images of the erotic frenzy portrayed by the Grecian urn paintings celebrated thousands of years later by Keats ("What mad pursuit... What wild ecstasy") drifted into my mind. As did the erotic mosaics of Pompeii, magically preserved from Aetna's wrath.

There was, even earlier, the Song of Songs, wherein the poet lovingly celebrated his lover's breasts in an ingenious device that vocalized her erotic longing in his words ("Let him kiss me with the kiss of his mouth... my breasts are like two young roes feeding among the lilies").

And I thought of the lonely, lovestruck Latin lyric poets and elegists of Rome throughout the ages—Propertius, Tibullus, and Catullus, to name a few—and my lonely nights freshman year at Yale wrestling with translating them and feeling a kinship with those poets, alone at night with their fantasies like Jacob wrestling with an angel.

Leaping over a thousand years there is Chaucer's "Troilus and Criseyde" and its exquisite "aubade"—the genre of the predawn poem, which mourns the first signs of dawn that will tear the lovers apart. So different from the cynical mockery of love in Shakespeare's play of the same name (though slightly different spelling), *Troilus and Cressida*.

But in addition to his 150 or so mainly love-tormented sonnets Shakespeare gave us, you can come across that one line so sad and heartbroken and heartbreaking and perfectly delivered by Sir Andrew Aguecheek, "I was adored once." Proof alone in its simplicity and complexity that love is not found in the singularity of a drive.

And there was the unforgettable night I saw Claire Bloom recite all of Shakespeare's epic-length narrative poem "Venus and Adonis" with the clarity of a pure mountain brook and the intensity of a fever dream of love in its evocation of the goddess of love, or should we now say the goddess of coke-like drives.

Don't remind me of the romance of Esther Summerson and Mr. Jarndyce in Dickens's *Bleak House*, which had me weeping

for years every time I recalled it. Still does. But no, not an emotion there, right?

Enough! I could go on but will stop with the daring evocation
of love in a handclasp on a stone sarcophagus that prompted
Larkin to abandon his customary gloom and exclaim, "What will
survive of us is a drive." No, I'm sorry, "What will survive of us
is love." We could survive as a species without landing on the
moon, but would we be recognizably human without love poetry
that invokes the moon?

So those are the stakes to me, the deep thrill inculcated by
the literature of love whose surface I have barely scratched, only
given some off-the-top-of-my-head memories and moments we
are now told can be dismissed as little more than an analogue of
sniffs from a line of cocaine.

Yes, some will say, it doesn't matter. But I think it not only
matters—it is a symptom of the dehumanizing encroachment
of science on what are aspects of our consciousness that made
us most human and their reduction to nonhuman particles,
whether molecules, equations, algorithms, or quarks. Not just
love, but justice, morality, evil.

It's like the proverbial hedgehog and the fox of Archilochus
again: The hedgehog knows one big thing (the single indistin-
guishable "drive") and the fox knows many things (the infinitely
variable emotions). That is what love poetry and song and story
are about: the differences, the different narratives of each love
affair. The physicalists want to empty us out of the cornucopia of
differences. Render us the "Hollow Men" T.S. Eliot wrote about.
And what is at stake in this battle I spoke of, the battle for the
soul of love, is not isolated. But rather analogues of the same
battle can be found in disparate areas of human experience, such
as the conceptualization of morality and even evil, also subject to
the blind invasiveness of brain science.

Blind? You may have read about the neuroscience team that used their favorite tool, the fMRI brain scan device, on a dead salmon—and got the same response as that of a living being. Not the fault of the salmon, but rather the fault of the machine and blind faith in its scientific trustworthiness. Neuroscience is an aggressive but not infallible science. Applying it to love is like using an electric power drill on a butterfly.

The many-fronted defense of love does more than just resist the materialist chemo-mechanization of love, but also deepens the appreciation and the beauty of love and its infinite variety, the forms that the emotion of love, such a shape-shifter, takes. The literature of love poetry and song and story that evokes an almost infinite panoply of loves. Evoking an array of, yes, emotions, not unitary drives.

So also for such numinous indefinable un-pin-downable concepts as evil. We know it's there but we can't decide what its boundaries or definitions are because it can't be reduced to equations or brain scans.

I wish I could ignore it, the assault on the soul of love—it will be difficult to challenge, much less reverse it—but I feel I can't stand by and watch that soul stolen. Stolen away from the poets, not just from literature, but from lovers, from serious thinkers and philosophers.

Even the loss of love affirms its painful reality at times. John Donne's own title "A Valediction: Forbidding Mourning" is in fact a beautiful affirmation of love disguised as a farewell. Indeed, for centuries—millennia, in fact—the experience of Love, from Sappho to Willie Nelson, was most beautifully evoked by its loss, by the hole in the heart it can leave behind, after an all-too-brief habitation, by an unexpected disappearance, an absence not just forbidding mourning, but permitting eloquence and elegance beyond crude chemical analysis.

Love—evoked so often in flight by poets and artists. Verbal and visual art whose multifarious ever-shifting subtle and wild colorations can capture the often all-too-brief and elusive experience of love, not merely the number of milliliters of certain neurochemicals in segments of the brain.

The metrics of the neuroreductionists, the foremost new enemies of love who display an implicit contempt for such a numinous but gloriously cloudy conception as love by seeking to reduce it to an equation or an algorithm, or a neurochemical reaction based in the tunnels and runnels, the damp Venetian passageways of the brain. The brain, not the heart.

And it's not just love. It's important to point out, it's every numinous aspect of humanity—morality and evil, for example—subject to neuroscience imperialism.

Thus far challenged by a mainly subterranean or subtextual battle in North America where the opposition more frequently goes under the rubric of "neuroskepticism" or "neuroethics" (I recommend an MIT Press collection of papers on the subject called *Neuroethics* for those who wish to explore its American branch more deeply).

Did Hitler Have a Conscience, Ron?

I'd like to tell you how my thinking about this began with evil before love. It was while writing *Explaining Hitler* and its study of futile attempts to attribute Hitler's evil to various (conflicting) neurological complexes (and thus, however, inadvertently exculpate him from moral responsibility for his genocidal crimes: He couldn't help it, his dopamine went to the wrong cortical portal).

Yes, I had taken on SHAXICON, which attempted the reduction of what was "Shakespearean" to digitizable particles and it had alerted me to the folly of reductionism.

But the question of the neuroscientific reductionist explanation of evil took on saliency again for me the summer of 2010, which I spent in England on a Cambridge University fellowship that focused on the interaction and separation of science and religion. It was my introduction to the worldview of the "neuroskeptics," who challenged the determinism of the mainstream neuroscientists.

As it happened, there was, on the Cambridge "campus," crisscrossed by eight-hundred-year-old streets and alleys, this hole-in-the-wall gritty newsstand vendor shop across the street, as I recall, from the manicured emerald lawn frontage of Trinity College (once home of a "Third Man" mole, Kim Philby). A newsstand shop that offered what to me was a joyful selection of smudgy newsprint—British newspapers from the red top tabs to the sobersided broadsheets, an armload of which I would gather up each morning to delight in since hard-copy newspapers had just about died off in the United States and—there's a tragic love story—I love them.

I don't remember in which of these papers I first saw it, but I had been following a murder trial through the various papers' lenses, and in one of them—I think it was *The Independent*—I found a provocative spread about murder and neuroscience keyed to the trial of a confessed killer. A story that made the claim that punishing such killers judicially was wrong because neuroscientists had shown there were neural defects in their signaling apparatus in the brain—a missing or malfunctioning organic chip, in effect—that made murder if not inevitable, then not necessarily immoral, because the killers were incapable of controlling their acts. They lacked "agency," as it's said, lacked free will, lacked the proper brain chemicals for constituting a moral being. The dopamine signals did not ring the bell at the right portals in their cranium. And thus they shouldn't be punished. They didn't do it; their brain made them do it. It was an uncontrollable drive, not an emotional choice.

We've heard well-intentioned versions of this before, but here they were given a dodgy neuroscience rationale for abandoning any jurisprudential punishment, or accountability. Not just murderers, but anyone. No one was to blame for anything in this vast neurochemical behavioral wasteland.

At the same time I began paying attention to well-credentialed refutations of brain-based neuro exculpations by "neuroskeptic" thinkers such as Dr. Raymond Tallis, who wrote often on the subject in the London *Times Literary Supplement*. Who made the case that neural circuits' defects did not obviate the notion of immorality, intentionality, or the consequent need to punish evil, free-willed choices.

In fact I wrote a paper for the Cambridge fellowship that summer that used that particular murder trial as a case study of the question of the existence of evil or, as U.K. philosophers often preferred to call it (to single out some of the most opprobrious, willing, knowing acts of evil), the archaic-sounding term "wickedness"—not just evil acts but conscious, knowing evil (read the works of the U.K. philosopher Mary Midgley on "wickedness," for instance).

The Cambridge fellowship fellows encouraged me to study such things as the reductionist abolition of evil. It was something I had seen in "Hitler studies," mosquitoes and all, but the paper I wrote was prompted by a question from Sir Brian Heap, a scientist fellow of the Royal Society. "Did Hitler have a conscience, Ron?" he challenged me.

. . .

The paper I wrote appeared later in somewhat altered form in the Catholic journal *First Things* (despite my atheist-adjacent agnosticism, there were some things we agreed on, such as the reality of wickedness in humans, regardless of the being or non-being of God or the devil).

And when I got back to the States I wrote about the neuro-skeptics (for *Slate*) and began to realize that the problem of evil is adjacent to the problem of love, neither being justly subject to neurochemical reductionism. But that hasn't stopped the neuro-reductionists and their popularizers like the ruling figure of love science, Dr. Fisher.

Consider this paragraph from a University of Pennsylvania professor that appears in a collection of neuroskeptic papers published by MIT Press under the title *Neuroethics,* which I introduced in my essay for *Slate* this way: "The 'Brain Overclaim' paper by Stephen Morse of the University of Pennsylvania's Neuroscience Center," I wrote, "is a tongue-in-cheek 'diagnostic note' on the grandiosity of the assumptions of the brain-book fad, books like David Eagleman's *Incognito: The Secret Lives of the Brain.* Morse is mainly concerned with the way they have been creeping into jurisprudence. The way fMRIs have made their way into a Supreme Court opinion that year, for instance: Justice Stephen Breyer cited 'cutting edge neuroscience' in his dissent to a ruling denying the right of California to ban violent video games, because the otherwise-pro-free-speech justice was alarmed at neuroscientific studies that claim such games could create neural pathways for actual violence."

"'Cutting edge,'" perhaps, but not well established.

But Professor Morse's critique extended beyond the jurisprudential and went to the heart of the failure of current neuroscience to explain or "replace" evil. Popular neuroscience has claimed to find the neural locus of love and God and evil, but

Professor Morse points out a fundamental flaw in its logic—and the logic of the neuroscience of love.

"Despite all the astonishing advances in neuroscience, however," he writes, "we still know woefully little about how the brain enables the mind and especially about how consciousness and intentionality can arise from the complicated hunk of matter that is the brain.... Discovering the neural correlates of mental phenomena does not tell us how these phenomena are possible." In other words, we know where love and evil may "take place" in the brain but not where they come from, why, or what they are.

Feelings are not chemicals. Chemicals are not feelings. According to Dr. Fisher, love can be "found" in the "ventral tegmental area" and the "caudate nucleus" of the cortex. But she fails to explain beyond incessant citing of dopamine how or why the feelings as opposed to just the chemicals got there or what the feelings, the qualia they induce, are. Or why the same chemicals can produce wildly variant feelings.

It's the hard problem of consciousness again, the hard problem of love. And despite the optimism of my friend Errol Morris and other philosophers I've studied, the claims that consciousness is an "emergent phenomenon"—the latest attempt to explain how the brain meat generates consciousness—all fail to explain the transition from meat to thought because they can't answer what consciousness *is*, what particles or quarks if any it's made up from, and thus are unable to tell us anything useful about it.

Still the media from print to broadcast and cable and You-Tube have not been able to even think of challenging the simplistic claims of the love scientists that proudly pretend to have answered these basic questions or rush by and elide them in toto.

The "Trait Constellations":
The Great New Revelation

I woke up one day in November 2019 to find an illustrated Twitter ad promoting a feature in the otherwise serious-minded *Wall Street Journal* that was written by their relationship reporter and credulously presented Helen Fisher's newest simulacra of love science as revealed truth. And went on to go beyond what I had seen of her claims before to what seemed to me a level of absurdity that demanded exposure, I believe, of the foolishness that popular love science had become.

The article opened with a line drawing of a winsome young woman in a leotard sitting cross-legged in a yoga-like pose with the headline:

"Are You a 'Testosterone' or a 'Dopamine'?"

And the subhead:

A brain-based personality test helps people understand themselves better and why they are attracted to certain other personality types

Specifically, "why do we fall in love with one person and not another."

The article answered it with a solemn recitation of what Helen Fisher called her new method of analysis, "trait constellations"—note the word "constellation," which almost seemed a deliberate link to what is offered by astrology's reckoning of the meaning of the actual starry constellations (or "houses"), although even astrology offered more complexity—twelve houses as opposed to Helen Fisher's four "trait constellations."

The *Journal* feature is not shy about claiming Helen Fisher had discovered the secrets of life as well as love.

All revealed by fifty-six-question questionnaires that are supposed to link your answers to one of four brain chemicals that define your "trait constellation." In other words, the great new achievement of "brain-based" love science is to reduce the vast panoply and perplexity of human complexity to just four personality types. Chemical types that determine who you can or should fall in love with.

Apparently since Dr. Fisher wants to keep these questions closely held for some reason (monetizing them for sale to corporations who seek "science-based" analyses of the personalities of possible hires? One of the questions I emailed her about was how many corporations have downloaded them. No response). And the *Journal* article, which is totally focused on the so-called eureka-like breakthrough in love science, is reticent about them. The writer, who apparently has seen the magical questionnaire, refused point-blank to show it to me. Nonetheless, as we shall see, I was able to winkle out a dozen of the magic questions from the published material in one of Fisher's articles in a peer-reviewed scientific journal called *Frontiers in Psychology*. The questionnaire answers apparently do double duty—determining both your love type and what kind of employee you'd make. I believe there is no better place to focus an examination of reductionist love science than this *Journal* article, which has been promoted and repromoted and republished online at least twice by the paper (whose serious reporting side, I should emphasize, I admire as I do much of its cultural coverage meant—unlike this—for adults) ever since it was first published back in November 2017, and indeed I saw no less than three illustrated promos for it on Twitter in 2019 and another one in 2020. Rather unusual for the business-oriented broadside unless you consider her apparent attempt to target corporate hiring departments with her personality analysis.

Furthermore, one of the emailed questions I sent Dr. Fisher was whether or not there was anything in the *Journal* article that shone such a bright spotlight on her work that she wanted to add or subtract. No response. No corrections. The *Journal* feature professes to offer the very latest in the very greatest of popularizers' new repertoire of love science metrics and matrixes. Not just what chemical constellation trait you are, but how to talk to humans from other traits almost as if they were aliens new to the planet.

But before revealing these alleged secrets of love and life, I'd like to pause and consider a more fundamental question about the "science of love" or "the medicalization of love." I'd been following the website Academia.edu, which notifies me of citations of my work in peer-reviewed journals (five hundred or so as of this writing). They had been publishing a series of papers on the pros and cons of "Love enhancement," usually meaning the use of "Love drugs," from prescription medications to X-rated compounds like Ecstasy. An argument over whether, in certain cases, a married couple whose love life had become routine and who wanted to rekindle the old flame or who were having trouble igniting it in the first place were justified in adding chemical enhancements to their diet beyond champagne, say. Needless to say, this chemical tinkering would depend on, if it were to be taken seriously, a base of scientific reduction of love chemistry of the sort Helen Fisher propounded to show what needed tinkering with what chemicals. Find the right molecules rather than find the right many-faceted elements of the interpersonal, metaphorical chemistry of intimacy.

The controversy drew mainly Oxford and Cambridge philosophers and I was particularly drawn to a quotation in a *Cam-*

bridge Quarterly of Healthcare Ethics compendium of responses to an article by Oxford neuroscience philosopher Brian D. Earp, one of the most nuanced savants engaged in the matter.

It was a response from one of the philosophers, Sven Nyholm.

Earp had cautiously suggested there might be carefully modulated, regulated cases where "love drugs" might be used. He was not talking about one-off, one-night-stand uses of such chemical assists like Ecstasy (nor was he puritanically dismissing that out of hand for those who only wanted that).

But Nyholm had a deeper objection that I thought applied to the kind of "trait constellation" classification that Helen Fisher does, almost like racial categorization.

Nyholm argues that "there has been too much focus on the good or bad consequences of love's medicalization and not enough on the way in which there may be something intrinsically regrettable about the medicalization of love" in the first place. "To treat it," as Helen Fisher does (though he doesn't mention her specifically), "as a scientific or medical issue is to make an evaluative category mistake."

In other words, even if love could be reduced to four "systems" or four "constellation traits" based on chemical analysis, or eight or ten, "there would still be reason to object to bringing love into the realm of science or medicine" because to do so would be "inherently" confused or mistaken and invite treating something numinous as divisible into racial-like traits/categories and thus invite chemical or medical tinkering on the assumption that the human essences had been scientifically established. When, in fact, love was "inherently" something that evaded scientific categorization, something intrinsically un-pin-downable. A recently published book by Raymond Tallis called *Freedom: An Impossible Reality* makes the same case against scientific reductionism at greater length.

I'd take it further and say scientizing love is potentially destructive to love.

It seems to me that love's authenticity is imperiled by chemical alteration, an authenticity that can never be recovered once tinkered with. And when the project itself becomes acceptable to a conservative outlet like *The Wall Street Journal*, when we are instructed how to alter ourselves, alter our love language, on the basis of chemistry, the project deserves close examination because it brings us closer to a brave new world where no one will know whether what they feel is the product of their true selves or chemically based intervention or determinism. Love itself will no longer be able to be identified for who one is but for whose chemicals one plays to. Love itself, love "intrinsically," love "inherently," will no longer be identifiable, in effect will no longer exist as a freely willed phenomenon.

A Confession

I must, however, make a confession at this point. There was a time several decades ago when I wrote a credulous article about a so-called "molecule" of love, in this case a now nearly forgotten compound known as "phenylethylamine" or PEA (like "the princess and the pea"), that gave it as much precedence as Dr. Fisher did dopamine (and now three more brain chemical molecules).

What can I say, I was in love at the time and perhaps my mind was clouded, but I wrote a profile of Dr. Michael Liebowitz, a Columbia University scientist who had been getting publicity for what had been called "the molecule of love."

Reading about this early pre-fMRI instance of love science at a time when I had fallen in love made me vulnerable to the feeling I *had* been chemically dosed by some internal brain chemical and so I went along with it. Curiously, though, one rarely hears of PEA anymore. It has been supplanted by new candidates for preeminence as "molecule of love."

First there was oxytocin (not OxyContin, the opioid known in other circles as "hillbilly heroin"). No, this is the all-healing, all-beneficent "moral molecule"—the actual title of a book about it. Indeed, there is a coterie of U.K. philosophers and psychoanalysts who believe oxytocin might be used for "love enhancement"—chemical intervention—to save marriages from what neuroscience has convinced them is the inevitable decline in passionate love in post-ESIRL life.

Of course, there were some, shall we say, "off the menu" candidates for love enhancement. In the sixties there was LSD, which Timothy Leary cannily promoted as enabling you to have orgasms a thousand—or was it a million—times stronger than ordinary, but that was mainly sex, although, who knows, it's making a comeback in "microdosing" as a kind of love drug.

And in the seventies there were Quaaludes, which I have to say have gotten a bad name (or a worse-than-deserved name) from Leo DiCaprio's famous 'ludes-disjointed crawl to his car in *The Wolf of Wall Street*. Yes, too much could disable you (I'm told), but a single pill could induce a sense of erotic romantic euphoria that gave rise to the popular saying at the time after two strangers met and mated: "Was it love or was it 'ludes?" Unfortunately people got addicted. I covered the case of a young ambitious *Time* magazine Hollywood reporter, David Whiting, who fell in love with the actress Sarah Miles, then called by *Vogue* "the most beautiful woman in the world." He was eventually found dead with the British version of 'ludes, Mandrax or "Mandies," scattered all around him on the floor of Sarah Miles's room in a desolate motel on a movie set in the tiny heat-blasted desert town of Gila Bend, Arizona. (Probably an overdose, although

Sarah's costar, Burt Reynolds, was thought by some to have had a role in knocking him unconscious—unfairly, I came to believe.)

It was a kind of warning, I was Whiting's age at the time.

Then of course in the eighties, there was X—Ecstasy, the popular name for a family of chemicals, mainly MDMA, which had a similar erotic, euphoric, sometimes romantic effect (I'm told) but had some dangerous downside side effects.

In the nineties there was Alexander Shulgin, a kind of psychedelic, polymathic Wizard of Oz who crafted a molecule known as 2C-B, still popular on underground websites as a go-to love drug. Shulgin was said, by one of his disciples I interviewed, to have created hundreds of 2C-B-type molecular love drugs, tweaking them regularly as soon as the DEA could identify their chemical composition and "schedule" (outlaw) his latest creations, forcing him to make another tweak to stay one step ahead of DEA prohibitionists.

Though he didn't make claims that love could be reduced to a science, merely "enhanced," like the U.K. philosophers seemed to advocate to promote something to recall the ESIRL stage of love in marriages that had lost that hot glow. Was this existentially worthy? It's a big unanswered, perhaps unanswerable, question, at least among the Oxbridge philosophers, an uncertainty that calls into question what "true love" really is. Is it unadulterated "natural love" or "love plus," so to speak? What the "real" self was, or is, is called into question by chemical manipulation.

I once interviewed a disciple of Shulgin the aphrodisiac maker who gave them away to friends and was skeptical of whether they in fact "enhanced love" in a lasting way. Frankly, I'm skeptical of any kind of aphrodisiac "enhancement" beyond good champagne.

I mean, if you're deeply in love, what would "enhancement" feel like, or would there be a danger of side effects like increased possessiveness and jealousy, even stalking? And if you're not deeply in love, maybe try to enhance the feeling by finding someone with whom you could be? Rather than someone you could dose up together with.

Although what is champagne if not that kind of temporary enhancement? But I'll stick with music, with Marvin Gaye and Tammi Terrell, Motown's brief, beautiful duo who sang, convincingly, "ain't nothin' like the real thing, baby."

Which brings us to Helen Fisher and her initial molecule of love, dopamine.

By the turn of the century, Helen Fisher's dopamine/drive hypothesis had seemingly driven the competition out of the field, enjoying as it did the supposed imprimatur of hard science. What was more, she had the confidence—or hubris—to say she had answers. And after five thousand years of fluctuating emotional ambiguities about the nature of love, there was a hunger for answers about love, answers with the simplicity or simplemindedness of "it's a drive." If we can get to the moon, why can't we solve the moonlit "problem" of love?

What makes the *Wall Street Journal* article so distinctive and so worthy of "close reading" is that the *Journal* article seemed to indicate that Helen Fisher abandoned dopamine's singularity and declared there were no less than four brain-based molecules of love.

It was almost like a romantic breakup. Or a shift to polyamory. No more brain drug monogamy for her, although the *Journal*'s relationship reporter didn't seem to realize—when I asked her—what a radical shift Dr. Fisher's love science, as she presented it now, was.

Dopamine was no longer the prime open-sesame key. Perhaps

after nearly two decades of flogging dopamine, Fisher felt she couldn't get media attention from repetition of same-old same-old single molecule of love focus.

There was an audience out there eager to hear about new love drugs and new love "science," and she had ridden the wave to lucrative consultancies with dating sites and distinguished professorships at Rutgers and the Kinsey Institute. (Yes despite all the scandals surrounding Kinsey and his b.s. sex surveys, Indiana University still maintained his institute. I spent some time with the scientists there, earnest but a bit backward; the ones I spoke to seemed not to have heard the news about the vagus nerve and its third pathway to orgasm that went from "the secret parts of fortune" through the heart to the brain.)

But dopamine-centered love science had to make way for Helen Fisher's new version of love science—the "trait constellations"—which she first unveiled in the journal *Frontiers in Psychology* in 2015 and began popularizing as early as 2017, although only *The Wall Street Journal* as far as I could tell (outside of academic journals) decided to give its imprimatur to the complexities involved in the new love science matrixes Dr. Fisher unveiled.

I believe that the *Journal* article is the first place she disclosed to the wider media world this new wrinkle, this earthquake in her "brain-based" love science. So I don't think it's unfair to focus on the remarkably credulous *Journal* article; it seems to be the summa so far of Dr. Fisher's new reductionist love science. After all, Helen Fisher's theories have captured the discourse of the culture. So attention must be paid. And it's worth repeating that one of the questions I emailed her was whether she'd want to add or subtract anything from the *Journal* piece about her and her new "constellation trait" science. No reply. So the story must be considered gospel regarding her new love science.

. . .

In the long *Journal* feature one gets the full Helen Fisher experience, complete with "Helen's Tips" for romantic success based on the astrology-like "trait constellation" pretensions to science.

"Why," the *Journal* asked, "do we fall in love with one person and not another? This question has vexed philosophers, psychologists and poets for generations. The theories—proximity, pheromones, timing—don't fully explain the mystery. We can be in a room full of attractive, available strangers—and be open to love—and still choose one person over all others.

"A decade ago, the biological anthropologist Helen Fisher set out to answer this question of how we choose whom we love. Dr. Fisher is known for her research scanning the brains of people in various stages of love, and she went looking for neurological clues.

"She found them."

The Sacred Questions

Or did she?

What she found were the four "trait constellations," sometimes called "the four systems," that a questionnaire—the sacred, secret fifty-six-question quiz Helen Fisher devised that enabled her to divide not just humans but (almost) all living things into straitjacketed categories. Like the four "humors" of ancient philosophers.

Here is *Journal* writer Elizabeth Bernstein's description of Dr. Fisher's "four trait constellations":

"We all have all four systems—as do humans, monkeys, lizards and birds." Yes, it bears repeating that Dr. Fisher's love science applies to birds and lizards.

"'This is a new way of understanding personality,' says Dr. Fisher, the author of several books, including *The Anatomy of Love*." She claims that a fifty-six-question quiz administered to a sample whose identities (race, economic position, education, sexual preferences, etc.) we are not told supposedly verifies this breakdown to four—just four types of humans.

Not only are we not told, but nor, apparently, are any demographic breakdowns taken into account. All humans are just replicas of her dating site subjects. Their experience of love, like their experience of poverty, racial hatred, and other life-altering factors, is of no consequence or at least little interest to this new iteration of love science. The questionnaire with its fifty-six questions (actually, I was able to discern just fourteen questions with four multiple-choice answers), which supposedly identify which chemical "house" system or "constellation" you belong to, tells us everything we need to know.

That these questions can comprehend all of humanity and divide all of humanity into just four types supposedly based on four brain chemicals is just assumed. Although—and this is important—we are never told in the *Journal* article exactly how answers to quizzes can identify the chemical categories that determine romantic preferences and indeed entire personalities with any certainty.

The relationship reporter is not evidently curious about the link between checking boxes on a questionnaire and the complex chemistry of the brain. Perhaps because, she tells us, she even took the quiz herself and found much to flatter herself about, which seems to have satisfied her curiosity. As for the rest of us:

"The four types are each associated with distinct traits. People high on the dopamine scale tend to be adventurous, curious, spontaneous, enthusiastic and independent. They have high energy, are comfortable taking risks and are mentally flexible and open minded."

And guess what? That's her, she tells us.

On the other hand, serotonin types are "very social, traditional, calm and controlled, conscientious and detail oriented. They love structure and making plans."

In other words, boring control freaks in comparison with her spontaneous adventurous type.

Testosterone types (which can be either male or female apparently) are "direct and decisive, aggressive, tough minded, emotionally contained, competitive and logical. They have good spatial skills and are good at rule-based systems such as math or music."

If you took every cliché about men from the 1990s bestseller *Men Are from Mars, Women Are from Venus* and herded them together, you would get a testosterone "trait constellation." This seems less like brain-based science than brain-based stereotypes.

On the other hand, the woman who is classified by the sacred oracle as testosterone is typed with masculine "traits" in their constellation. They are denied the freedom to be other than their chemicals type them. The inherent misogyny of this typology is confirmed by the so-called trait constellation of the "estrogen trait" (again, not confined to either male or female) and the fact that two traits are based on brain chemical "trait constellations"—dopamine and serotonin—and two are based on sex hormones is a puzzling apples-and-oranges mix, and, what do you know, "estrogen types are intuitive, introspective, imaginative, empathetic and trusting." Again very *Women Are from Venus* gender stereotypes.

Frankly I was stunned that the replication of weary old conventional stereotypes was being presented here as the—celebrated!—fruit of "brain-based science," supposedly revealed with fanfare and precision by a quiz. It should be noted that gay or trans or nonbinary people do not appear to be considered in this theoretical system.

Can Helen Fisher not be aware of the tiredness of a replication of simpleminded aspects of the male—drawn to math and "spatial skills" (all those qualities that "estrogen types" lack, supposedly)? It's the kind of typology of women that got former president of Harvard Larry Summers in such trouble for replicating these stereotypes of women's relative lack of STEM skills that he was forced to resign from his job.

The *Journal* writer just accepts that there is a scientific basis for dividing "monkeys, lizards and birds" into "four trait constellations" as well. Did the lizards take the fifty-six-question test? What did their answers to the quiz say about the nature of lizardian romantic love? Was it like a scaly version of human love, the "scientific" analysis of which Helen Fisher was so celebrated for? Similar sections of their brain may show excitation but we have *no* access to lizard qualia.

Those questions surely must be humdingers to extract constellation traits from monkeys. Do I have to point out that monkeys don't willingly take written quizzes, and their answers are not translatable from monkey language to English? More important, there is no persuasive evidence cited that human answers to the fifty-six-question quiz are translatable to certain corresponding brain chemicals in humans and tell us anything about love. Remember, she is the love "scientist."

. . .

The awed *Journal* writer makes the questions the "open sesame" to human *character,* human nature, human love, and yet in all her thousands of words she never discloses a single one of the secret, sacred questions that unlocks the mysteries of love and character.

So I did some digging and found a dozen of the questions from one of Dr. Fisher's publicly available peer-reviewed papers, the one underlying her trait constellation analysis. Such a discovery about the scientific key to human romantic love and personality should be shared with the world, should it not? From what I can tell there are only fourteen statements each with four possible responses, thus somehow fifty-six "questions."

The magic questions: Here now is the discovery I made: Buried in the trappings of supposedly serious science in a Fisher paper abstract are twelve of these profound questions. Read them closely; I have bolded the trait types buried in the boilerplate. They are actually questions in the form of statements with options to agree or disagree strongly or weakly. Below are excerpts from "Four Broad Temperament Dimensions: Description, Convergent Validation Correlations, and Comparison with the Big Five," published in *Frontiers in Psychology* by Helen E. Fisher, Heide D. Island, Jonathan Rich, Daniel Marchalik, and Lucy L. Brown—bolding is my own.   .

[Questionnaire]: "Using factor analysis," Fisher and her colleagues write, "we developed a 56-item questionnaire, the FTI" [Fisher Temperament Inventory], the subjects of which were "39,913 anonymous members of a US Internet dating site." [!] Fisher names four trait constellations; each of the four categories consists of 14 items in the FTI questionnaire. Yes, only 14 statements on which to build a grand personality analysis that tells all about love, too. The paper clarifies that "the response options reflect a four option… agreement scale with a score of 0 for 'strongly disagree,' 1 for 'disagree,' 2 for 'agree' and 3 for 'strongly agree.'" "The Curious/Energetic [dopamine type] scale included statements such as, 'I am always doing new things,' 'My friends would say I am very curious,' and 'I have more energy than most people.'" Later, the survey posits that "The Cautious/ Social Norm Compliant" scale [which the *Journal* article calls the "serotonin type"] included statements such as: "'People should behave in ways that are morally correct,' 'My friends and family would say I have traditional values,' and 'In general, I think it is important to follow rules.'" The third of Fisher's scales is "The Analytical/Tough-minded scale" [surprise: the "testosterone type"], statements of which include: "'I enjoy competitive conversations' [mansplaining], 'I am more analytical and logical than most people,' and 'I understand complex machines easily.'" Finally, Fisher's study enumerates the qualities of "The Prosocial/Empathetic [estrogenic] scale," the statements of which include the following: "'I like to get to know my friends' deepest needs and feelings,' 'I highly value deep emotional intimacy in my relationships,' and 'Regardless of what is logical, I generally listen to my heart when making important decisions.'"

And needless to say, these statements are so gameable: Who is going to respond "I don't value emotional intimacy"? Or "I don't care about being 'morally correct'"?

So these are the magic revelatory quiz questions. They are so removed from the reality of love. About as sophisticated as the side-street basement "clairvoyant" who gives readings about love and money and says she will remove the curse on your money if you hand over your wallet.

But let us soldier on through the new claims the "trait constellations" have generated according to the *Journal* article.

Here we get into the stratosphere of "love science," Helen Fisher's "Tips" about how you should talk to another person from a different "trait constellation." I really feel we are now at the very core of the absurdity of the reductiveness of love science so I don't want to stint on the comic foolishness it entails.

"Helen's Tips," the *Journal* proclaims in bold type.

Helen Fisher's tips on how to communicate with the four personality types on the Fisher Temperament Index:

When interacting with a dopamine type:

Do: Be energetic, optimistic and enthusiastic. Be flexible, spontaneous and creative. Explore new information and ideas. Speculate and theorize. Give them variety, possibilities and choices. Be daring.

[I must say it sounds exhausting. On the other hand, Helen's Tips warns you:]

Don't: Smother them with details. Go heavy on process. Require rigid schedules or routines. [Don't] moralize.

[Don't say, "Don't steal that car, honey."]

(Avoid "ought" and "should"). Don't spend too long on one point. [Don't] Be repetitive.

In other words, rather than try to establish honest intimacy, involving your authentic self, whatever it may be, create or stage-manage a trait-compatible version of yourself: It's all about how to manipulate those with alien traits.

Did you hear that? "Don't moralize," because you're with a dopamine type and he or she might well be a cocaine addict.

Next on the menu of "Helen's Tips":

When interacting with a serotonin type:

Do: Discuss concrete topics. Be orderly and calm. Make and stick to schedules and plans. Emphasize the "right way" of doing things. Accentuate tradition. Minimize risks and uncertainties. Emphasize details.

[Don't worry if this makes you sound like a dreary stick in the mud. You never know, some people like the stolid, boring types.]

Don't: Present an unsubstantiated point of view. [Don't] Give unfounded theories or speculations.

[Wouldn't these admonitions be good advice for all four trait constellations, even love scientists?]

So much obvious advice here. But it's science! Or on the other hand, good advice for everyone who loves clichés, but ridiculous to assign the clichés as if they were only good for just one of four specific types.

But we're not finished with your instructions for dealing with alien "trait constellations." (Admittedly, it sounds a little confusing at first.)

When interacting with a testosterone type:

Do: Be direct and tough-minded. Get to the point. Focus on the goal. [Women are so easily distracted, aren't they?] Be logical and unemotional. Avoid sustained eye contact. Give the big picture first, then details. Disagree and debate, backed by facts. Engage the person's sense of fairness. Give orders clearly.

In other words, be a stupendous mansplainer. Give orders? Give orders! What is this, a recipe for mansplaining to escort girls? Or mansplaining to men? It's all so confusing. So the point is to make yourself into a domineering martinet to mimic your date's testosterone-type stereotype?

But there's a lot of long-evolved wisdom here. People love following orders. It may remind them of being brutalized by top sergeants in Marine training camp ordeals or the time they spent in lockdown solitary confinement in penitentiaries or mandatory rehab centers. COVID quarantine.

Avoid eye contact? Look sneaky? The very essence of love is eye contact! But not according to Helen Fisher's "brain-based science." Instead, she recommends when dealing with this "testosterone trait constellation" that you be servile in an unthreatening, lowered-eyes way. And whatever you do, don't get all "emotional." You know males, they hate emotionality, talking about feelings, and all that noise. Didn't you read *Men Are from Mars*? Overflow with gratitude when they fix your plumbing, things like that instead.

On the other hand, "Don't: Be self-deprecating or minimize your achievements or rank." First of course you need to brain-scan them to be sure. But what if you are supposed to act eyes-cast-down in modesty? Should you also *not* be self-deprecating? Both? How can the *Journal* author (a fun, adventurous, dopamine type) not have worked out the set of conflicting instructions? Some men like the charming confusedness that women allegedly display. Maybe that's what they're going for.

To conclude advice for interacting with a testosterone type:

[Don't] Apologize unless appropriate. [Don't] Make moralistic statements (avoid "ought" and "should").

In other words, stick to trivial topics; don't venture into serious matters. So says *The Wall Street Journal* (if you want to be loved). "[Don't] Be long-winded, redundant or effusive. [Don't] Talk about theories without linking them to facts."

I'm really getting confused. Can/should women do "mansplaining"? If you wonder why I am including so much from "Helen's Tips," it is only because seeing them in their full splendor is the only way their alleged "brain-based" science can be appreciated or evaluated.

When interacting with an estrogen type:

Do: Think contextually and long-term. Balance facts with feelings. Give theories and use ancillary data. Find points of agreement. Appreciate the person's contributions. Express caring. Reveal your feelings. Sit facing them and use an "anchoring" gaze. [That "anchoring gaze": sounds scary, a bit stalkerish.]

Don't: Be competitive or confrontational, aggressive or blunt, or impersonal or aloof. [Don't] Interrupt. [Don't] Push for a decision before the person has explored all the options.

In other words, forget all feminism's rhetoric about self-empowerment—expressing an opinion will make you one of those "pushy women" and we don't want that. Bite your tongue if you want to interrupt a nonstop error-filled flow of mansplaining; it will hurt their tender sensibilities. Be a modest little mouse.

In other words, women as a type can't handle direct talk but must shyly and coyly look away. Whatever you do, don't confront a male type, however idiotic he is being. What century is this, again?

"Helen's Tips" seems to me a reification of outmoded stereotypes. Though probably comforting to the disproportionate number of men in boardrooms who don't want any silly girls making objections to their big, stupid destructive plans.

These antiquated clichéd typologies are an insult to science. They are an insult to love.

The "166 Cultures"

Nonetheless, following Helen Fisher's path to her current reign over love might be instructive. In the course of following it, I realized something about one of her claims.

In several of her biographical descriptions it has been commonplace to say, as one Harvard medical school article puts it, "More than 20 years ago, the biological anthropologist Helen Fisher studied 166 societies and found evidence of romantic love—the kind that leaves one breathless and euphoric—in 147 of them." Love, in other words, is "cross-cultural"—that is, virtually alike all over the Earth, and thus her fMRI studies of dating site types are true from Borneo to Tajikistan. (We already know from the *Journal* article that she seems to believe romantic love is cross-species—the lizards, etc.)

Let us look more closely at this cross-cultural claim, though.

It began with Fisher's many anthropology degrees. After graduating from NYU in 1968 with a BA in anthropology and psychology, Fisher pursued multiple graduate degrees in anthropological studies: an MA in physical anthropology, cultural anthropology, linguistics, and archaeology from the University of Colorado at Boulder in 1972 and a PhD in physical anthropology, human evolution, primatology, human sexual behavior, and reproductive strategies from the University of Colorado, Boulder, in 1975. At the very least she seemed to have the academic ground covered.

At this point, however, there is what at first seems a surprising claim. It was in her degree-laden cursus honorum through academic anthropology that Helen Fisher turned her attention to love. Specifically to the anthropology of romantic love and then, with the help of the newly developed fMRI machines, to the neurophysiology or brain-scan investigation of the neurochemical dynamics of love, the study of which would make Helen Fisher famous and change the cultural discourse about love.

But there was something in the anthropological foundation of her study that aroused my curiosity. It was the repeated propensity to make claims about the cross-cultural nature of romantic love. Repeatedly in her lectures and in the brief biographical encomiums to her that magazines, books, and TED Talks and the like offer, the claim is made that a "study of 166 societies" proved that romantic love was "cross-cultural," in the sense that it was present in 147 of these 166 societies. Furthermore, in the 19 other societies, "no negative data was found"; it was, rather, the fault of the anthropologist "who asked the wrong questions."

At first I just breezed by it. The implication, in other words, was that no matter where you'd go in the world you'd find that romantic love presumably among couples was basically the same.

I think the only reason I came to be skeptical of the implication that she "studied 166 cultures" was my good fortune in having studied basic anthropology under the great Margaret Mead when she was a visiting professor at Yale.

Mead, of course, known best for her book *Coming of Age in Samoa*, made a point of telling us students that one had to spend years living in a culture to hope to get a real understanding of phenomena like love and how they were expressed.

So let's do a little math: 166 cultures; if Helen Fisher "studied," say, maybe two years, even less, each one, she'd have to be over three hundred years old, wouldn't she, to have covered that many with Mead-like depth?

Something sounded improbable when looked at closely, either the meaning of "study" or the number 166 and the conclusion that most of them (precisely 147) were cross-cultural or thought of and acted out, felt love in the same cross-cultural way we here in the United States do.

Maybe it was an innocent, unintentional misunderstanding on my part that allowed the impression to linger of her in a pith helmet and tribal garb speaking to young Pacific Island adolescents, Margaret Mead–style.

But we are talking about a big statement about the nature of love planet-wise—about someone who has single-handedly changed the way popular culture here looks at love and has used her persuasive powers to convince the media that this was true, worldwide science.

I had entered into an email correspondence with anthropologist David Price, author of several books on the subject and a professor at the University of Pittsburgh.

When I asked him about Helen Fisher's anthropological theories about romantic love's cross-cultural universality, he said they reminded him of theories bruited about by his students on supposed signs of UFO builders of ancient civilizations (the von Däniken "ancient astronaut" theory) and he referred me to a serious peer-reviewed paper on the anthropology of love that just happened to enumerate the number of cultures academic anthropologists had studied firsthand over the years with regard to romantic love.

And what do you know, that paper on the number of cultures the authors found specified that the number of cultures studied (by others) was 166—and that 147 of them had some evidence of romantic love. The paper, it turned out, could be found in one of Helen Fisher's bibliographies. So it turns out that I, like the Harvard med school buildup—and much of the admiring media—had gotten a misleading impression. Dr. Fisher had not studied all those societies firsthand; she wasn't claiming that; rather, she'd studied a *paper* that amalgamated 166 firsthand studies (of unknown quality) by *others*.

That paper ("A Cross-Cultural Perspective on Romantic Love" by William R. Jankowiak and Edward F. Fischer) raises an important question. Is "romantic love just a western phenomenon or perhaps even restricted for centuries in most western societies to a privileged elite who had the leisure their slaves and serfs gave them to indulge in?"

In fact, the celebrated scholar of family structure, Lawrence Stone, insists that "if romantic love ever existed outside of Europe, it only arose among the nonwestern nation-states' elite who had the time to cultivate an esthetic appreciation for subjective experiences." I'd suggest it existed but not as a uniformity that could all be reduced and defined by the same quantitative analysis.

I think Price and Stone are calling into question whether all classes in all realms of the world have the same feelings necessarily about love, in love, and therefore if one measures such feelings in Western dating site patrons, as Helen Fisher has done, the conclusions may not be good for the rest of humanity. And, consequently, one mathematical or chemical formula can be said to represent "the science of love"—or even the same "trait constellations" in all 147 societies.

Even accepting the 166 or 147 that supposedly believe in what

Helen Fisher calls "romantic love," "what that is isn't necessarily what *we* have," Professor Price told me. In other words, the 147 cultures may be talking about 147 different things though they may call them the same thing. Some kind of different feeling from the ordinary or routine but different feelings that differ from each other. That certain feeling, those special "qualia," may be "talking about 147 different things that are incommensurable," Price told me.

Which poses a problem for the fMRI science with which Helen Fisher has made her name. The chemicals the fMRI scan traces surging in the brain to areas receptive to "romantic" excitement may look (chemically) identical and yet the qualia of the excitement they ignite might be radically different in different cultures. Shaped as much by culture as by chemicals.

We need to talk about the fMRI, the magnetic resonance imaging machine that Helen Fisher and neuroscientists use to back up her claims. You probably know that the hemoglobin in the blood bears iron molecules and so a machine that registers the magnetizable volume of the iron in the blood can trace the intensity and the path of blood bringing excitation to the excitable centers in the brain.

But is this excitation the same as love? And do these blood flows cause love or are they caused by love?

It may be that the differences between what is called romantic love can be so profound and deep that no useful conclusions can be drawn from a single one of them beyond their shaping by the parameters of each culture. Dr. Fisher assumes but fails to prove that love as a feeling is a cross-cultural universal.

Especially as her early experiment made no distinction between those who were presently in love with the person in the photograph shown them in the fMRI and those who were shown photographs of those people who had dumped them. It's all excitation, at least in the early peer-reviewed paper in the *Journal of Neurophysiology*. But no proof that the excitation subjectively *feels* the same.

Her claim was that, theoretically, the fMRI tells us what was going on in the minds of a people who could previously only be studied anthropologically from the outside—but she did not ask the crucial chicken-or-egg question. Were the surges of neurochemicals of excitation causes or correlations of love? Did elevated levels of PEA, for instance, cause one to fall in love or were they the product of falling in love? It's a question I failed to ask in my "PEA" story. I no longer believe that was a "cross-cultural" answer. It is a question I could not find an answer to in Helen Fisher's work or the work of other "love scientists."

Conclusion: Love has defeated the foremost "scientific" attempt to pin it down.

CHAPTER 6

Love in the Age of Oral Sex

Can Love and Pleasure Conflict?

I'm fascinated by singular moments in cultural history that signal tectonic shifts beneath the surface. Not superficial external fashion changes on the outside—miniskirts to maxi skirts—but alterations of some of the most profound aspects of human nature, inside.

Love and pleasure, for instance—and their relationship. Can one subvert the other? A note of warning: Some may find the sexual explicitness of this chapter's exploration of these relations shocking, or even offensive, but I've found that it is in the details of human interaction, often erotic interactions, that larger patterns of phenomena such as love can be discerned. I would argue that discussing the interrelations of love and pleasure is not inconsequential or sensationalist but often profoundly significant.

Love and pleasure. Their distinction. Their synergy and their conflict. How we speak of them and where we speak of them influences and shapes how we feel them, how we experience them, how we translate, how we legislate and police them.

Love and pleasure. Are they in some way antithetical? Can

the oft deplored humdrum routine of marital or coupled sex (gay, straight, or nonbinary) leave any of the parties open to the attractions and distractions of previously unknown heights of pleasure with a relative stranger, the thrilling dramatic moments of dangerously addictive desire that could disrupt the trust, the bond, built up over, say, twenty years of monogamous love? (And—for many years in many states with laws still on the books that threaten practitioners of "illicit acts"—with jail.)

On the other hand, could monogamous love and the often celebrated beauty of its bonds inhibit the exhilarating plunge into the throes of pleasure and potential self-awareness one might attain if one were only free to disregard the vows (or their equivalent) of monogamy once one's appetite for the sharp knife of pleasure was whetted?

Love and pleasure. Must one be sacrificed for another? Dangerous are the temptations that new and allegedly more intense variations of pleasure offer. Or, within limits, can love and pleasure play synergistic roles?

Is pleasure an enemy of love? Or is love an enemy of pleasure? Is it possible we should welcome the rise of a new(ish)—or newly public and publicized—mode of pleasure (and relative convenience and orgasmic efficacy) afforded by oral sex, for instance? Must we concede that in some ways a new sexual dispensation supersedes previous emotional parameters of love?

I found myself thinking of a question like this when looking more deeply into the relatively well-known aphorism—or jest?—attributed to Virginia Woolf, who wrote, "All human nature changed in December 1910" upon the utterance of a single disruptive word at one of Ms. Woolf's aristocratic Bohemian soirees in her glam flat in London's Bloomsbury where avant-garde tastemakers in literature and art congregated.

Many literate people are familiar with this "December 1910"

declaration, few with the so-called secret word that brought about—or signified—such alleged Richter scale disruption.

I love the romance and mystery of secret words and societal changes. And this is a book about Love, and so much of the literature and lore and reality of love is about secrecy.

I can trace my fascination with secret words from my childhood, watching Groucho Marx, the great wit and comic film star who had a second-tier TV quiz show toward the end of his career in the 1950s that featured a "say the secret word" gimmick. If a guest happened to utter the word so denoted (disclosed to the audience but not to the guests at the beginning of each broadcast), a duck (not a real duck) would come dropping down from the rafters, fake feathers flapping, and he or she (the contestant, not the duck) would win some kind of prize if he or she happened to utter the secret word. It happened more often than you would think. I wonder why.

In any case, I always have sought such a reward, the metaphorical duck; perhaps it was the secret motivation for my pursuit of the "secret word" that so jolted Virginia Woolf and signified the cultural shift she claimed it betokened.

First of all, I discovered that she made her remark not in December 1910 or thereabouts but in 1924 in a periodical essay called "Mr. Bennett and Mrs. Brown." And it seems the date upon which the secret word was actually uttered was closer to 1907 than 1910. Be that as it may, the identity of the man who uttered the word that rocked the dinner party—and the culture that sustained it—was Lytton Strachey. Strachey was a familiar figure in the Bloomsbury set, famous at the time (and still fairly well known) for his scandalous group biography *Eminent Victorians*, a collective portrait of several Victorian and Edwardian notables. Not really scandalous by our standards. But his snarky takedowns of some turn of the century's role models like sainted nurse Florence Nightingale and General George Gordon, embodiment of heroic masculinity, stung.

To put Strachey's utterance and Woolf's deliberate hyperbole in context, here is a more complete version of her response: "On or about December 1910 human nature changed"—she wrote. "All human relations shifted," Woolf continued, on the utterance of a single word, "and when human relations change there is at the same time a change in religion, conduct, politics, and literature."

She was not saying there was some insidious evil culture-deranging radioactivity in the word itself. In part, it was the setting in which it was uttered. Many of the men at the soiree that night might well have heard the word in the changing rooms of men's cricket clubs, for instance.

But it was unlikely to have previously rattled the fine china at Ms. Woolf's digs. Unlikely to have been uttered amid the mixed company sipping sherry in harmonious literary fellowship.

And what was that single word with such mad seismic resonances? Not surprisingly, it was an erotic word or, to be more precise, a sexual term—some might not find it "erotic."

I don't want to make too much of a literary historical mystery about that word, that seismic—or seminal—moment (actually, of course, I do).

So without further ado, the word that left Virginia Woolf so discomfited, nonplussed, the word whose utterance was the herald of a new age of sexual license and the crack-up of centuries-old sexual morality that ensued, was—according to Woolf—"semen." Or, to be exact, the word in the inquisitive mode—"Semen?"

Strachey had just entered a drawing room where Virginia and her sister [Vanessa] sat and, pointing to a mark on Vanessa's dress, casually and explicitly inquired as to its origin. Strachey simply but mischievously asked: "Semen?" And according to Woolf, "everyone burst out laughing and a new age was born.

The age of anything goes." As she puts it in her autobiographical *Moments of Being:* "All barriers of reticence and reserve went down. A flood of sacred fluid seemed to overwhelm us. Sex permeated our conversation..."

It's the semen apocalypse! Or so it seemed. (It now seems to me that she was employing sarcastic hyperbole rather than Mrs. Grundyesque grumbling, but that does not diminish her sensitivity to moments marking cultural change; instead it suggests a more tolerant attitude. Though nearly a century later tolerance was not the keynote to the eerily similar discovery of a spot of semen on a blue dress that nearly brought down a government here in the United States.)

Back then, I felt I was witness to an allegedly earthshaking pronouncement as a youthful reporter covering the anti-war movements/riots in the sixties and seventies. The phrase you heard a lot from the leaders and theoreticians of "The Movement" was a quote from Plato's *Republic* to the effect that "when the mode of music changes, the walls of the city will fall." Or something prophetic like that, which led the theoreticians to point to electric guitar rock 'n' roll (the new Dylan vs. the old folkie) as the altered mode of music that would bring the Establishment to its knees amid the debris of fallen walls. As you might have noticed, it didn't happen, though punk tried—mainly through tiresome braggadocio—to claim it did and that they did it.

All of this is preface to what I consider the contemporary equivalent of Virginia Woolf's earthshaking seminal observation: Just a few years ago as a kind of ironic punctuation to the idea of a boundary-shattering new form of art came that aphorism from the Canadian experimental novelist Sheila Heti, whose wit I've admired.

This time our Virginia Woolf didn't so much herald a New

Age as put a forceful end-stop, exclamation point upon the climax, the culmination of the evolution of what I have come to call "the Age of Oral Sex." A period of gradual but ultimately radical change in all the fields Virginia Woolf cited—"a change in religion, conduct, politics, and literature." A change whose dawning and evolution, whose birth, I was witness to from the time I impulsively dropped out of Yale Graduate School, abandoned my Carnegie Fellowship in English literature, and first came to New York to become a writer.

It was decades of observation (and, yes, a bit of participation) later that I stumbled upon Ms. Heti's rather daring tongue-in-cheek mock celebratory (or was it?) declaration that put a period—no, an exclamation point—to that era and crystallized my sense that I had been witness to a change in sexual norms I came to call, retrospectively, "the Age of Oral Sex." Rather than a one-word remark—"Semen?"—it was a one-sentence declaration delivered in the early twenty-first century. It may have made the rounds in the small world of literary publishing (an equivalent succès de scandale of the august *Partisan Review* publishing the most rebarbative masturbatory [raw liver] fragment of *Portnoy's Complaint* in a prepublication excerpt), but it had certainly not become common parlance as I spent considerable time asking literary knowledgeable types I knew whether they had heard it and suffering embarrassment when they stared at me in wonder.

It was an offhand remark, not a theoretical statement, that Sheila Heti made—almost like Virginia Woolf—in her half-joking, at least jocular, assertion. Her declaration was this: "Every age has its own art form. And we live in an age of some really great blowjob artists."

Wow, it makes you think: What kind of art is it akin to if the comparison is taken seriously? Something delicate and tactile like Japanese brush painting? Where the tip of the tongue does the work of the whetted tip of the brush?

One thing you think of is the word "blowjob." The word "blowjob" itself and in any and all variant spellings is stupid and misleading on its face (so to speak). I just can't figure out the etymological evolution of such a botch of a word—slang usually has at least a grain of wit at its heart; here none. Why its universality and apparent popularity? Where did it come from? It's just not descriptive of the act. Perhaps there is some obscure forgotten Kama Sutra–like technique lost in the mists of time that justified the term. But why hasn't anyone asked or answered this question?

And why is "blow" a description of an act of love and, at the same time, a universally accepted term of obloquy ("the Knicks blow this year")?

And then there was the strange software veto I experienced the very first time in the very earliest draft of this chapter in which I used the word "blowjob." As soon as I hit the final "b" my computer shut down. Shut down flat—I had to reboot everything. My theory is that I had mistakenly gotten some software with child safety protection built in so no nasty words could cross the kid barrier.

But I didn't want to risk losing more of my draft so I decided on a tech technique I'd seen other writers half-jokingly employ: substitute the numeral 0 for the letter o as in "p0rn" to elide digital censorship. And since I knew I was going to have to employ the word frequently—if I were discussing what I'd come to think of as "the Age of Oral Sex"—I'd soon run out of polite euphemisms, I'd rather have that comic but deliberate type-botch than the studiously (ridiculously) "correct" word studded throughout my text. This way I could, without seeming like Mr. Bowdler, highlight the transgressiveness of referring to the act. But I was talked out of it. Call it fellatio and forget it.

"Blowjob" is, in some circles, a stigmatized way of expressing an often transcendent and loving human experience, yet reference to the practice as an insult, after all, goes back to the ancient obscene Roman epigrams of Martial, Catullus, and Propertius; in that era a blowjob was almost always used as a sign of male-to-male denigration. An assertion of your power—power to make your enemies kneel before you, demonstrating their submissiveness, their subservience to you. Not a loving desire to give pleasure.

And I know that in the mostly working-class culture of my high school on the South Shore of Long Island in the mid-sixties the usage was not very different. There was an acknowledgment that female-to-male oral sex existed—somewhere—but the only references to blowjobs were mocking and derisive accusations of male submissiveness. Weirdly, the epithet "blow me" was considered the height of hostile insult among cisgender men (and perhaps a disguised form of same-sex longing, for all I know). It's a mystery when it can be an act of surpassing tenderness between men and women, and men and men, of course. But the power of misogyny prevailed—it was the kind of thing women, seen as promiscuous, lower-caste beings, sex workers, did in the back of a car in the waterfront district of cities.

So to sum up, there's no blow, no blowing, in a blowjob that I know of. And more to the point, in my experience—despite having a couple of affectionate girlfriends in college, neither seemed "into" oral sex of any kind and it seemed to me to be a strange uncharted territory where, if not "there be dragons," there was not a lost paradise of sexual pleasure. I was happy, amazed at the "ordinary" or "vanilla" sex I had and didn't feel any insufficiency that oral sex could fill.

Nor did they (the women), it seemed, and this was true of every girlfriend after that for a couple of years, most of whom must have been faking orgasms because when I finally read the pleading signals of the dancer in Brooklyn I was living with and "went down" on her, it was like presto-change-o, instant orgasm, and suddenly I was a master of sex. Not because of any skill or attractiveness but only because I finally did something I should have figured out she wanted some time ago and she was grateful—and more important, swiftly and intensely—and orgasmically responsive. Meanwhile, all across America marriages and families were breaking up because of differential preferences for oral sex, usually obtained outside the marital bond.

But why the apparent preferences for female receptive oral sex I was discovering in women? It's taken me a while and the explanation will take a while, too, but it boils down to two factors intrinsic to the act of "going down" on a woman itself: accuracy and intimacy. Accuracy and intimacy that oral sex, at its best, can offer. And a third wild-card factor that is sometimes allied with but not identical to intimacy—Love.

It was about then that it began to dawn on me, began to get through my thick skull, that women, many women, really wanted this, really liked this, liked it more, it often seemed, than "conventional" sex. But were often reluctant—in the early years of the Age of Oral Sex—to ask for it explicitly and men were often too arrogant and thickskulled to decipher the signals. At the very least it seemed to assure women the orgasm that exhausting and futile thrusting often did not.

It was in the seventies that I began to look around and take notice of how oral sex was portrayed in literature and intimate tipsy conversations and I realized the groundswell taking place.

Perhaps the turning point of what I will *not* call a "sea change." (A minor irritation, I know, but there has been much misunderstanding of that phrase, which comes from *The Tempest*, Shakespeare's late play. "Sea change" is not meant to signify a sudden change. Please recognize once and for all, but it's the cumulative effect of slow oceanic transubstantiation whereby, for instance, the bones of a drowned sailor are eventually metamorphosed into coral—"and of his bones are coral made" as the "full fathom five" song in *The Tempest* has it: a *slow* change into "something rich and strange.") The Age of Oral Sex was like that—something rich and strange to me, at least—though there were some hard-to-miss markers.

Slow Learner

Though I am a "slow learner"—Pynchon's title for a collection of his early prose—I nonetheless picked up on a couple of clues. For me the first jolt this slow learner apprehended was a passage in Philip Roth's *Portnoy*. Not the raw liver masturbatory encounter that aroused the initial sensation when that preliminary fragment from the book first appeared in the august pages of *Partisan Review*. No, it was a later passage in *Portnoy,* the one I've come to call "the Lexington Avenue pickup," that made me aware that something was happening and "You don't know what it is / do you, Mr. Jones?" as Dylan phrased it.

The Lexington Avenue pickup scene: Roth's Portnoy, a thirty-ish city assistant human rights commissioner, is crossing upper Lexington Avenue. But he stops dead when he spies an alluring, willowy blond model type crossing in the other direction and he's struck with a thunderbolt of lust.

He ventures a weak pickup line, inviting her for a drink. She sneers at him: "'A real swinger.'" And he decides to go for broke and tells her he wants "'to eat your pussy baby, how's that?'"

To his astonishment, she doesn't slap him or call the cops, costing him his job, at least (as it might in the #MeToo era). Her response: "'That's better,'" she replies amiably. "And so a cab pulled up and we went to her apartment, where she took off her clothes and said, 'Go ahead.'"

What makes this a Virginia Woolf/Sheila Heti moment in the punctuated evolution—or devolution, some would say—of the culture of romance is the matter-of-fact, loveless, once stigmatized but now regarded as merely pleasurable act—the casual acceptance of oral sex as the dealmaker, the game changer.

Even my predictive typing was shocked, changing on my laptop "I'd like to eat your pussy" to "I'd like to speak with you"— I swear this happened without my having a hand in the change. I began to think that my computer's software had developed a Rothian disapproving superego carefully scrutinizing my language, even though I know that was impossible, wasn't it?

What startled me was not the fact that people routinely engaged in oral sex but that Portnoy's approach was so low-key, so matter-of-fact, an assumption of default consent, no attempt to interest her in his work. ("Are you interested in human rights?") He just assumed that an attractive woman would in fact be flattered and pleased by the offer. It wasn't that he was movie-star handsome or had some offbeat charisma. Nor do I think Roth was boasting that something like that actually happened to him (though I think it probably did). In any case, it led to a rather long, occasionally tormented relationship in the novel.

So oral sex, asking for oral sex, had already been thoroughly normalized so that we were meant to believe there was nothing out of the ordinary in this encounter. I suppose if he had said, "I'd like you to give me a blowjob," it would have been a different matter, though.

What was also important in retrospect, as I came to realize

the Age of Oral Sex had already come of age, was that it was something that women wanted as much as or more than men.

Further validation of this observation came to me in what I think of as my "kitchen island eavesdropping" party experiences.

In my first couple of years in the city as a *Village Voice* staff writer, I kept getting invited to big parties where hardly anyone knew me. I would nonetheless stay to the end hoping for a magical connection, drifting around with an empty bottle of beer in hand. My main memory of those lonely party wanderings was an unusually illuminating dispute I got into with the writer Katha Pollitt, whose work I'd admired. We differed about the merits of Dickens and Trollope, she favoring the precise social realism of the latter, me the often hallucinatory iconic passages of the former, such as the death of Paul Dombey and all of *The Mystery of Edwin Drood,* uncompleted at his death. (I would later write a satirical novel whose main character was obsessed with discovering Dickens's most likely solution to that mystery.)

Eventually I learned to find the kitchens, where the fridge often contained unopened six-packs and I'd make a show of getting a fresh bottle, even though I didn't (then) particularly like beer. But it was there that I discovered the kitchen islands that were, I believe, a relatively new design feature of Upper West Side kitchen remodeling.

And I'd often find a gang of women giggling over something, often sex. And more than once I'd overhear one or more of them tipsily "confess" how she preferred guys going down on her more than the clumsy futile thrusting most of them had been treated to by men, which often required that they half-heartedly fake an orgasm to bring frustrating matters to a close.

It was shocking to me at first—I was twenty-five or so and did not have a sophisticated background—women admitting they preferred men to "eat their pussies"—but it seemed to have been normalized in polite society.

It took me a while to figure out that "going down" had those two advantages conventional penetrative sex did not: accuracy and intimacy.

Accuracy: Need I explain that when one's face is inches away from its goal, it's much easier to direct lips and tongue to the most sensitive spots.

Intimacy: The ability to look up from ministrations down there directly into the eyes of a lover can be an experience of transcendent beauty and value.

And of course there is pleasure. It was my firsthand impression that many women got more intense pleasure from the intimacy and accuracy combined. Something I judged by aural if not oral means.

And the exchange of loving gazes while giving each other such intense pleasure could be almost unbelievably intense. But was the exchange of pleasure mutual?

I recall a conversation I had with Abbie Hoffman, a buddy I knew from covering a lot of political demonstrations and marginally illicit activities. He was an early adopter of the "phone phreak" hacker techniques I had exposed in my story about "blue boxes" and the hacker underground. (He was also the only one of the Chicago Seven with a lively, sarcastic sense of humor.) We were on a plane to Chicago where he and his cohorts of the Chicago Seven who had been convicted of responsibility for the '68 Convention riots had won themselves a new trial and a sympathetic new judge. For some reason our talk on the plane turned to blowjobs and Abbie complained that, sure, he liked them in theory, but he found it difficult to come, to ejaculate, from whatever women were doing to him down there.

It's too bad because it was about then that I had begun learning just how adept some women had become in accomplishing that task. I had a girlfriend then, for instance, who had, as a teenager, picked up a copy of a book called *The Sensuous Woman,* whose author was only identified as "J." It was not distinguished literature but it gave effective advice.

It seemed that "J" had some very specific and very efficacious advice about how to defeat the gag reflex—to relax the throat muscles to allow deeper envelopment without serious discomfort to the woman.

Voilà: "Deep Throat." As a noun, a verb, and a sleazy porn film starring a woman who called herself "Linda Lovelace."

A woman I'd actually met at an embarrassing *Esquire* luncheon. The magazine had splashed Ms. Lovelace on their cover, dressed—as I recall—in an old-fashioned high-necked gingham dress and matching pioneer-style bonnet, and had heralded her as The New American Woman or some such snarky ironic title. She attended the luncheon on the tattooed arm of a ponytailed ex-con type called "Chuck" who had apparently taught her the trick that made her famous.

Soon "Deep Throat" became a much-snickered-about national sensation and later an iconic journalistic phrase, although I cringed when years later I learned that "Chuck" was more like her pimp and, according to her autobiography, would hit her and abuse her and force her to play the all-American blowjob artist against her will. The dark side of oral sex culture.

Nonetheless at the time Deep Throat was another sign of the normalizing of blowjob culture. And there were other "learning curve" points of sexual wisdom women were exchanging, which I will refrain from describing in detail but which involved recondite areas such as the frenulum. Poor Abbie Hoffman was just a bit late to the scene, which often involved women boasting about their own special "tricks" for making men come, like the wrist twist, the perineum finger curl, and such like.

Again, women ruled the roost, so to speak. Many knew more about male sexual response than men did. But trumping them all was the pneumatic technique. I say pneumatic not because it's a technically correct description but because of the piston-like action of a woman's mouth gripping the male member and pumping away up and down so vigorously that it seemed to create a pneumatic vacuum seal effect.

Personally I didn't find this particularly pleasurable, but I once did find myself in the care, so to speak, of one woman who was remarkably good at it. I remember her particularly well because we met at the funeral of a beloved cat sitter and somehow sharing that emotional bond made for rather rapid intimacy.

Really I scarcely knew what was happening when she did it, but it felt pleasant if effortful for her and always makes me recall a colorful line from a Robert Redford film, *The Electric Horseman*, in which Redford plays an over-the-hill bronc buster who turns to a suit of electric lights to entertain darkened arena crowds. Anyway, one of his down-and-dirty cowhand buddies who was appraising the talents of a certain woman accorded her this accolade: "She could suck the chrome off a trailer hitch."

Not my thing, but I remember it because the film made its debut at the very first Sundance Festival at Redford's ranch somewhere in Utah and I found myself seated next to squeaky-clean Mormon pop star Marie Osmond, and cringing mightily when that line was delivered.

But the pneumatic technique also incited a heated argument between me and the cat sitter fangirl. I was complimenting her skill in what I thought was a gentlemanly fashion afterward when she somewhat harshly reprimanded me: "You know, no woman really likes doing that. They get no pleasure themselves giving blowjobs, even if they're good at it."

Talk about nonplussed, I hadn't considered that, but she was adamant.

What about the exchange of loving gazes while giving another person such intense pleasure? Was there no pleasure obtained by women in giving pleasure, in giving blowjobs? She insisted that no woman ever enjoyed it. Was this possible? I thought of *Rapture,* the Susan Minot novel about a single blowjob from the point of view of the woman bestowing it. And how dutiful she made it seem—truly a job—and how for her it was all about the status of their (failed) relationship—could a blowjob rescue it? It was a brave book to write but not a pleasure to read, no evocation of pleasure by either partner, really. When I tried arguing from the evidence of loving mutual gazes, the cat sitter woman claimed, "Then they're faking it."

In other words, faking loving gazes during blowjobs was the new faking orgasms. The oral sex equivalent of Meg Ryan's Katz's Deli performance.

I don't know, I can't prove it, but I feel that at least some women gave such a convincing performance of enjoying giving that kind of pleasure that it might as well be real. Especially if it was done out of love.

I tried to make the case to my cat sitter client friend that some women might not feel physical pleasure but enjoy the metaphysical emotional communion of the intimacy a blowjob could afford, in particular the way eyes could be locked in a loving trance or some such blather I believed in.

"Then they're *really* faking it," she repeated with finality.

On the other hand, she did not deny that women enjoyed men going down on them. It had always seemed to me that the potential for accuracy—the proximity to the pre-orgasmic vibratory fluttering signs, and the ability to feel so directly the spasmodic orgasmic contractions—would disallow successful faking of the Meg Ryan sort, which depended on what you might call aural sex—the escalation of faked moans to shrieks that supposedly indicated the presence of orgasm. But I could not deny it was possible that the intimacy or sincerity could be faked. What was that old saying? Once you learn how to fake sincerity, you're capable of anything.

Still, I think—and this may be controversial—that on the whole most women experienced greater pleasure from oral sex than conventional "p in v" sex, as the feminist website Jezebel good-naturedly often called it. That still left open the question of whether women in general experienced greater, more intense pleasure than men from sex, oral or not. And if there was an imbalance, what were the consequences for love?

Nine Times

For that one almost has to go back thousands of years to the myth of Tiresias, which laid down a marker that was hard to ignore.

There was trouble on Mount Olympus, we are told. Zeus and Hera, the King and Queen of the gods, are having an argument and throwing thunderbolts around. The fight is over pleasure in sex. Hera says men owe women a profound debt since they get more pleasure from sex than women and Zeus responds by asserting women owe men a debt because they get more pure pleasure from sex than men.

The royal pair decide to settle the bet by asking the one person most qualified to judge: the seer Tiresias, who has lived his life as successively man and then woman and enjoyed sex as both (not at the same time). He started out as a man but then tangled with some minor god who changed him into a woman, lived as a woman for seven years, and then ran into another irritable god who changed him back to a male.

Which one of his sexual personae had a more intense experience of sexual pleasure? Zeus and Hera asked Tiresias. He probably should have kept his mouth shut, but instead he answered quickly: No doubt women have the most pleasure. Not just by a little but *nine times* more pleasure than men. (Don't ask me how he came up with that number.) But throughout the subsequent ages the judgment of Tiresias (which Hera punished him for by striking him blind) hung over the debate between the sexes. Is there some ancient truth embodied in the judgment of Tiresias? How did the ancients quantify it? Don't ask me.

But again the Age of Oral Sex seemed to provoke a reconsideration of that controversial question: It was an age in which women's sexual experience came to the fore in terms of knowledge and primacy of pleasure, or at least satisfaction. Of course if you look at the history, the transition wasn't entirely a smooth one, the transition from December 1910 and "semen" (said out loud in polite company) to 2010 and Sheila Heti's Woolfian declaration of the flowering of the age of great blowjob artists.

Sometimes things seemed to move backward. Self-proclaimed sexual liberationist D. H. Lawrence couldn't abide male-female oral sex and felt that there was something metaphysically inferior about it, or "p in v" sex was conversely superior.

In *Lady Chatterley's Lover,* Lawrence even called the clit a "beak." Think of that: "beak."

Freud at least would allow the clitoral orgasm a place in feminine sexual development, although he lacked the basic knowledge of women's anatomy, most especially the ruling role of the clit—not just its alleged early developmental role—a ruling role that was only discovered for certain in the year 2009 when the first ultrasound picture of the clit in living context was published.

Here is one of the great examples of misogyny in history: Thousands of years of "medicine" and "anatomy" go by before men have the slightest birds 'n' bees idea of what the clit really is for as a key adjunct of orgasm, not merely a little icing on top of the pleasure.

What the 2009 ultrasound picture (you can find it hidden on Wikipedia) revealed was that the clit was, relatively speaking, in contradiction to its frequent characterization as a little external bead, a relatively massive sexual organ whose external presence, that little beadlike protrusion on the outside of the upper vulva, was the tip of the iceberg, so to speak. That the body of the clit—90 percent of the clit—was beneath the surface and the whole organ was shaped like an octopus with the beadlike external part, like the very top of a cephalopod's head, visible externally and the invisible part beneath the skin a large body from which tentacle-like extensions draped. Tentacles that, when filled with blood upon sexual arousal, wrapped themselves around the tunnel-like vaginal sheath the clit was sitting on, and, as arousal and blood flow increased, tightened their grip around it.

It was this tightening of grip that caused the spasmodic contractions that were the vaginal sheath's attempt to expel the engorgement with blood. And these spasms—spasmodic contractions experienced as pleasure—were the orgasm. Class dismissed.

Simple, and yet for thousands of years men couldn't get the basic birds/bees right. Stand-up comedians still joke about male perplexity. When they finally did get it, it solidified the role of oral sex because (at least some) men knew what they were doing down there—aiming at things that mere blind thrusting often missed.

Thus accuracy was possible when men knew what the goal was. And accuracy facilitated intimacy. Intimacy often facilitated love. Intimacy when a couple made the physical connection down there that resulted in the metaphysical connection above the sheets between their gazes.

But as I said, the path was not always smooth. Consider the torment John Updike, soon to be known as Mr. Blowjob, chronicler of marriages broken up by the lure of external pleasure, had to go through to get a description of a blowjob into his breakthrough novel, *Rabbit, Run.*

There were a number of significant losing battles before then. There was Norman Mailer, who recounts in his memoir *Advertisements for Myself* that once in the mid-fifties he fought a tenacious but losing battle to give explicit verbalization to a blowjob in his Hollywood novel *The Deer Park.*

When an aspiring actress crawls under the desk of a powerful producer in Mailer's novel, Mailer was forced by his publisher to euphemize the act that ensued by describing the object of her oral attentions as "the thumb of power," which at least has a kind of thematic merit. It was about power not pleasure, in that case, anyway.

But the 1910 moment in quality lit publishing probably came in the last effort of an editor to subdue John Updike's euphemistic priapism. In the case of Updike, it came during the editing of his wildly successful *Rabbit, Run,* and I trust Adam Begley's deeply researched biography of Updike (2014) for the details we have.

Begley tells us that Updike was at that point permitted to use a single "climax" and not one "orgasm" in his book, although he was allowed a word never widely adopted, if at all: "orgasmatic." But he apparently felt it important, even if he were not allowed the word "blowjob" to appear in print to describe the act.

He evidently felt that this variation on conventional sexuality deserved, demanded, the place in his novel that it was assuming in culture and society. And in a work of sensibility it was an important inflection point in his chronicle of the sexual evolution of American middle-class culture.

In the novel, Ruth, the woman who broke up Rabbit's marriage, was willing to perform the act his wife would not, and it became the paradigm for the lost and broken marriages that began to dot the marital landscape of America, often leaving a legacy of one-parent latchkey children in their wake.

A situation that from all accounts many middle-class couples could relate to—the downside of the Age of Oral Sex—and such relatability may well have made Updike the best-selling middle-class author he became.

As Begley puts it, in *Rabbit*, "Updike again chooses to suggest the act rather than describe it. He arranges a tableau:

"'He takes his [clothes] off quickly.... Ruth undresses, kneels at his feet...'"

At this point, where a description of what Ruth does would be expected, the publisher and editor stepped in and demanded censorship—apparently out of fear of prosecution for obscenity (despite the federal court decision in favor of the unexpurgated *Ulysses* in 1933).

"At the time however," Begley tells us, "even to hint at fellatio was to court censorship. Particularly objectionable to the editors in 1970 was Ruth's reaction after the deed is done," without any details of its doing. After Rabbit has unchivalrously bolted "[w]hen the door closed the taste of seawater in her mouth is swallowed by the thick grief that mounts in her throat so fully she has to sit up to breathe." The sudden access of visceral accuracy, or at least visceral imagery (and the collocation in one sentence of the words "taste," "seawater," "mouth," "swallowed," and "throat"), was at the limit of the distaste contemporary sensibilities and censors could bear. Begley writes: "Updike's publisher [Victor Gollancz] circulated a memo which claimed 'I have never read a novel which approached this for absolute sexual frankness.'" The memo at once recognized the literary value of the novel and also foresaw the legal difficulty in publishing a book "'likely to be judged obscene by the powers that be.'"

What followed was a bitter scrap in Gollancz's offices wherein he predicted jail for him and Updike. It was not to be, but clearly the ne plus ultra, the furthest limits then possible for serious literary fiction, had been reached or perhaps breached. By oral sex.

It was a literary/cultural turning point. Updike was forbidden to describe the actual act of a man getting a blowjob and was relegated by editor and publisher to a somewhat strained euphemism for the aftermath in a woman's mouth. Indeed, one can almost pinpoint the dividing line, the moment of death of the Old Order in that account of Updike's struggle with his publisher over the blowjob issue.

In Begley's biography of Updike, we see the already well-established author still forced to bow to pressure by his publisher to remove an explicit description of the act from the manuscript. What results is an unsatisfying observation that makes the woman seem like she's experiencing shame, sorrow, regret, and degradation after the act. That it's intrinsically demeaning. Just like the Hays Office used to insist on unhappy endings in movies for those who might have had happy ending sex.

Updike's woman character waits till he's gone to describe the clearly unpleasant nature of the experience of swallowing to her. Of course different people—different men and differing women—have differing feelings about what is essentially (forgive me) a matter of taste.

Uncle Junior and the Stigma

Now we must address the Uncle Junior problem, a different kind of stigma.

As late as the nineties there was, at least among a certain niche group of manly men, a stigma about "eating pussy." Many people will remember the *Sopranos* episode involving "Uncle Junior," as the O.G. gangster was known. Uncle Junior and his Miami goomara (mistress). How he took a couple of weeks off for some Florida sunshine and romps in the hay with the bleached blonde manicurist, Bobbi, who was his longtime hookup.

It seems she was so overwhelmed with gratitude for his oral sex talents that she made what was a fatal mistake: telling her salon girlfriends, who loved hearing of her pleasure since they apparently had to put up with lame gangster guys' unsatisfying conventional sex. Anyway, one of her girlfriends told one of her gangster boyfriends and the story of Uncle Junior eating pussy made the rounds of the O.G. social clubs back north that were his chief habitat.

And one of those social club guys made the mistake of making a joke about Uncle Junior and his sexual predilections with his Miami girlfriend (in his presence), which left the humiliated, stigmatized Uncle Junior no choice (in his world, anyway) but to shoot the loudmouth. Nobody gave him any trouble after that.

But it's a reminder that the great groundswell of the Age of Oral Sex had some troubles, some eddies. It was not entirely a smooth shift but one led by sophisticates and demimondaines whose practices may have spread to (or from) hookers and men of lesser wealth for whom oral sex was an economic compromise— a quickie in a car versus a hotel room, which drove the price up for more than a blowjob. It was a class thing. The role of economics has yet to be closely studied.

Nonetheless, shift it was, for a variety of reasons, pleasure being only one of them, though a not inconsiderable one to some men.

So pleasure of the oral sex variety may not be an enemy of love, but an accelerant and potentially thrilling manipulation of skin-to-skin contact. One must take into consideration a third factor that rivals both oral and penetrative sexual contact. The sensitivity, the inside a woman's private parts. I wouldn't have brought this extremely intimate matter up were I not struck dumb—not that I was chattering when it happened—by a passage in the third volume of Hilary Mantel's utterly absorbing Thomas Cromwell trilogy, *The Mirror and the Light*. One that described master politician (under Henry VIII) Cromwell's downfall at the end of a fifteen-hundred-page trilogy that ensured his place among the defining anglophone fictional/historical characters.

But until that penultimate moment he had little to say explicitly about sex or romance beyond the political implications of royal bridal choices and imputations of infidelity that affected them. But in this very late passage, written of course by a woman, he is depicted talking with a boatman who is rowing him across the Thames in the midst of London. The boatman is speaking of a friend who has some sort of sexual encounter with a libidinous princess of the realm. He tells Cromwell, "That little lass of the Duke, I hear she is spoiled. There is one in the Duchess's household boasts he had his fingers in her cunt. He says he has felt it in the dark but that he would know it among a hundred."

Cromwell scoffs at the boatman's tale but can't get it out of his mind.

Mantel tells us that for the next few weeks he can't help muttering to himself. "Among a hundred." It felt so, so astonishingly

memorable to the touch. Shocking in a fifteen-hundred-page
trilogy that often alludes to sex but rarely this lubriciously.

Cromwell, who has had wives and mistresses but never in the
fifteen hundred or so pages has spoken of a woman like that,
takes the image in silently but for some time afterward is unable
to shake the erotic charge of this memory from his mind. "One
hundred!" he repeats to himself, "one hundred!"

Strange, not entirely understandable, that Mantel decides
to give him this highly charged gift of sensual memory shortly
before his gruesome death by beheading, which his enemies
have connived for him.

Is it a gift, or rather a barbed reminder of what he'll be
missing—the exquisite sensuality of life about to be snatched
away from him by the executioner's gleaming blade, the reward
for all his own conniving? A reminder, if not intentionally, that
sex is not just one method but can consist of several variations
in the realm of pleasure.

I have to admit I've been mystified—still am mystified—by
the unexpected intrusion of that shocking sexual passage. I'm
not easily shocked. But I almost feel like Cromwell, who can't get
the image out of his mind. "One among a hundred," he repeats
to himself.

There's a two-word phrase my Chaucer professor liked to
use in discussing how the technique of "close reading" could
open up, disclose previously overlooked vistas of signification
beneath the surface of a poem or a prose passage's lines. The
phrase was "conspicuous irrelevance." I think what we have
here in that boatman's obscene evocation is a classic instance
of conspicuous irrelevance. It seems irrelevant to all the court's
political intrigues that have preoccupied the previous fifteen
hundred pages of Mantel's trilogy, which acknowledged but

never described sexual matters in the flesh in such detail. And yet in a way it's a disclosure—a flash cut, in cinematic terms—of what really lies beneath all those intrigues. It's a disclosure of what's been hidden, covered up, what lies unspoken beneath all the frantic scheming and conniving in the pages that precede it: the raw, naked electrifying attraction of exorbitant sexual pleasure promised and gifted by power.

The academic move is to seek power relations beneath the sexual ones; I suspect Mantel is giving us a glimpse of the sexual appetites beneath the power appetite. What Cromwell has repressed with an iron will, but suddenly escapes, flares up to inflame him. If you read *Wolf Hall,* the first novel in her trilogy, with its ravenous, appetitive title, you'll see the red thread of how Anne Boleyn uses, among her wiles, a certain sexual technique—known then as "French methods"—to facilitate her rise to power, to become Henry VIII's queen after she was able to arouse, tease, and, it was said, ensorcel Henry's sexual appetite in her campaign to break up his marriage despite the proscription against divorce of the mighty Roman Church, the Pope (and his secular ally, ruler of most of Europe, the Holy Roman Emperor).

That "French" technique, the one that contemporaries believed won Anne Henry and a Crown: oral sex. Anne's purported introduction of "French methods" to Henry (and his courtiers) is assumed to be true or regarded to be true by Henry's courtiers and court enemies. And has become a fixture of popular myth as evidenced by this witty Longreads excerpt I came across by Anne Thériault:

At the French court, Anne learned all the skills necessary for being a good courtier—including (allegedly) the art of the blow job which was (again, allegedly) unknown in England at the time. While this last part is entirely apoc-

ryphal, it is my favorite rumor about Anne Boleyn. I have
so many questions! What did it feel like to introduce la
beej to an entire nation? Do you think she later demonstrated it to her own ladies-in-waiting so that they, too,
could spread the gospel of "buccal onanism"? What were
they even doing in England before Anne taught them the
joys of fellatio? The mind boggles.

"Buccal onanism"! A new one to me. As is the mock French
la beej for b.j. or "giving head," as it's now commonly called in
America.

Can we rely on this? Mantel writes fiction but is serious about
getting the big things about her big historical characters right.
Here (on page 302 of *Wolf Hall*) she has Sir Henry Wyatt, whose
son has had a sketchy canceled betrothal to Anne Boleyn, reflect-
ing on what he knows about her: "By the account of drinkers in
Kent ale houses and backstairs servants at court (the musician
Mark [Seaton, real person, later executed for fornication with
Anne when she was queen] for one) Anne has done Thomas
Wyatt [his son, the poet] all the favors a man might reasonably
ask, even in a brothel."

"'And do you know what they do in France?'" a noble named
Brandon asks on page 363. "'My lady wife told me . . . she wrote
it down for me in Latin.'" What follows (in English) is the most
graphic description of the "French method" you can imagine,
which I blush to repeat here. I'm inclined to take Mantel's word
for it on the principle enunciated at the close of *The Man Who
Shot Liberty Valence*, the classic John Ford Western, whose penultimate words are, "When you have to choose between history
and a legend, print the legend." Only in this case the legend—true
or false—had profound geopolitical, historical ramifications.

Anne's legendary reputation as a witch, a succubus, a whore

who used "French methods" to bewitch the English King, fac-tored into the Pope's refusal to approve their marriage and his subsequent excommunication of Henry, which resulted in a his-toric blowup. Henry went ahead with the marriage to Anne, beat down the Church of Rome in England, incited later wars with the Holy Roman Empire, but, more important, more lastingly established an independent "protestant" church that did more than sack abbeys and monasteries, leaving what Shakespeare called "bare ruin'd choirs." You may know this—I didn't—but it was Anne Boleyn who was prominent among those who secretly promoted the radical step of permitting distribution for the first time of an English translation of the Bible—Tyndale's—previously only accessible in Latin or Greek, in the three years before she was beheaded for multiple adulteries in 1536.

Many scholars see the Bible translations as the first step in the evolution of English liberty, putting the word of God in people's hands, not the Church's, thus engendering dissent, giv-ing birth to sects who pressed for freedom from state church dictates—for separation of church and state, for greater individ-ual liberties—all ideas Protestant sects brought over to America, whose colonists ultimately demanded more individual liberty at gunpoint in 1776. And so, do we trace our precious American religious liberties as far back as Anne's French methods? Is the "Age of Oral Sex" then actually more than five hundred years old? Yes, that's probably hyperbole, but one thing that could be said about Anne Boleyn and those liberties: She gave her head for them.

CHAPTER 7

Angels Flying Too Close
to the Ground

I THINK I OWE YOU some love stories. I know the gravamen
of this book has been what has been done, what is being done,
to Love. Still, I think I should offer some account or accounts of
what love has done to me. Especially now, since for reasons glad
and a little disorienting I've come to the end, time has run out,
and just in time.

I've found my last love, the love of my life. Not a moment too
soon. At this point in my life there would be no point in looking
further and I've found what I dreamed of, someone unlike anyone else I could imagine who loved being loved and loving me.

That doesn't make these few past stories I've cited inconsequential. I learned a lot about love and loving from them. To me
the memories that were their legacy served as stepping stones,
or rather a stairway to heaven, on the path to where I've arrived,
to figuring out if not how to do everything right, then to avoid so
many things I'd done wrong. Apologies to all.

And if it's not obvious now, one reason I chose to write this
book as opposed to any other—I was tempted to write more
about Shakespearean scholarly controversies—was being in love
like never before, experiencing it more intensely than I could

have imagined. Let me begin, though, with one night in Brooklyn and Two Questions. About something I learned from an affair in the past.

The bistro was getting ready to close. The last few diners were settling their checks and the waitstaff was beginning to sweep the tabletops, breadcrumbs and all, of empty tables, revealing the broad, polished wood beneath.

The restaurant, located in deepest Brooklyn, called itself Lodge and had an Adirondack rough-hewn décor motif. Exurban gentrification.

We were the last couple left and had a kind of ceremony to perform after we'd finished dinner: It was my birthday dinner and Maya (name changed) was about to give me my birthday present, the day and the present being the reason for our outing, Brooklyn the locale because she had friends in Williamsburg who often put her up on her visits to the city. She'd arrive from Washington down the Acela rail line, where she and her family—ex–husband and children—lived.

D.C.—I used to love going down there as a reporter. But the idea of leaving New York I found upsetting, which was one of the problems that had ever been underlying our otherwise enchanting—though initially clandestine—romance. (She claimed the night we met she was in the *process* of getting a divorce, reducing my hesitancy since I'd always been rather puritanical about intruding on marital bonds, however shaky. If it's not clear by this time, let me make explicit that, however old-fashioned it seems, I believe in monogamy in love, at least sexual fidelity, though it is not for everyone—live and let live and I don't claim moral superiority, more a temperamental preference.

When I say I blame D.C., that is perhaps too strong a word,

but my D.C. girlfriend gave a lot of parties and it was often torture for me: the exquisite boredom of hearing gray-souled D.C. careerists natter on about nothing, exhibiting a shocking ignorance of literature. Few books aside from the latest political tell-alls were ever mentioned and only the rare writers and reporters there had a sense of humor.

And yet I had been pressured into a reluctant assent to moving down there to live with her among all the gray people as a condition of continuing my otherwise lovely romance; she was the only one I had considered sacrificing New York to be with.

In case you're wondering why I'm telling you all this—and this is just the beginning of the story of that night, which will include the fateful two questions and the revelation that was their consequence—I've been feeling that in a book called *In Defense of Love* it would be a mistake not to offer at least one personal love story, perhaps more than one, and preferably one that doesn't defend love as nothing but the alchemical quintessence of pure enchantment, but Love in its encompassment of pain and loss and grief. Love that goes counter to any Hallmark stereotype. I will offer one indelible memory. And something I learned, or should have learned, from the dinner that night.

It's true that I have in previous chapters offered anecdotal snatches from my past that may leave the misimpression of pure rhapsodical memories (or promiscuity); "a defense of love" must not be an exaltation of Love from one of those lucky ones for whom love has always been nothing but intervals of unmitigated romance. I still seek the answer to Larkin's implicit question: What becomes of love when it is lost? If "what survives of us is love," what is the locus of that survival when it departs the hearts of lovers? In what celestial storage cupboard can lost love be found, if you've been in love more than one time? Or is there only one time that has been *real* love? Which one?

In any case, I haven't wanted to seem above the battle and to have escaped the pain of love, of going from enchantment to enchantment. Do you know the Chrissie Hynde song "Back on the Chain Gang," which seems on the surface to be about separated lovers whose attraction brings them resignedly together again?

Recently I found myself discussing it with my current, longest-lasting love. I had always loved the song, loved Chrissie, but we both had been depressed by the "chain gang" metaphor for love's renewed attachment.

But this time, in this talk about it, I came to feel that there was a possibility she, Chrissie, was using the phrase—"back on the chain gang"—affectionately, ironically, a bit abashedly for an attachment she just can't—doesn't want to—renounce forever. As opposed to the surface affect of sullen resignation "chain gang" evokes. Perhaps it partakes, we agreed, of both ironic affection *and* resignation to a power greater than either of us—very Shakespearean in its ambiguity. The ambiguity of Sir Andrew Aguecheek's "I was adored once."

Hail Chrissie Hynde for capturing the mystifying dividedness, the two-sidedness that the almost violent attachment of Love can bring. The closeness of enchantment and enchainment.

Indeed, a more than passing retrospective glimpse of my own experience with love, some of which—this one, that night in Brooklyn, for instance—does not come off all too readily as a one-sided argument that Love has always been about pure delight. A recognition of the dark matter seems important.

In this case, and the one that will exceed it in life-and-death primacy later in this chapter, love can encompass beauty and courage, as well as pain and drama.

So this chapter is not the pure encomium of a poet, more a confession, a narrative of a realist, an investigative reporter turning on himself. Of course for the sadness to have the lasting depth and effect, the ache of a lasting wound, there must have been a period of oblivious joy whose interruption and vanishing left a scar. Be assured I have the scars.

And also what I'd call grateful sadness, a hurt, endings that would never have healed had they not followed upon beautiful beginnings and middles that still had resonance in remembrance of flings past. And things learned. I've felt I learned some things about myself—that's why I want to tell the story of the night at Lodge and the two questions.

Those complexities are a reproof to the reductionists' claim that what we think of as love is nothing but algorithmically predictable, chemically identical products of the interaction of particle-based chemical "trait constellations" that can be reconciled by "Helen's Tips."

A reminder that our love lives are subject to unpredictable, unforeseeable, unmathematical, non-algorithmic, non-particular intrusions of mystery and painful memory. Of "dark matter," as the physicists now call it.

This state of uncertainty has prevailed for centuries. Just glance at the five-hundred-page section on "Love-Melancholy" in Robert Burton's vast encyclopedic seventeenth-century *The Anatomy of Melancholy*, a compendium of all the causes, effects, and cures of love melancholy that thousands of previous years of sages, alchemists, and quacks have prescribed upon. A book whose subtle answer is that there is no single "anatomy" of such a ghostly form possible. This doesn't stop me from reading it obsessively when I get melancholy over the matter. The voluminous futility of conjectures and cures somehow lifts the spirits in demonstrating the endemic bafflement that has afflicted millennia of sages seeking the key to—the cure for—love.

Remember the ridicule hapless Prince—now King—Charles

suffered when asked to respond to Diana's marital promise to "Love honor and obey."

"Whatever love is," he said, stunningly unchivalrously, obtuse and yet possessing a grain of truth about how little we know. We still don't know what it is, we only know what it isn't, what it somehow makes us do, the nature of the supernal reward or shattering disappointment it offers. But nothing else can match it.

I take heart that the great student of the matter was a doctor, Chekhov, who knew how each body had, has, its own individual story to tell, its own idiosyncratic responses, and that cumulatively individual autopsies of Love's body (as forgotten sage Norman O. Brown called it) refute generalizations and reductions. Love is the indecipherable signature of human individuality and dignity. Each love has its own fingerprints, just as each snowflake its incomparable crystalline latticework.

Speaking of autopsies, I know I finally learned something important and new from the aftermath of that dinner, though only after years of thinking about it. Years of autopsying my love life. Every account of a love affair is a kind of autopsy probe into the darkness of the dark matter. An autopsy of things past. So there. Yes, I guess I've been forestalling getting into the heart of the matter, but it's painful to recall.

Back to the Lodge

The night was meant to be a celebration. Two years! Two years from the night we met at the Tribeca loft of the editor to whom I was delivering the last section of my book on Shakespearean scholarly controversies. She, Maya, a writer and reporter, had been a longtime friend of his whom he'd called to congratulate on her scoop on an Afghan war scandal—the involvement of women both as U.S. guards and Afghan victims of abuse and torture.

In their conversation, my editor had invited her to the party that he was giving for Nobel Peace Prize winner Shirin Ebadi, a brave crusader for human rights in her native Iran, where she'd faced down the regime at great peril. The party was to celebrate the release of her memoir, which he had edited.

The woman in question, the one I met there, was now sitting across from me at Lodge after two years of two-city romantic love. I had been drawn to her more than anything, I now think, by her Degas-like poise, standing alone amid the eddying party crowd, alone but dignified, embodying grace. I watched various men make tentative approaches and withdraw disappointed. I had the luck to run into her and strike up a conversation as we were both getting our coats to leave.

I had managed to maneuver her, after several failures, away from her admirers, out of the loft into the rainswept Tribeca cobblestone evening, from which we found shelter from the storm in the romantically shabby artist bar called Walker's, and we spent the next five hours talking, drinking beer, and gazing at the reflection of the traffic light colors on the rainy wet cobbled streets, pretending we weren't interested in more than talk.

It was great talk, though. Consciously nonromantic: Although I thought about kissing her almost for all five hours, I did not try. Despite or because she was still married then I hesitated about making romantic overtures.

As the dawn approached and we finally, reluctantly, said farewell, she made a conspicuous effort to erase all trace of anything more to our connection by inviting me to dinner with her husband in D.C. I thought she had made a decision that I was not worth the risk, not until the divorce was finalized, anyway. But there was something there, something more than discussion of media gossip—which *Vanity Fair* reporter threw a fit because she had to fly economy to Afghanistan—like that. The meaning of "A Whiter Shade of Pale."

Silence between us followed her departure, but after two months she emailed me and told me she was coming to New York and asked if we could meet and see the Truman Capote film. Journo stuff. I was quietly ecstatic and the night we had dinner she told me her divorce had gone through. I unconvincingly mimed sorrow and that night we took a long walk that ended with us sitting on the damp stone steps opposite the UN after 3:00 A.M. Finally I leaned over and kissed her. For two years after that we became closer and closer, or so I thought.

The Two Questions

Let me cut to the chase. The question beneath the two questions put to me that night at Lodge was this: What does it mean that one can fall in love more than once, indeed, in some cases, many times, and each time feel that it is forever? Does each successive time just make greater and greater fools of us and our illusions, or do such repeatedly refuted beliefs in eternity summon up a ghostly congregation of lost lovers to appraise and approve, perhaps? Can any current love offer an answer to Larkin's questioning "What will survive of us is love"? Does that mean every love is "One Love" (props to Bob Marley)? Every love? Every love that lasts two years or more? Or two weeks but feels like two years?

If what will survive of us is love—Larkin's hesitant final affirmation in "An Arundel Tomb"—must each successive illusion of permanence of survival mark a greater and greater "learning experience" but still something less than the *telos,* the Singularity, the ultimate attainment of the love so perfect that it "will survive us"—or is every lesser love a greater and greater delusion about something less than love?

Seeing the bistro closing for the night, and that it was time for my birthday present, Maya opened her stylish purse and, as I recall, removed a parchment-like envelope and took from that envelope another smaller one with my name inscribed on the front with childlike formality: "To Ron from Maya."

And inside that envelope was a single sheet of parchment-like paper, the candlelight giving it a waxen glow, on which I could see displayed her bold cursive handwriting in black ink.

"This is from a page I copied from my diary," she said. "Two questions."

I knew she was a veritably religious diary keeper and indited her deepest thoughts in it, for which reason, I now suppose, she never let me read it.

What was the state of our relationship at this point? On some level we both knew we were treading on thin ice, the thinness inhering in the question of why she should commit herself to the first person she fell in love with or who fell in love with her after she left her marriage. Thin ice precariously supporting our dual weight.

But she had not given me any particular reason for fear or suspicion because of that unique circumstance, at least after she had succeeded in (lovingly) extorting from me a promise that we would sooner or later live together in Washington, D.C., although it turned out we had different ideas of "sooner," "later," and "together."

I had sincerely prepared myself (or deceived myself) that I was ready for what I knew would be a major sacrifice, a major life change, because I felt I was truly, deeply in love with her and would do anything, including set my way of life on fire, not to lose her.

But I was truly, madly, deeply in love with New York City, too. "Two Lovers," as the great Mary Wells sang.

I would change my life and accept the consequences, though it's true I did find a succession of reasons to postpone taking the big step immediately. And she, it turned out that night, had found one reason to worry about my commitment.

I had no doubt of her love, nor she mine, albeit subject as it was to long access interruptions due to its two-city nature.

To me the interruptions made the reunions all the more romantic, even cinematic—the times I arrived early at Penn Station awaiting the arrival of her D.C. Amtrak train, heart pounding when the train would arrive late, drawing out the suspense and elevating those moments when she'd finally emerge with the other passengers from the sublevel tracks beneath the big hanging two-faced (two-sided) arrival/departure board in the huge waiting room, the board all the waiting lovers had been gazing fixedly at (I assumed those waiting and staring were, like me, all waiting lovers).

When at last she would emerge from the underworld, my Persephone, glance around, and find me, and our eyes would meet with "we'll always have Paris" fervor, and she would smile casually as if her life, unlike mine, had not been hanging like a thread up 'til that moment of mutual recognition. You probably know what I mean. Don't you?

That arrival recognition smile, nothing could ever seem more unforced, casually undramatically genuine. Nothing performative about it.

So was her smile that night at Lodge as she handed me the parchment envelope with the two fateful diary questions.

The first question in cursive black ink was, as I remember it: "Why is it I'm so in love with Ron?"

Well, I couldn't help being happy, thrilled, by that. At first. Couldn't be improved on. Although I later realized it could be interpreted as "Why on earth am I so in love with Ron of all people?"

Still, that candlelit moment would admit no such doubts. So far so good, I remember feeling. The next question in my "present," not so much.

The next question she had written was: "Why is it that Ron's relationships never last longer than two years?"

Not exactly my idea of a "present," even in conjunction with the first question, but it didn't trouble me unduly at the moment— I didn't see the implication for *our* relationship—although I rarely saw the end coming when it roared toward me like I was Anna Karenina on the tracks.

I did worry that I had been too free with remembrances of flings past. Most of which she seemed to enjoy hearing about as well as my assurances that we had something none of the others did. So, right, nothing to worry about.

Opinion was not unanimous on that point. "She said *that*? On your birthday?" a close woman friend made a point of asking me sternly a few days later. And I'll admit I did have some transitory doubt about where she was going with that second question, but I was much more caught up in the first "question"—"Why do I love Ron so much?"

As to the second question, I thought to myself, a little too quickly, *"That's not entirely fair"* (as if fairness was the issue). I felt compelled to take issue with the summation of my checkered past in that second question. I had a defense.

"Wait," I said as the waiter placed the check on the table and she grabbed it and began searching for an appropriate credit card in her purse. "That isn't entirely fair. What about my marriage—three years after a year getting to know each other."

I later calculated that there were the nine times I had been in love for as long as a year, almost evenly divided between the relationships where I left and where I had been left. All of this cumulatively an answer to question number 2 in Lodge that night. Nine times. Over decades (by now). Was that too much or not enough?

I would like to say that I got better at it, but I'm not sure. I recount these stories because love in a way has its own learning curve. I'd like to say I didn't make the same mistakes, anyway. But it took me years of learning before the love I'm in now, which has lasted (as I write) more than seven years. It took me that long, that many ultimately broken entanglements, before it dawned on me why the previous nine had ended.

A word about the specificity of "nine." I have spent considerable time thinking about it since that night when I was asked about why my relationships rarely lasted more than two years. There always seemed to be a good reason. It took me a while to realize the underlying reason for all of them.

But ultimately, years later, while writing this book, in fact, the penny dropped, as they once said. I believe I found an answer to question number 2: Why so often? Why so (relatively) brief?

To put it shortly, I realized at last I was a loner at heart. Or let's say a self-deceiving loner. Believing each of the eight previous loves could be forever because I was so ecstatically happy sharing love when it was good, I neglected something about how brief that period of unadulterated bliss could be.

But—I think, like Maya—many of the women involved sensed what I thought of as permanent would only be temporarily permanent. Sensed I was not ready to give up permanently my freedom to do what I wanted with my time. I'm not asking you to admire it but to understand it. I know I'm not the only one afflicted with this temporary stars-in-the-eyes blindness, but some men (and some women) hide it better than others.

Now that I've had time for productive introspection, my response to the Second Question that night is no longer as defensive as it initially was. But more melancholically realistic. Alas, I later realized she had a point. It was a legitimate question: why there seemed to be a built-in sell-by date. Something that required a serious answer. Especially in a book called *In Defense of Love.*

The realization I came to in the years after that night at Lodge, the answer to the question, was not unimportant. What I learned about myself since then paved the way for what I now regard as my final attempt at permanence, the one I'm involved in now as I write this. Made me realize what a treasure each moment could be, not a prisoner serving out a sentence, a prisoner, yes, maybe, but a prisoner of love looking *hopefully* at the possibility of serving a life term.

What brought me to the realization was something I figured out about a commonality between my relationship with Maya and the one I'm in now. Both were with women who, as it happened, had children and were beginning new lives as single mothers after having been disappointed by men, by husbands. And both had boyfriends (me) who were to some extent *loners*, happy to spend time reading when they didn't have time for me. I was in a polyamorous relationship with the woman and the printed page.

But I had the privilege of seeing the love they bestowed on the kids in their custody. A love I could not ever presume to, or want to, compete with, it was so beautiful. It decentered me in the relationship, you might say, while bringing me into a larger, more intense orbit of love. Not having to feel responsible in a way for being the sole object, the sole bringer of love into their lives, the way their kids were, as well as living tributes to their skill and wisdom. I have lasting images of them tending to a sick kid, just holding and calming them. My God, it was so beautiful.

Not presuming to be the only object of their affection but a sharer in it made a difference. I think this current arrangement works because she has other things to think about than me. And I have no grounds for demanding more of her time than she can give and still be fully loving and attentive to the kids and her work. And I have plenty of time to myself.

Of course, it was knowledge not accessible to me in my youth, a knowledge of a love inextricably entwined with responsibility, not just to the woman in question but to the souls of the children I would always in some way feel responsible for: It was love no longer solipsistic, narcissistic, or not *primarily* those things.

Love and Oncology

Enter Ann.

The next story I'm going to tell in this interlocked, interwoven learning curve skein is a difficult one. My memory is sharp—in both senses of the word: clear and cutting.

It's about my relationship with a woman, during the course of which she developed stage 4 metastatic cancer and thus had something that both brought us closer and made me more and less a factor in her life. More capable of being a source of happiness at times. And a source of pain at others. Love was a real, dark matter we both had to avoid and to deal with. But I feel I first need to disclose some more about what I learned about myself from that dinner at Lodge in the interim.

What I realized after the letter at Lodge that caused me a long-overdue autopsy of my heart was that I might not be fit for long-term love, that I might always be a disappointment to those looking for it. Also to myself, who couldn't understand why I couldn't find it. And I was left wondering what will survive or had survived of us—all those I had loved and lost or abandoned—what had survived of us, was love, the love that had seemed so real, now gone. For good. Why?

It wasn't because I wanted the free time to go out and drink and wench, as they say. It was more about reading. Seriously. For better or worse, I almost would say I craved, loved, reading almost as much as I loved living human beings. I was an addict.

It took me nearly ten years before the truth dawned on me—the answer to the second question that night, the one about why my relationships didn't last more than two years: the fact that I was a loner at heart. Not always precisely that—I loved being in love, but I loved being alone with books almost as much. And eventually at some level the woman involved would become aware of it, and recognition of this doomed the future permanence they wanted.

That's my story and I'm sticking to it. After all, I have accumulated a library of some forty-five hundred books.

It probably began before I even learned to read, when my mother spent hours and hours reading to me. I grew up craving reading. From the summer when I read the thousands of pages of the complete works of Dickens to the periodicals I loved that were *about* reading, most notably the London *TLS,* which I began reading decades ago and never stopped. There was one moment I recalled when my *TLS* absorption converged with my romantic life. When the much-adored cult writer Veronica Geng (now gone) confessed that she developed a brief crush on me when I was able to solve the *TLS* literary quiz by knowing that the answer to one question was "Chaucer's Retraction." And during the pandemic, one of my great discoveries when I finally cleaned out a closet was a tranche of *TLS* issues from 2009, more than ten years old. I read or reread them all; it was an exhilarating experience—again like Keats's "On First Looking into Chapman's Homer."

And of course I read all three early printed versions of *Hamlet* and all three versions of *Lear,* tiny variations and all. I must admit that reading gave me almost—almost—a physical pleasure as great as sex. Well, no. But I had a craving to learn about the world that reading and investigative reporting offered, and love not always did.

I probably only became a writer because I was such an insatiable reader. Being a writer meant I'd always have something new to read, even if I had to write it myself.

Only after Maya brought it so abruptly to my attention, only after she left me because I had not fulfilled my theoretical agreement to leave New York and move to D.C., did this realization dawn, for which I'm grateful to her.

Reading and romance were always struggling for primacy in my life and women found the books a formidable rival. Eventually, they recognized before I did that I was a loner despite being the kind of romantic who sent them flowers on every minor holiday. Yes, I was a loner, a reader who rarely was able to coalesce my romance and reading obsessions.

Although there were those occasional blessed times when I

could share reading. One summer the woman who eventually left me for a banker in Cornwall and I would take canvas chairs out to the crumbling dock piers by the Lower West Side waterfront and read *Bleak House* and those other gigantic Dickens novels *Little Dorrit* and *Our Mutual Friend* together, though nothing could compare to discovering the realization of love that ultimately climaxed *Bleak House,* love between smallpox-stricken Esther and the gruff but benevolent Mr. Jarndyce of the *Jarndyce vs. Jarndyce* lawsuit.

Was all this necessary as an explanation for my romance with Ann, the cancer-stricken woman I fell in love with before I knew about the cancer?

Yes, I said, yes.

What linked them in memory were the piers, in particular a love song played by a broken-down brass band on the sleazy "amusement pier," the Brighton Pavilion, on the seaside a hundred miles south of London.

Have you been to Brighton? Another Graham Greene venue, in his somewhat insane religious gangster novel *Brighton Rock*. Love brought us to Brighton. Love and cancer, to be precise.

I didn't know Ann had, or had had, cancer when we first were introduced. I thought her short, almost buzz-cut hair was a fashion model thing, having seen the crew-cut look on models that season and knowing she worked for a glossy. I thought that she did it, had it cut short and kept it that way, because on some women—she was one of them—the super-short hair framed the face and brought out a kind of punky beauty. It looked so good, so foxy, it didn't occur to me what it really was. That it was, rather, a case of her hair growing *back* after post-surgery chemo left her bald, and she took a fairly long time to tell me. By that time, it didn't matter, or it did on another level.

I don't know if it would have made a difference, knowing it

from the start. I know I was lovestruck by her look and her idio-syncratic sense of humor from the first night a couple who were mutual friends brought us together for dinner at a downtown Mexican restaurant.

I didn't know about the cancer when we had our first date shortly thereafter, seeing a charmingly silly movie featuring the then hot duo "Kid 'n Play" (Where are you now, Kid? Where are you, Play?). There was a long, long dinner afterward at a place on Ninth Avenue not far from where I lived (London Terrace) when I was married. We talked and talked and felt ourselves click.

I didn't know that the next morning she called up the woman from the couple that introduced us and actually told her, "I've met the man I'm going to marry." Not even "I *think* I've met the man"; she was always very definitive. I never thought of myself as having that effect, but I wasn't going to argue.

I mean, it might have been hyperbole, though; Ann (name changed) could be a very determined woman. And surprisingly wily, I guess, is the word for someone with that face of angelic innocence.

I didn't know it then but she set out to make her initial mari-tal declaration come true, hiding her objective from me of course to avoid scaring me off as I found myself falling more and more under her spell even after—or because—I learned about the can-cer. She thought, she had been led to believe, that after the small biopsy-like incision and the chemo, her recurring lab readings showed her lymph nodes cancer-free. She had been led to believe there was no reason she wouldn't stay that way, although with cancer there were never any guarantees.

And so we led a relatively carefree life as close friends going to screenings and parties together.

Until the day the lymph node readings changed and she

was told after ultra-thorough reexamination that cancer has migrated, metastasized to other places in her body, and all bets were off as far as survival, length of time, degree of pain, all those things we now had to think of together. All those things that forced me to make a choice, or did I have a choice? Or did she, as in her own subtly escalating way, press me to make a choice?

And so I did make a choice.

After, or because, she told me it had metastasized.

A big change. It hadn't made much of a difference when she first told me she had had breast cancer. I'd been through that before with other women and this time the doctors had said the tumor was small, didn't require radical surgery, and was not likely to come back. Or so the doctors told her.

Still no guarantees with cancer, I'd been with other women who'd had scares before. With one whose biopsy was found to be malignant. I was waiting by her hospital bed when she came back from biopsy/surgery with that news. I think she mistook it for a death sentence because it changed her sense of herself and left little room for me in her life thereafter. It took a few weeks. She let me down easy but it was hard. Like a country song. Broke my heart.

Something I could understand, it took courage to live with it, although she's still alive last I checked, decades later. Looking back on it, though, I confess that experience with cancer, even at one remove, probably was a factor in my initial reluctance to consummate my relationship with Ann. We became very close friends, though it became clear that she wanted more, would have welcomed my physical advances.

Once you're in it with a "cancer babe," as she liked to call herself, there was no getting out without the shame of cowardice, the fear of grief to come, the fear of taking something away from her, a possible source of pleasure and hope, when everything might be on the line. But the extended time with sexual tension and not sex also had the effect—whether I intended it or not—of bringing us closer, drawing each other into our mutual self.

Still, when the news came of the metastases, the stakes leaped to a whole other level.

For a while I couldn't get past what a commitment I might have been entering into, from friend to lover. The sex would have sealed the deal, the kind of deeper responsibility and peril to my own emotional life from that past episode, and I was not sure I was ready for it. Once it was done, there was no going back, no loner's life. But she wasn't going to take no for an answer. She wouldn't let me be a coward. She even consulted her shrink, I later learned, for advice on how to seduce me, but for a time at least I didn't allow myself to be seduced.

There was even that memorable moment in a crowded doctor's waiting room when she'd read in some periodical that a friend of hers had been given her own imprint at a major publishing house.

In response to which she said out loud, "I'm going to get her to give me a million-dollar advance for a memoir and then you'll have to fuck me."

Believe me, heads turned. Even though she meant it, I think, as a joke, she was a very determined woman.

Later she disclosed her shrink's advice. That we should spend more time in our habit of lying on her bed watching television at night and that eventually I would not be able to resist her.

The shrink was right. Of course I was incredibly attracted to her from the moment we were introduced, so it was just a matter of time and bodies touching while TV watching on her bed, time needed to overcome my defenses. And I remember how glad I was that I finally let myself succumb and stop thinking about what the future might bring because I might never have moments as beautifully intense and meaningful as these, no matter what the future brought.

Things proceeded from there and we became a normal couple in love. Normal as could be, considering one of us was facing death from a stage 4 disease 24/7. The cancer came back with a vengeance, metastasizing to her bone marrow.

At that point there was no going back, and emotionally I was honestly falling more and more deeply in love with her and her courage in facing what might be an even more uncertain future.

Not that she didn't have a million friends; it seemed everybody loved her, guys I thought were my friends came on to her in front of me, but those million didn't know the whole story. It didn't show.

Then there began a series of crises interspersed with respites of love. There was one night when we were sleeping apart and she suffered a kind of seizure and couldn't get out of bed without paralyzing pain. When she tried and failed to reach me by phone she called her ex-husband, who, fortunately, lived nearby, and he raced down and broke down her door before the ambulance arrived.

He was, apparently, still in love with her despite what she'd told me had gone on between them before they split. In fact, after her death, he maintained her Facebook page for years with photos and memories of a younger, pre-cancer woman. She had that effect on men as well as demanding a lot from them.

I played my part the next day, after her seizure and ambulance rescue, when she still hadn't gotten a bed in the overcrowded hospital and was on a lonely gurney in a hallway in great pain and I called a friend of a friend who was on the hospital board and threatened to write a story about the way it failed her, a cancer-stricken patient, a threat that got her moved to a private room designed, I think, for a Saudi prince donor, pronto.

Was I being journalistically unethical? Was I being fair to others without connections? I didn't care. I didn't think about it. I only thought about the terror she must be suffering.

After she recovered, partially, at least, from that incident, the intensity of our love and her peril grew; there were further scares, worse and worse bouts of pain as the metastases invading her bone marrow spread and began to fracture her bones from within. Things couldn't be more dire.

We frantically researched treatments and trials; her parents were Christian Scientists and didn't then come to her side in the hospital, believing that only God's perfect love could heal and that modern medical intervention made things worse. Well, for a long time it didn't make things better.

Fortunately she had an uncle down in Virginia, a physician, not an oncologist, but a really smart guy who loved her, and he joined the team and we became convinced there was a trial of a new radiation therapy at Duke Cancer Center she should get into immediately rather than continue the failing standard treatments of New York's cancer centers. The doctors there who didn't want to let her go would, it seemed to me, almost rather see her die than let another medical team have a shot at saving her. My rage was unfair and irrational, I know.

The Duke trial, as I understood it, had the advantage or the purpose of permitting a patient to receive more than the usually permitted lifetime dose of radiation that had excluded her from other trials and protocols.

The uncle who had money opened his wallet and got a med-evac jet waiting at Teterboro Airport in Jersey to fly her—and me as well—down to Duke. He insisted I go—I wanted to—though my role was mainly to hold her hand through the painful flight through the stratosphere down to Durham, North Carolina. Never found out how much he laid out, but it was stratospheric, upward of $25,000, which insurance wouldn't cover, way upward, but he felt time was of the essence. The expert compassionate flight crew had hooked her up to a morphine drip before we took off so she was barely aware of the clouds we were sailing over.

That night I think I may have saved her life, at least temporarily.

When we got her checked into a bed in the Duke Cancer Center ICU wing, her pain had grown from intolerable to unbearable or vice versa even with the high levels of morphine. When I read out the level to her uncle standing by on the other end of a phone line, he whistled despairingly and said, "That's world-class bone pain."

She was scheduled for her first radiation treatment first thing in the morning, but it became a question of whether she would make it through the night. Whether she wanted to make it, to endure the pain for that long with no promise of relief.

This was the insoluble problem: They could keep increasing the morphine level to make the pain barely tolerable. But the higher the level of the drip, the greater the danger that the morphine would depress her respiratory function to the point that it would kill her.

It became a kind of race between her need for pain relief and the question of whether she could survive even with huge infusions of supplementary oxygen to keep her respiration functioning.

Her uncle and I couldn't at first figure out why there was a sudden spike in pain levels at Duke that brought things to a dread decision point. But there we were. The attending doctors were home in their beds asleep, and the hospital was asking us whether we wanted to go up another level of morphine and risk her life-giving respiratory function—or, implicitly, allow her to perish from pain or its underlying cause itself: the metastases in her bone marrow breaking her bones from within. (Ann herself was mostly out of it and later had no memory of the whole crisis.)

It was then that the investigative reporter in me kicked in and I questioned the night intern about whether there had been a change in her medication protocols from her New York hospital to Duke's. Bingo! It turned out, after a close reading of the charts, that there had been a small but, it turned out, significant change. In New York she had learned—and instructed the doctors there—that she'd had a bad reaction, a bad hyper-painful reaction of some kind, to one drug (I'll call it ****), which they'd given her at Duke instead of a slightly different, older medication, which she tolerated well.

But when she tried to tell the attending doctor at Duke not to give her ****, he had not taken her seriously and refused to vary from the Duke protocol, which called for ****. (Neither was an anti-cancer drug, but the Duke doctor had, without any basis, somehow assumed she wanted **** because she was some kind of druggy, which didn't make sense and was in no way true, especially since she'd been in AA for years.

But doctors can be arrogant. The sacred protocol, no matter what the patient says about her experience with it, and when that turned out to drive her pain to the edge of death—he blamed it on her. Don't get crosswise with the arrogance of (some) doctors.

I made a scene in protest. I was outraged. But since I had no official status (her Christian Scientist parents being hands-off), my protests were ignored.

For a couple of terrible hours there was a standoff, but at last the arrogant attending physician left to sleep and one very bright and compassionate (and brave) overnight intern took the time to listen and look at the chart and agreed to try to swap out the **** for ****. And while the pain was still unrelenting, it became bearable and didn't call for a life-or-death decision about raising morphine levels.

The pain subsided enough to make it unnecessary to raise the morphine to potentially fatal levels, got her through the night, and, mirabile dictu, the next morning the experimental radiation protocol began to work, at least temporarily, and over the course of two weeks succeeded in shrinking her metastases to some extent.

After the struggle to keep her alive was over, in the predawn hours I took a brief walk outside into the woods adjacent to the medical center. On the way back I hit the wrong button on the elevator and it took me down to the basement, a place like I'd never seen before and never want to see again. An all-metal hell.

My thirty-year-old memory could be wrong, but I believed it was the "firing range" for the radiation therapy "guns" that targeted tumors, a vast-seeming place; in my memory it was made entirely of titanium or some gleaming metallic material. I thought I was alone, but wandering around groggily looking for the exit, I came upon another human. A bald kid maybe six or eight years old who, I imagined, had escaped "custody" somehow and was visiting or revisiting the place where he'd been irradiated.

We didn't speak but I'll never forget the smile he gave me that must have come from a deep well of intuitive, life-affirming generosity. Love.

If I was down there, I'm sure he thought, I had most likely shared or was sharing what he had gone or was going through.

I'm not sure why but I totally lost it then, broke down, sobbing quietly, knew I couldn't hug him because he'd likely be too immunocompromised and vulnerable to infection. I had somehow displaced my grief, my fears and tears for my loved one several floors above there, which would only have made things worse, and then let them spill out down here in the presence of the poor kid. Love can just wring you dry.

Brighton

Cut to a month later or more, when she'd recovered sufficiently that we decided to risk taking advantage of an offer from one of the PR people she dealt with as editor of the travel section of her magazine.

She knew it was probably unwise but we were both thinking too optimistically about the future we wanted together and wanted a taste of what life could be like had cancer not denied it.

The offer was to do a story on a chain of five-star European hotels, including stays in their London, Paris, and Vienna branches. She wanted to keep her job, she wanted to keep working as long as she could, and so we took advantage of the super luxe palaces on offer. I remember so many things about that jaunt—the side trip we took to view the vast Rubens canvases in the Vienna Kunsthistorisches Museum and how I teased her, making up semi-porno stories about the rubicund goddesses Rubens loved to paint.

And after our five-star stay in Paris we decided to stay on for a couple of extremely romantic days in a small Left Bank hotel after being overwhelmed by the Paris palais. And I'll never forget that at the end of the day we'd spent crossing and recrossing the Seine, she turned to me and these were her exact words:

"This is the best day I've spent in my life."

If only we could have stayed at that peak, that plateau of pure joy. We deserved it. She deserved it, anyway. Love owed us it. It's what makes this not just a cancer story but a love story as well.

But the time came to an end. Back in the States we became for a while like an ordinary couple sometimes having ordinary or extraordinary fights exacerbated by the stakes for her and the remorse I felt not being able to be always available because of my work. Remorse I feel more now. Remorse I felt at not being able to make her always as happy as she was that day in Paris.

All good things, all ordinary things, must come to an end when there's cancer involved, and the following year it happened to us.

I think of it as our Devil's interval. Do you know about the Devil's interval? It's a term musicians, mostly guitar virtuosos, know about, as I understand it. An interval between chords, I think. I learned about it from Linda Ronstadt, who told me over a dinner when I was interviewing her about how as a kid she and her friends used to toy with some combination of chords that had a bad, virtually supernatural, reputation for summoning evil.

"We were all scared of it," she said. "It still makes me shiver."

As it happened in this interval, Ann still had to undergo periodic radiation treatments and blood tests, always finding that waiting to hear the results was unbearably suspenseful.

But she was incredibly brave; it was hard to tell from her intact wit and beauty that she was locked into stage 4 from the metastases but there came a time when things seemed to settle down and we were able to take up an offer from the doctors of a long weekend respite from hospital corridors and tests and treatment. The Devil's Interval.

I think it was the July Fourth weekend, but whenever it was, we decided we needed a break—however brief—from each other.

When I say it was a moment's respite, it was a brief interval we were apart after the Duke doctors (God bless them—all but the arrogant one) gave her some more time to live.

I had flown to London, where I had a deadline given to me by the London branch of Sotheby's, the giant auction house that was handling the disposition of the posthumous papers, books, and incunabula of the "spy of the century," Kim Philby, an enigmatic cancer within the anglophone intelligence community about whom I was writing a *New York Times Magazine* piece.

Sotheby's had offered me a preview of their still-secret auction of the posthumous papers, which, after the auction, would likely disappear forever into the hands of a Saudi collector. (Kim's father was a Lawrence of Arabia type.) I was in the midst of rummaging through mole memorabilia in their Sotheby's office. And she had a chance to experience some bucolic peace away from the ICU wards.

She had been enjoying some mountain air in her relatives' place in rural Pennsylvania when the call came.

The call. Anyone who has known someone whose life has been lived on the edge of a medical precipice knows what "the call" can mean. The doctor analyzing the latest blood samples, tissue samples, finds something, a marker, or a level of markers, that hadn't been there, often a simple but potentially deadly change in lab results that now can't be ignored and must be addressed with all due speed.

Ann called me in London. I told her I'd fly back immediately.

She said no, the doctors gave her a weekend before she'd have to "go back in." She wanted to fly to London to be with me for what, for all we knew, might be the last time.

I met her at Heathrow. We checked into a small hotel we'd stayed in before (Brown's, I recall). She wanted to go to the National Portrait Gallery. I said I needed to finish up Philby study, although I must admit I was not a fan of portraiture. I will always regret that. Regret that she was disappointed and went to the National Portrait Gallery alone. I wish I had a time machine for that.

But for that night I had gotten us tickets for the Donmar Warehouse *Hamlet* everybody was talking about. We barely saw it, holding each other through our tears.

With most of the weekend left, we decided to take a jaunt to Brighton, figuring that the seedy seaside Victorian-era resort town famous for its amusement pier might lift our spirits.

I remember the train, a Victorian-era steam engine that took us down there from London, had once-posh, now-torn red velvet cushioned seats. It was a short walk to the pier. We took what we thought was the Tunnel of Love, which was a rickety old thing with threadbare pop-up horror figures. I still am not clear how they were related to love. In fact, it was a threadbare Tunnel of Horror. Perhaps the Devil's interval was animating them.

We emerged and sat on a bench eating fish and chips and gazing at the relentless inflow of gray ocean waves like time running out, or running in.

But—and this is what I'll always remember, this is what music can do for you—or to you—there was an antiquated brass band, just one tuba and maybe a trombone and organ that played and then played and played again a song called "When I Grow Too Old to Dream" and we hugged each other so tight, we were nearly inside out each other and vowed we would never grow too old to dream of these moments we shared.

Here are lyrics from the 1934 song, which I found by googling:

We have been gay, going our way
Life has been beautiful, we have been young
After you've gone, life will go on
Like an old song we have sung.

When I grow too old to dream
I'll have you to remember
When I grow too old to dream

Your love will live in my heart
So, kiss me my sweet
And so let us part
And when I grow too old to dream
That kiss will live in my heart.
When I grow too old to dream...
Your love will live in my heart.

In the years afterward, when she was gone, there were times when I needed to hear that song that had been playing over and over in my mind. I remember the first time when I googled it and unfortunately Google served up a Linda Ronstadt YouTube version of the song, and though Linda is a special favorite of mine, in this YouTube version she was singing it to Kermit the Frog backed by a chorus of Muppets. One can't have everything; the song was like some nuclear-hardened rock. It triumphed over the context.

Don't laugh (I know you will). Even the Muppets couldn't break that song's hold on me.

Sadly, a couple of years later we stopped dreaming of each other or she stopped dreaming of me. I couldn't be the lover and healer she wanted.

Happily, she lived on for some dozen years after we broke up and wrote two books that received accolades.

Once we almost got together again—her choice—but the timing was wrong. I had gotten involved with someone else and couldn't just change partners and dance, so to speak. We had dinner, we clicked again, but when she asked me back to her apartment I had to say no. I'd feel I'd be betraying my then current girlfriend, whom I lost anyway.

Two days later I got a letter from her that said simply, "Please do me a favor and never contact me again." In a way, after all the love, after all the rancor, all I had left was that song. And that letter. For better or worse. For better *and* worse.

But that song, the memory of dusk on the Brighton pier—and that brave six-year-old bald kid, somehow—have never vanished from my consciousness.

And it was always painful. Well, not only painful—it was also at times joyful, which involved a lot of forgetting. But I can't deny that for years afterward the memory of the song kept our love alive. What will survive of us... sometimes just an old song. I couldn't bear the idea of loving like that again and losing. The song was a trigger that sent an arrow straight to the heart. I learned from the whole experience that maybe you never learn anything worthwhile about love until you find the very last one. The one who answered the question of why Ron's relationships never last longer than two years.

In fact, as I write, it's been seven years with my current love and I never want another. I only want more time than I'll get with this one, who just wrote me a note lamenting we didn't meet years earlier and saying she would have kissed me right away. Ironic because it took me two years before I had the nerve to kiss her, knowing I could never bear being rejected.

We are all "angels flying too close to the ground" in the grip of love's beautiful, inexorable gravity.

Acknowledgments

I wouldn't be surprised if many—if not most—writers faced with the acknowledgments page experience FOLO, let's call it. FOLO, not YOLO or FOMO, or POMO, but FOLO. Fear of Leaving Out the names of any of the many people who deserve mention, heartfelt thanks, and the small recompense of such a recognition for their help in making this book a reality—and helping me get through some difficulties, including serious illness, along the way.

I know that acts of gratitude should be gratifying, and they would be, were it not for FOLO haunting me. So, a preemptive apology if your name is not here and it should be. And an assurance, on the other hand, that I have sought not to disclose the names and identities of any of my past partners in love. But I do feel gratitude to all of them, no matter how things ended up—gratitude for what I learned from them, acknowledgment of all the mistakes I've made and how those mistakes shaped and reshaped me. The reality of what we once shared convinced me of the need to write a defense of love, and a lament for the way love is being reduced to equations and algorithms.

I had a lot to learn, and you helped me.

As to the book itself, one thing I can be confident about saying is that this book has been unusually blessed in that it's had the benefit of not one, but two gifted editors. The first being Gerry Howard, top-notch literary essayist, biographer of Malcolm Cowley, as well as far-sighted editor who helped me see what I was doing. And his successor—after Gerry's retirement (long planned, *not* due to the difficulty of working with me)—the formidable and wise Thomas Gebremedhin, who saw what I was in the midst of doing, helped make it better, and brought it home.

So many at Doubleday deserve my praise and thanks, from publisher and editor in chief Bill Thomas, to copy editor Muriel Jorgensen, fact-checker Mervyn Keizer, and legal counsel Daniel Novack.

Special thanks to my editor Thomas's assistant Johanna Zwirner, who handled every aspect of publication, from typescript to book, with meticulous thoroughness and thoughtfulness. My name is on the cover, but the book wouldn't be the book without this team.

Another essential person was my longtime friend and now literary agent Chris Calhoun, with whom I started talking about such a book as this even before Gerry told me to read Tolstoy's *Father Sergius*. Chris Calhoun is a gentleman and a scholar, sharp as a tack. I met him for the first time years ago (along with future Doubleday publisher Bill Thomas) at a nameless dive in Little Italy where, to the mystification of its O.G. owners, many other young people serious about writing would gather to grapple with grappa and drink to niche favorites such as Terry Southern, Eve Babitz, and Charles Portis. The dive has disappeared, but this book feels almost like a reunion with Bill and Chris, and with the spirit of that place.

I owe a special debt of gratitude to an old friend, Jeff Greenfield. Just as I was beginning this book, a serious illness (pre-COVID) hit me, and Jeff rounded up a posse of friends and strangers to help keep me afloat until I mostly recovered (though I still deal with serious medical issues I refuse to call Stage 4).

Thanks to all of you and the others like Jeff who got me through that time: Jessie Sheidlower, Gil Roth, and Emily Yoffe, among others. FOLO alert!

And a friendly nod to Laura Kipnis, whose book *Against Love* I've praised in the text. Because of our apparently contradicting titles, my *In Defense of Love* should in no way be considered an "answer" to hers, which in its own adept way is itself a defense of love, I think she'd agree.

Three of my Yale classmates deserve special mention here for staying in my life all this time. Mike Yogg, a valuable interlocutor ever since we shared a postgrad beach house; Richard Burling (and his wife, Jan), a faithful friend since we were freshman roommates; and Steve Weisman, with whom I shared a still-influential Milton seminar and the singular wisdom of the late scholar of the metaphysical love poets Michael John Kenneth O'Loughlin, one of those teachers whose influence has lasted a lifetime.

Speaking of literature, I also owe a lot to the great director Peter Brook, who opened a portal to Shakespeare for me with his life-changing production of *A Midsummer Night's Dream*, a once-in-a-lifetime theatrical realization of collective and personal love. In my long talks with Brook about Shakespeare, I left feeling lit up—he could always say something revelatory about love in and out of Shakespeare.

I sometimes wish I could be a Boswell to my longtime friend and philosophical interlocutor Errol Morris, the brilliant documentarian and author, always a source of provocative ideas and hilarious aphorisms that made every dinner with him and his sharp-witted wife, Julia Sheehan, a one-of-a-kind feast. And, I should add, their talented documentarian/scientist son, Hamilton, who has become a valued friend and source on questions of consciousness. As have Prof. David Price and Daniel Reich at the National Institutes of Health.

A special place of honor to Mark Steinberg, patron of literature and baseball historian, for playing an important role in my life after the inception of my illness.

I have an archivist, Alex Belth, an omnivorous reader, thanks to whom I've been able to keep track of the scores of stories in magazines and periodicals into which I often poured book-length efforts; I'm so glad they won't be lost in the mists of back issues. I've had four hardbound books of my collected stories, but here, for instance, are a trove of some favorite, mostly uncollected periodical stories Alex has saved on his website, stacksreader.com. These are a sample of pieces that have defined me as a writer: http://www.thestacksreader.com/the-essential-ron-rosenbaum-part-one and http://www.thestacksreader.com/the-essential-ron-rosenbaum-part-two.

And there is my old friend and onetime editor, novelist Betsy Carter, who started me thinking and writing seriously about love when she assigned me a Linda Ronstadt portrait a dozen years ago (nor should I neglect her super-smart husband, gentle giant Gary Hoenig).

And there is Rosanne Cash, who I learned can speak with casual eloquence about the thing called love as well as conjuring it up in songs like nobody else, and who made me think more deeply than before about such questions as quantum entanglement as a metaphor for love in the multiverse.

I will always be grateful to the late great Peter Kaplan, who made writing my *New York Observer* column "The Edgy Enthusiast"—made writing itself—a joy for ten years. And his talented brother James, peerless biographer of such musicians as Irving Berlin and Frank Sinatra.

Other editors made me feel their love for writing, among them the late Dan Wolf, Lewis Lapham, Harold Hayes, Jonathan Karp, and the late Harry Evans (the Hitler book), and David Ebershoff (the Shakespeare book). My editors Meghan O'Rourke, Julia Turner, and Jacob Weisberg at *Slate* gave me latitude to explore everything from my critique of neuroscience to my celebration of Sofiya Tolstoy's long-hidden novella. Nor can I forget Tina Brown, who made 15,000-word investigative nonfiction stories a thing again, as did Jack Rosenthal at *The New York Times Magazine* and David Remnick at *The New Yorker*. I feel their varied influences in everything I write.

I want to mention Jonathan Bate, the gifted scholar with whom I had the privilege of making a small contribution to the edition of the Royal Shakespeare Company's *Complete Works of Shakespeare* he oversaw—in addition to being one of the smartest and most readable contemporary scholars I know (read his Ovid book).

Another scholar I must thank is Yale and Oxford's Brian D. Earp, who was helpful in testing out my ideas on love science. Sometimes I felt a bit alone in my critique of neuroscience reductionism of the Helen Fisher variety, and I only recently discovered his early paper on "neuro reductionism" in a Cambridge University journal, which supports my skepticism. For those who want a more academic take on the matter, you can find it here: http://journals.cambridge.org/abstract _S1477175614000128.

I can't forget my sister, Ruth, superb psychologist; super photographer Nina Roberts; my longtime previous agent, friend, and source of wisdom Kathy Robbins; along with smart guy David Halpern and the TRO crew who continued to be supportive of my back catalog.

Closer to home, a patron of the arts and artists named Ross Wisdom: I wrote the books; he and his predecessor Noah Kimerling kept the books.

A shout-out to all my former writing seminar students at Columbia, NYU, and Chicago, whom I hope I helped a little somehow. I love to watch them rise up the media hierarchy.

Thanks also to Helen Whitney, with whom I shared the Columbia-Dupont co-writing award for the documentary *Faith and Doubt at Ground Zero.*

So many more people helped in so many ways, each a short story, or indeed a novel, and they've meant so much to me in irreducible ways. So, in mostly random order:

Craig S. and Alison Karpel; Catherine L. Nichols; Richard Molyneux; Virginia Heffernan; Susan Brownmiller; Clark Whelton; Ed Fancher; Sally Kempton (and her late father, Murray Kempton, whose prose I'm still in awe of); Dan Kornstein; Stan Mieses; Jack Shafer; Blair Sabol; Joe Conason; Sharon English; Daniel Weber; Robert Vare; David Black; Julia Vitullo-Martin; Rebecca Wright; Sarah Kernochan; Lauren and Jim Watkins; Lisa Randall; Josiah Thompson; Maggie Topkis; Daniel Mendelsohn; Nadia Sultana; Rob Boynton, the late Isaac Bashevis Singer, pandemic companion; the late Hilary Mantel, same; most of my 7K Twitter followers (@RonRosenbaum1) even if the "hellsite" is no longer around when you read this; and many of my 3K Facebook "friends."

And my one true love, X. Who made me believe in love again.

Permissions

ABOUT THE AUTHOR

Ron Rosenbaum was born in Manhattan and grew up on the south shore of Long Island. A graduate of Bay Shore High School, he earned a Phi Beta Kappa degree in English literature at Yale before becoming a staff writer and White House correspondent for *The Village Voice*. He went on to write for numerous periodicals including *Harper's, Esquire, The New Yorker, Vanity Fair, The New York Times Magazine, Slate,* and *Smithsonian,* while also writing a column for the *New York Observer.* He is a member of the editorial advisory board for *Lapham's Quarterly* and has been on the publications advisory board for the Royal Shakespeare Company.

Rosenbaum's books include *Travels with Dr. Death, Explaining Hitler, The Secret Parts of Fortune, The Shakespeare Wars,* and *How the End Begins.* Married and divorced, he has a sister, Ruth, and has had three beloved cats, Smoochie, Stumpy, and Bruno.